IMAGES
of America

MENOMONIE

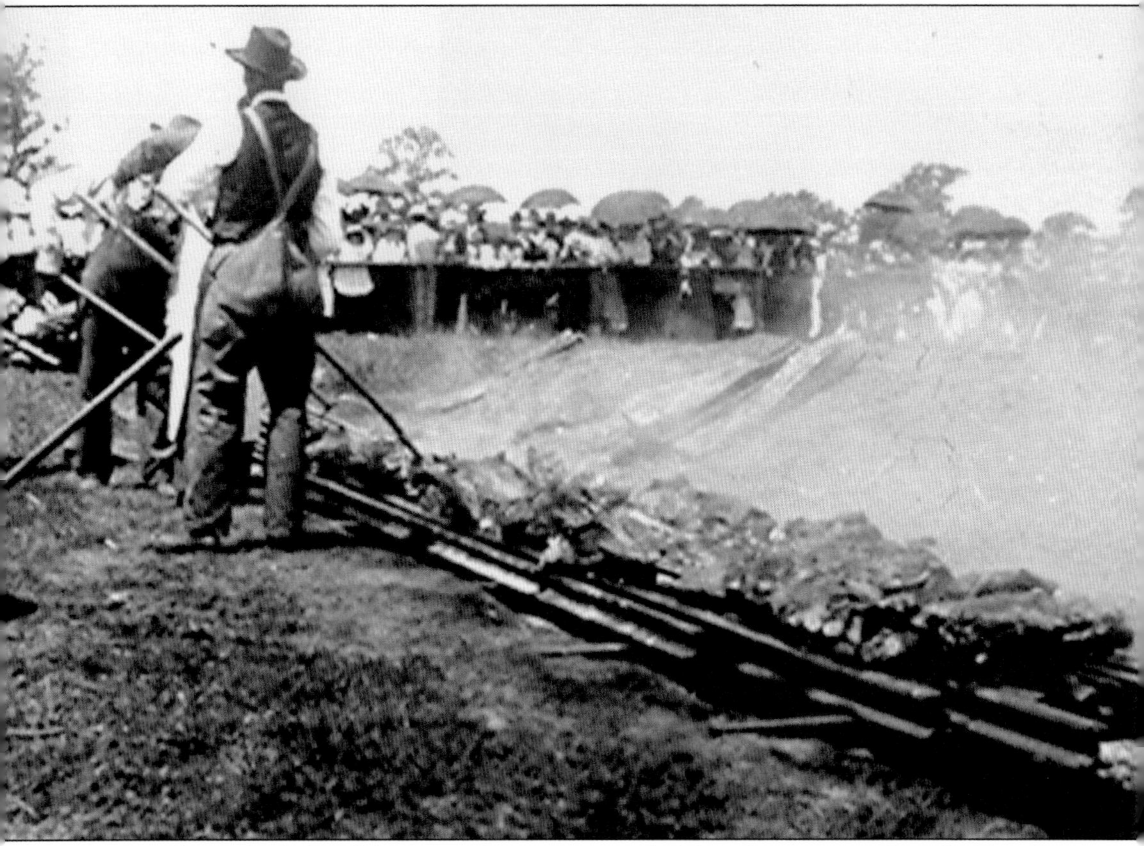

A good Fourth of July celebration in Menomonie included cooking on outside grills. Here, James H. Stout takes his turn at the cooking. (Courtesy of University of Wisconsin Stout Archives.)

On the cover: The inside of Ben's Corner Market, 1124 South Broadway, was organized, well-stocked, and always ready for the many customers who came to buy goods or just spend time discussing events of the day. Pictured here are Ben and John Metling in 1945. Ben Metling and his wife Melissa (Lierman) Metling owned and operated the small grocery from 1945 until 1961. (Courtesy of Mary Galvin Shows.)

IMAGES
of America

MENOMONIE

Ann Christy Dybvik

ARCADIA
PUBLISHING

ISBN 978-0-7385-4127-3

Published by Arcadia Publishing
Charleston, South Carolina

Printed in the United States of America

Library of Congress Catalog Card Number: 2006932981

For all general information contact Arcadia Publishing at:
Telephone 843-853-2070
Fax 843-853-0044
E-mail sales@arcadiapublishing.com
For customer service and orders:
Toll-Free 1-888-313-2665

Visit us on the Internet at www.arcadiapublishing.com

This book is dedicated to the people who had the foresight and initiative to document events of the past. Photographs capture the foundations upon which our present and future are built. May the tradition continue, and may others desire to capture and share what is so vitally important to future generations.

Contents

Acknowledgments

The images in this book came primarily from the collections of ordinary citizens. From one person hand-carrying a special photograph to the door just days within the publisher's deadline, to scrapbook collections lovingly arranged and explained, to collections from the University of Wisconsin–Stout, Menomonie citizens contributed their historical memories and images. True to the spirit of community so prevalent in this area, men and women responded to the call to share their own unique piece of history through family photographs. Their trust and honesty is overwhelming. Most of the names of the past residents are lost to history, but their photographs live on, preserved by relatives, friends, neighbors, or formal public and private institutions. Without these images there would be no pictorial representation of the passage of time, no way to see what the land, people, and buildings of the area once were. Generations beyond ours will learn from this generosity and understand the unique characteristics that make Menomonie an important place on earth.

The following individuals must receive individual credit, because without their assistance this book would not exist. Kevin Thorie and Marty Springer at the University of Wisconsin–Stout offered unprecedented access to the photographs in their collections. Ryan Miller, student assistant in the University archives, spent hours scanning photographs from the collection. John and Jackie Dotseth, lifelong Menomonie residents with a passion and dedication to preserving the past, shared their knowledge, time, and photographs. These two citizens, along with their son, Tim, are valued members of the city and deserve recognition for the Wilson Place Museum and Olde Towne meeting hall, to which they now dedicate their lives.

Sofi Doane, mother of three and avid collector of historical photographs and objects, was the first to answer the call for photographs and continued to offer new images throughout the writing process. Mary (Galvin) Shows, former resident, sent photographs from her home in Washington, having read my call for photographs in the *Dunn County News*. In fact, it is one of her photographs that graces the cover. Alta Vasey Morgan, dedicated historian and active community volunteer, Kathleen Rulka Hathaway, and Gary Hinrichs, also answered the call. Each of these people shared what they had with trust and enthusiasm; they have all added dimensions to my life as they entered it. Without the efforts of people such as these, records of the past would be lost. To them I extend utmost thanks.

Jeff Reutsche, editor at Arcadia Publishing, provided guidance and patience throughout the writing process. Your ties to Menomonie made this even more of an inspirational journey. And finally, last but definitely not least, to Bruce Dybvik, patient and willing partner, a sincere thank you for your photography skills, expert technology insight, and support. This is truly a team effort.

INTRODUCTION

The most recent book published on the history of Menomonie, Wisconsin, is now over 10 years old. It was a community effort, published as part of the sesquicentennial celebration of 1996, spearheaded by a group of interested citizens and officials, and edited by local historians Larry Lynch and John Russell. *Where the Wild Rice Grows* now occupies an important place on the bookshelves of many Menomonie residents. Unfortunately, it is out of print and unavailable to anyone else wishing to learn about this beautiful, quiet, yet progressive place in the heart of the Midwest. *Where the Wild Rice Grows* is a rich collection of facts, dates, stories, and images. Its predecessor, *1925 History of Dunn County*, was a thick, textual collection of facts, impressive but daunting to those wishing only to learn a little and view a lot.

The area now known as Menomonie began in prehistoric times as a sea that occupied space across most of the United States. This is notable because the cliffs that still remain today, along the Red Cedar Trail, Paradise Valley Road, and other spots around the town, are remnants of this period, millions of years ago. A bike ride down the beautiful Red Cedar Trail reveals limestone cliffs, teeming with wildflowers and native vegetation. Every season along the trail yields new natural discoveries and adds to the intrigue of the ride, whether it is to Irvington, Downsville, Dunnville, or Eau Claire.

Much of the documented history of Menomonie begins with the lumber era. People grew wealthy here from the natural resources of the Red Cedar Valley. Yet many gave back as much as they took, and their legacies live on in buildings, natural spaces, and institutions. Lumbering took front and center in industry for over a decade, but was not the only industry that claims Menomonie as home. Brickmaking filled a gap when the lumber era ended; breweries began, pianos were built in a factory that originated in Minneapolis but moved to Menomonie, cigars were handcrafted, schools were established, and inventors created such things as submergible electric motors and mechanical parts for dams.

Images of America: *Menomonie* is meant to fill the gap in historical records that exist; a gap that many visitors, residents, prospective community members, and businesses have requested be filled. It is a collection of images gathered from citizens both young and old, keepers of stories and collectors of the past. The photographs they provide give glimpses into the lives of past citizens and places. We see the well-known lumber barons carving roads out of thick forests, using natural resources to make a fortune, create work, develop a town, and leave lasting legacies. Some of their homes still stand, the wood from trees felled many miles up north still grace many buildings in town. The Mabel Tainter Theatre, a centerpiece for the arts in Menomonie and the surrounding area, looks much the same as it did when it was built in 1890. The ornate interior creates an atmosphere both of elegance and comfort. Seats come in three different sizes to accommodate anyone wishing to enjoy an intimate evening of song, theatre, or discussion. Weddings held here create lasting memories. Two blocks up the street, the former Knights of Columbus hall still stands, its beautiful Menomonie brick marking over 100 years of existence.

After this much passage of time, many stories are lost or half-recalled. Yet the opportunity to see what once was offers readers a chance to reminisce, compare, or imagine. The "wild rice people" of Menomonie continue, in the spirit of those that began the journey.

For photograph credits, the following abbreviations will be used throughout this text: University of Stout Archives (UWSA) and University of Stout Media Center (UWSM). Private contributors will be acknowledged by name.

One

WHERE ON EARTH

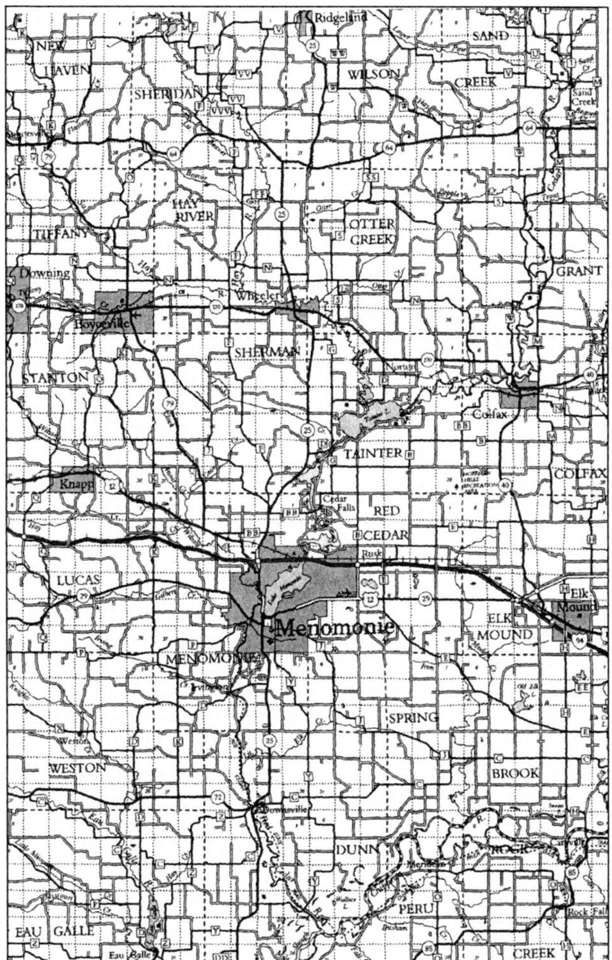

Shown here is a map of Menomonie and the surrounding area.

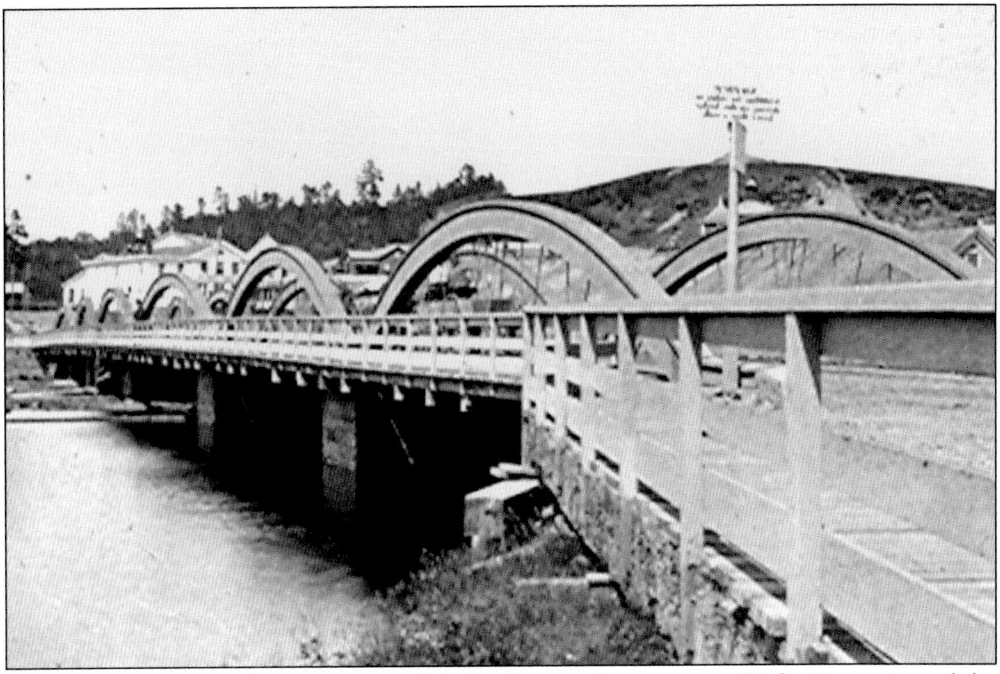

Semi-circular bridge railings once graced the bridge over the junction of Lake Menomin and the Red Cedar River. It was replaced in 1942, when the new bridge was dedicated. Updates to the structure continue, since it is the primary link between north and south Menomonie. Building a dam across the river was first attempted in 1851, but was not successfully accomplished until 10 years later. (Courtesy of UWSA.)

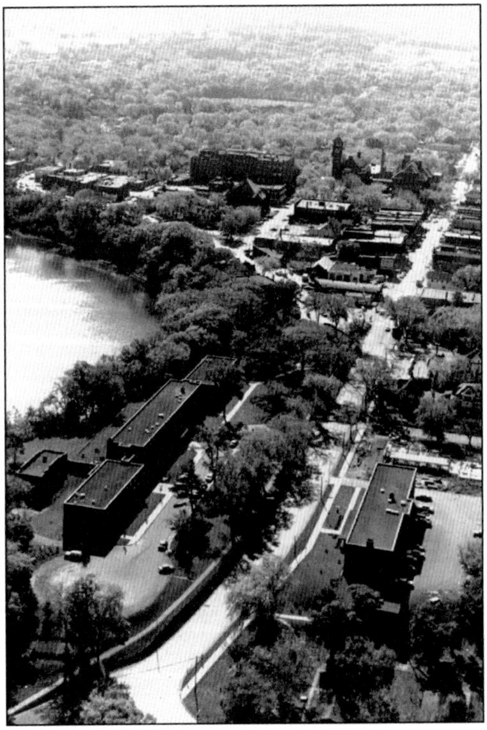

An aerial view of the downtown area shows two sets of dormitories facing each other across Broadway Street. Initially the Jeter-Tainter-Callahan complex, on the left, was for women, and Hovlid Hall, across the road, was for men. A footbridge now crosses Crescent Avenue and makes it easier for students to walk to the main Stout campus. A new dormitory was completed in 2006, behind the dorm on the right of the photograph. Note the Stout Tower in the center of the photograph with Harvey Hall across from it. (Courtesy of UWSM.)

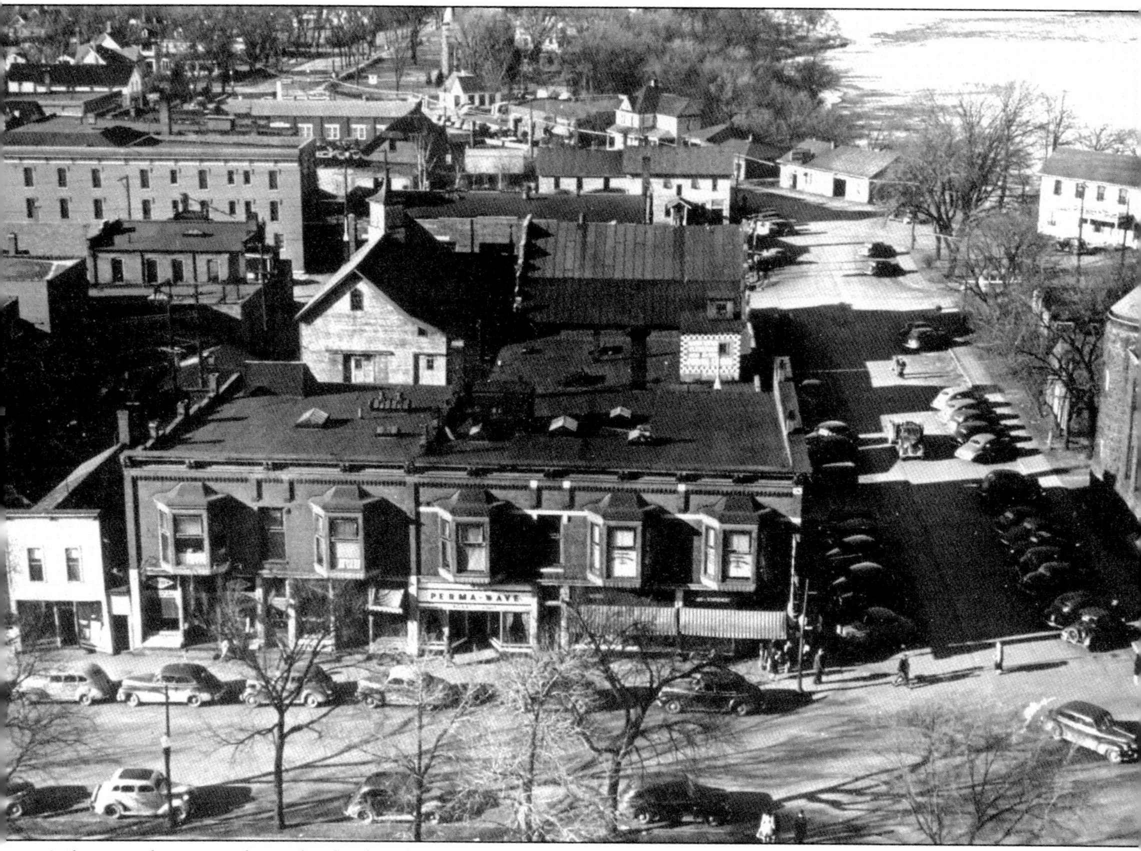

A brave photographer climbed either to the top of the Stout Tower or the roof of Bowman Hall to take this picture of the building across the street, in the 100 block of Main Street. The beautiful bay windows on this classic brick building have been removed, but Lee Drug Store, a mainstay in downtown businesses, continues to operate out of the corner retail space. On the west side of the building is a mural painted in the 1980s. This mural was painted from a picture taken of the people who built the theatre. (Courtesy of UWSA.)

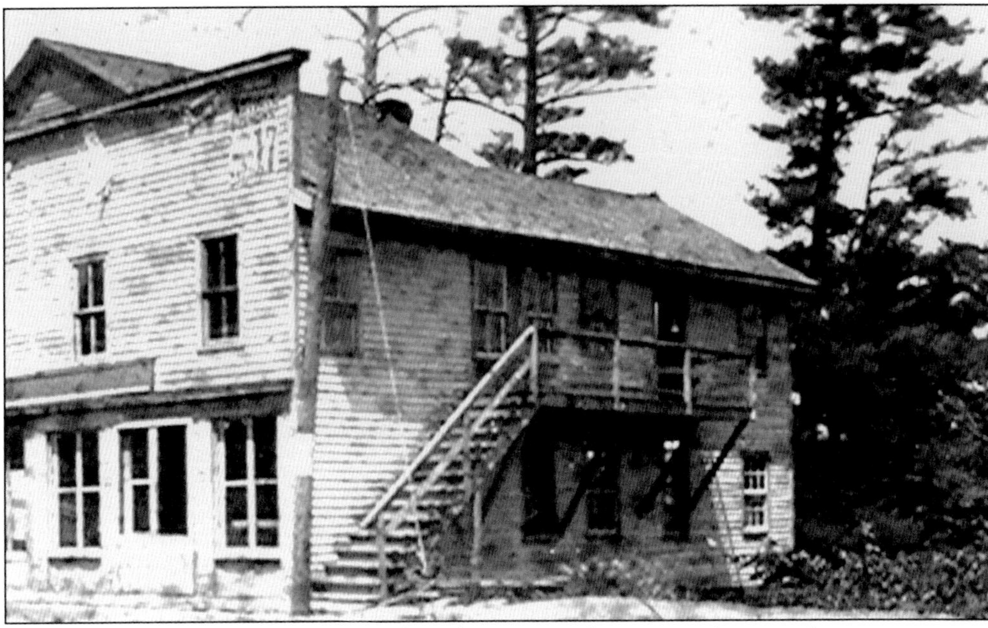

This wood frame building once stood at the corner of Crescent Avenue, the main entry to downtown and a view of Lake Menomin. The corner of Crescent Avenue and Broadway Street is now a busy intersection, with the Louis Tainter Smith house on the left, adjacent to north campus dormitories. (Courtesy of UWSA.)

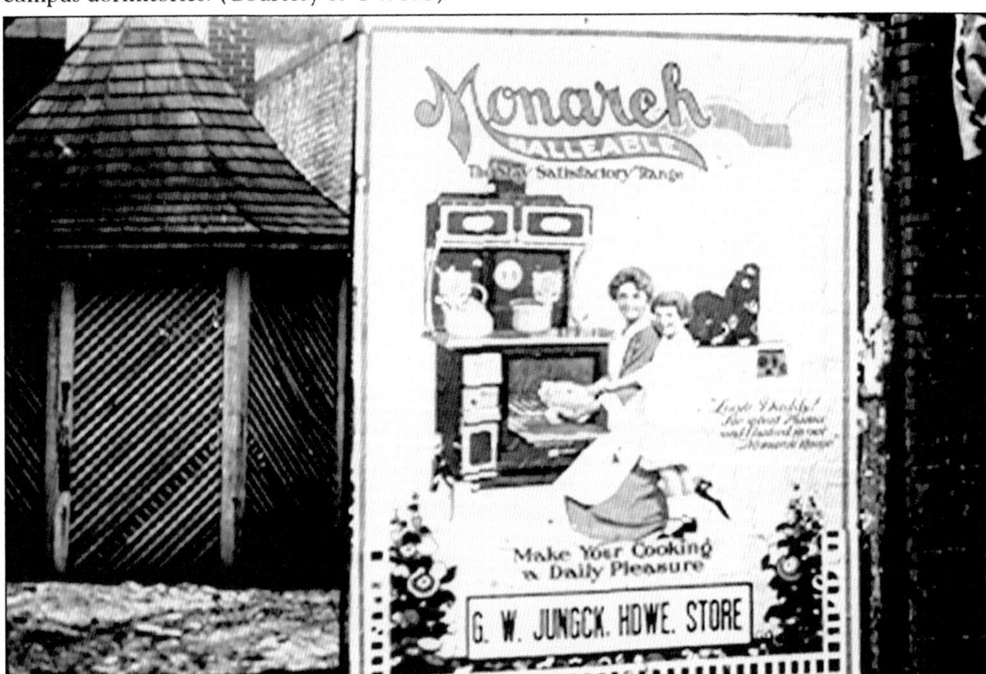

Beautiful Monarch wood cookstoves were prominently advertised on the outside of the local hardware store downtown. This store was located in the 700 block of South Broadway. During the lumber boom and beyond, downtown was the hub of retail shopping for Menomonie and the surrounding towns. (Courtesy of UWSA.)

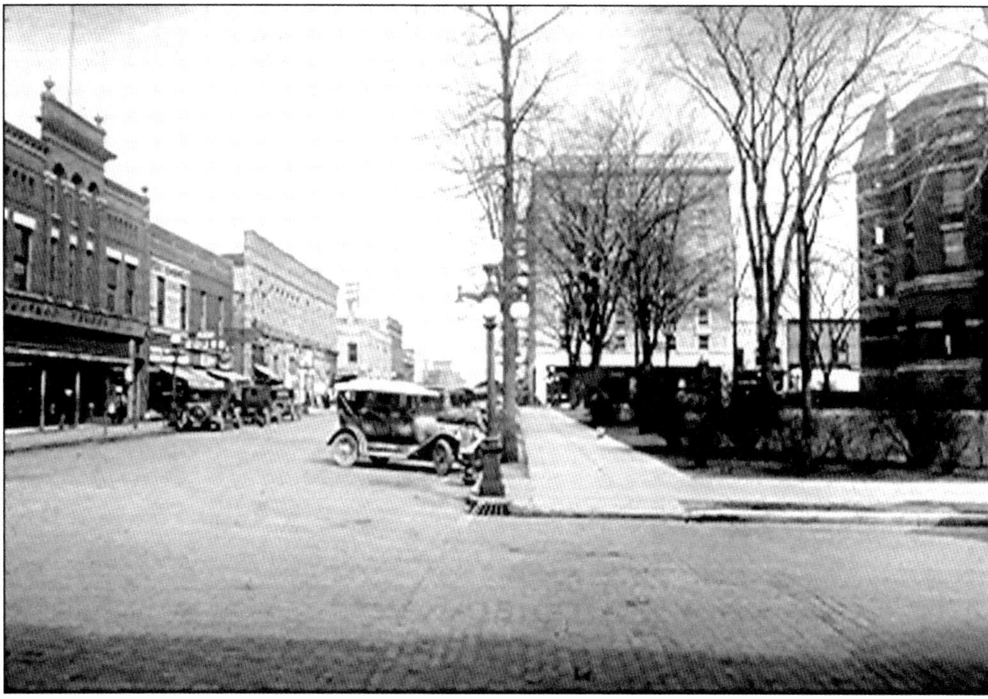

Brick paved streets were commonplace in Menomonie, where at one time, five brickyards thrived. (Courtesy of UWSA.)

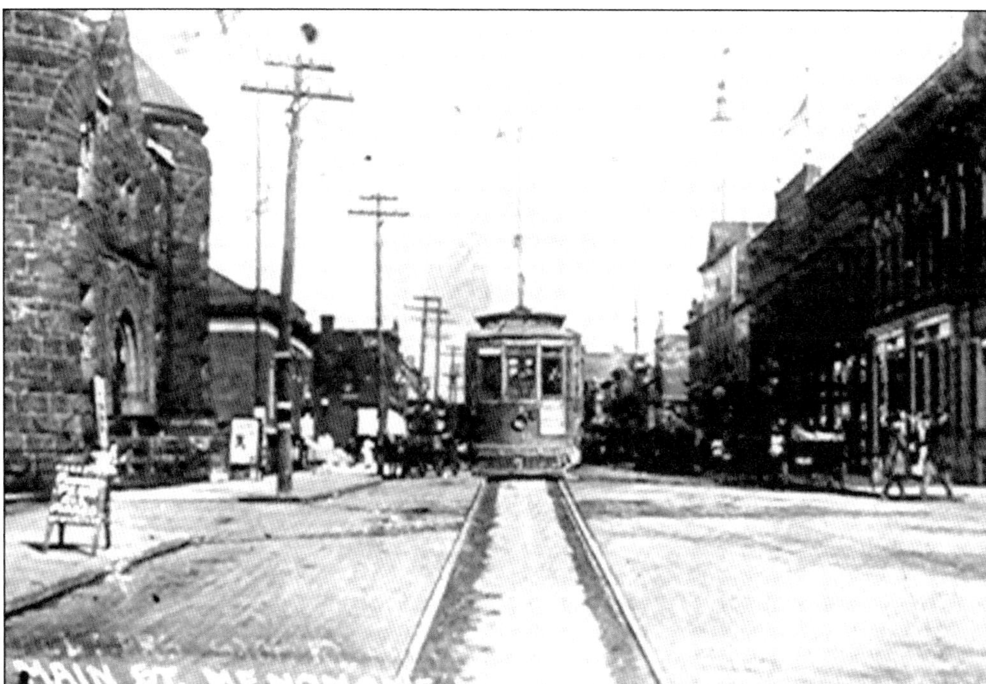

A trolley runs through downtown Menomonie? This postcard was a hoax, but many people bought it and believed there was a trolley that ran down Main Street. (Courtesy of UWSA.)

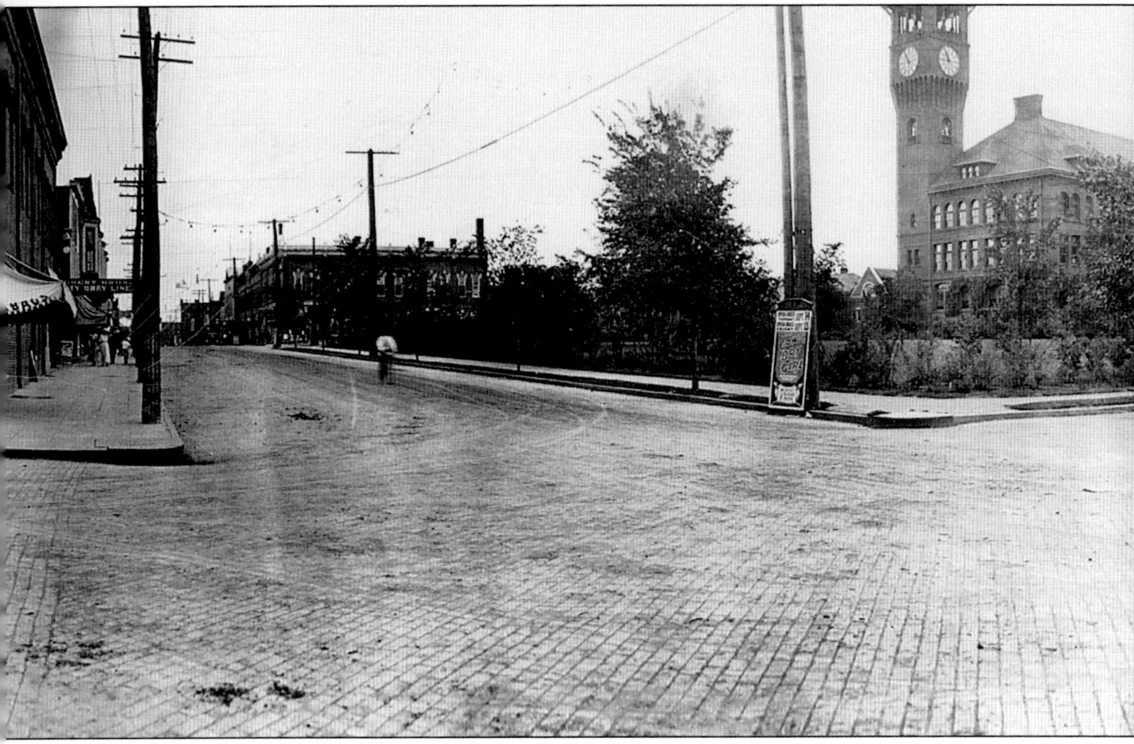

Pictured here is the corner of Main and Broadway Streets. The two brick buildings are a part of the first Stout Manual Training and Domestic Science School and Central School.

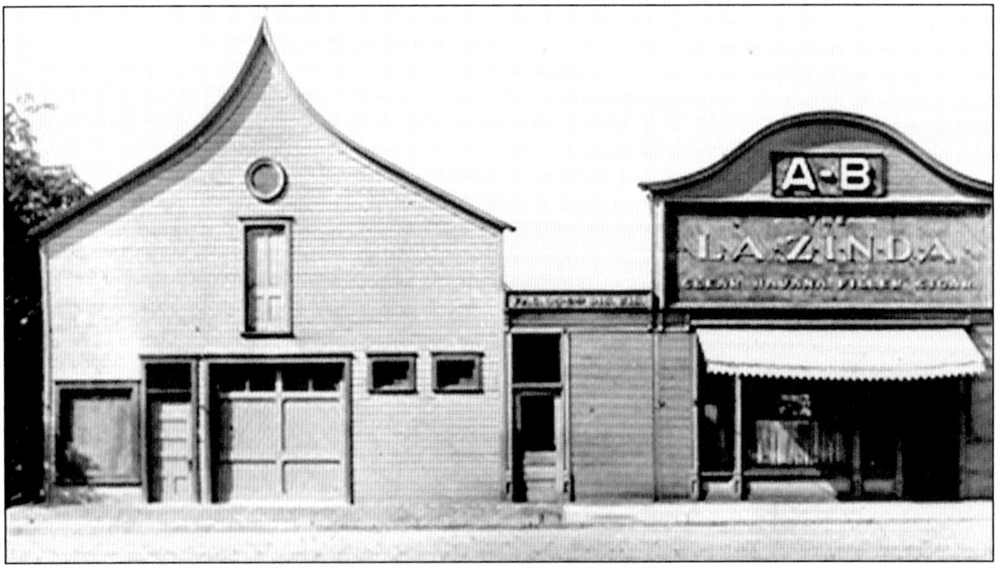

It is not known where these buildings once stood, but the roofline on the building on the left is worth noting for its distinctive slope. (Courtesy of UWSA.)

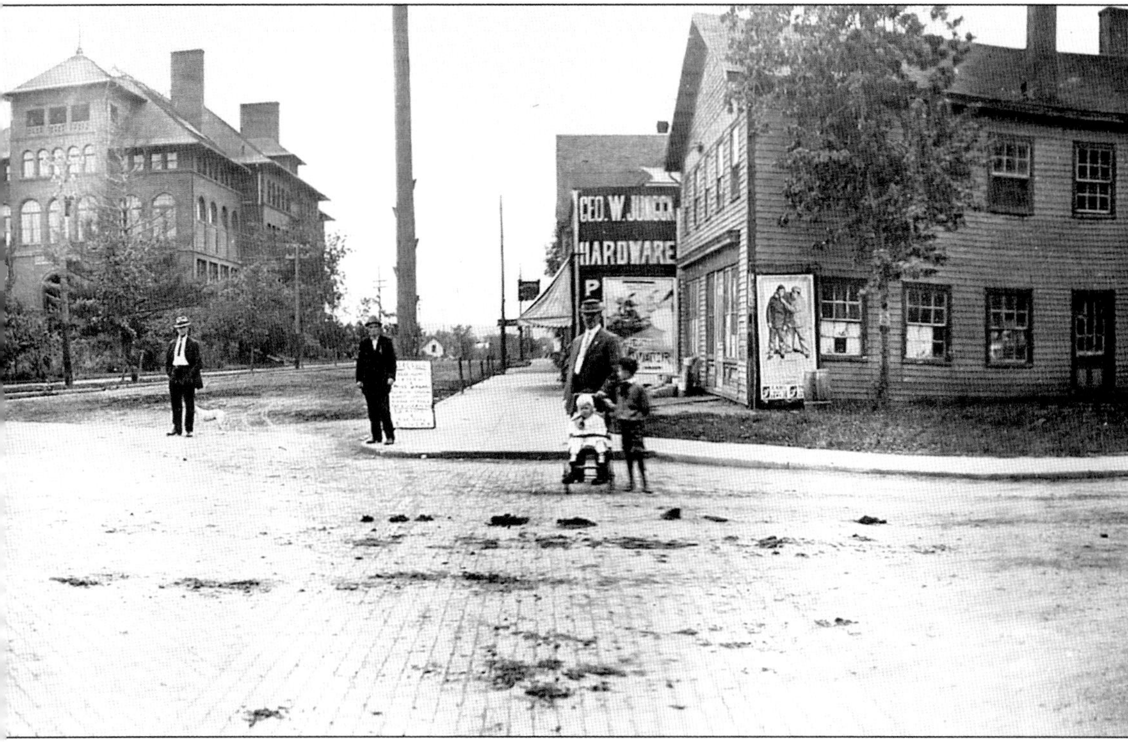

(Courtesy of UWSA.)

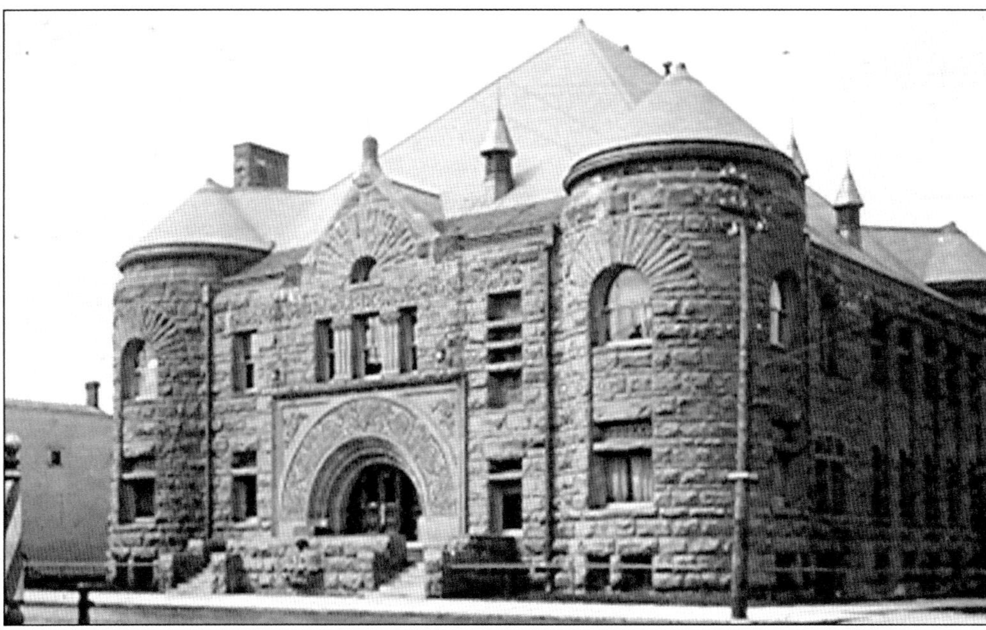

The beautiful Mabel Tainter Theatre still looks the same today as it did in 1889 when it was built. Andrew and Bertha Tainter commissioned Harvey Ellis of Minneapolis to design the building in tribute to their daughter who had passed away at age 19. (Courtesy of UWSA.)

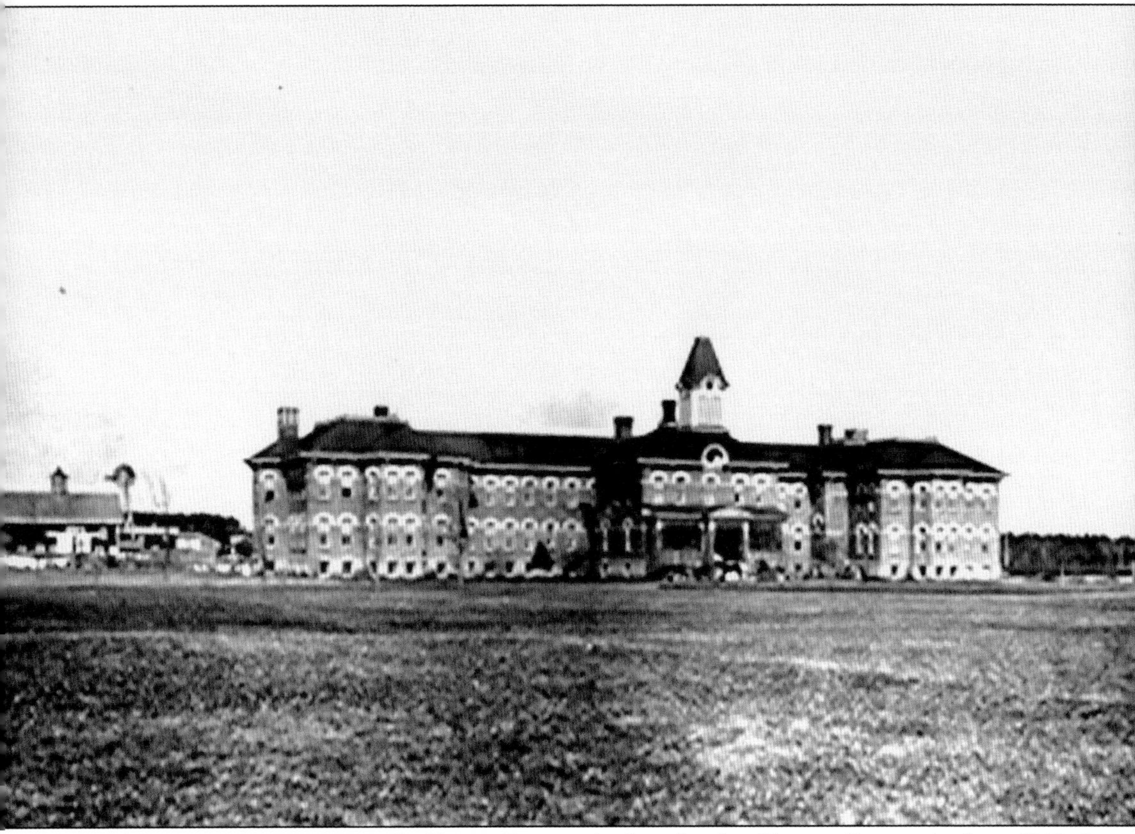

This imposing structure is the Dunn County Asylum for the Chronic Insane, built in 1892. It was a source of pride to residents and administrators in the county, because it was created not as a way to make money but, as a former trustee stated in the *1925 History of Dunn County*, "to provide a comfortable wholesome home where the unfortunate charges placed in our care may be made happy." The institution was self-supporting and consisted of a basement, two floors, and an attic. The first patient was received on February 10, 1892. For 25 years, Dr. N. L. Howison was the medical attendant. (Courtesy of UWSA.)

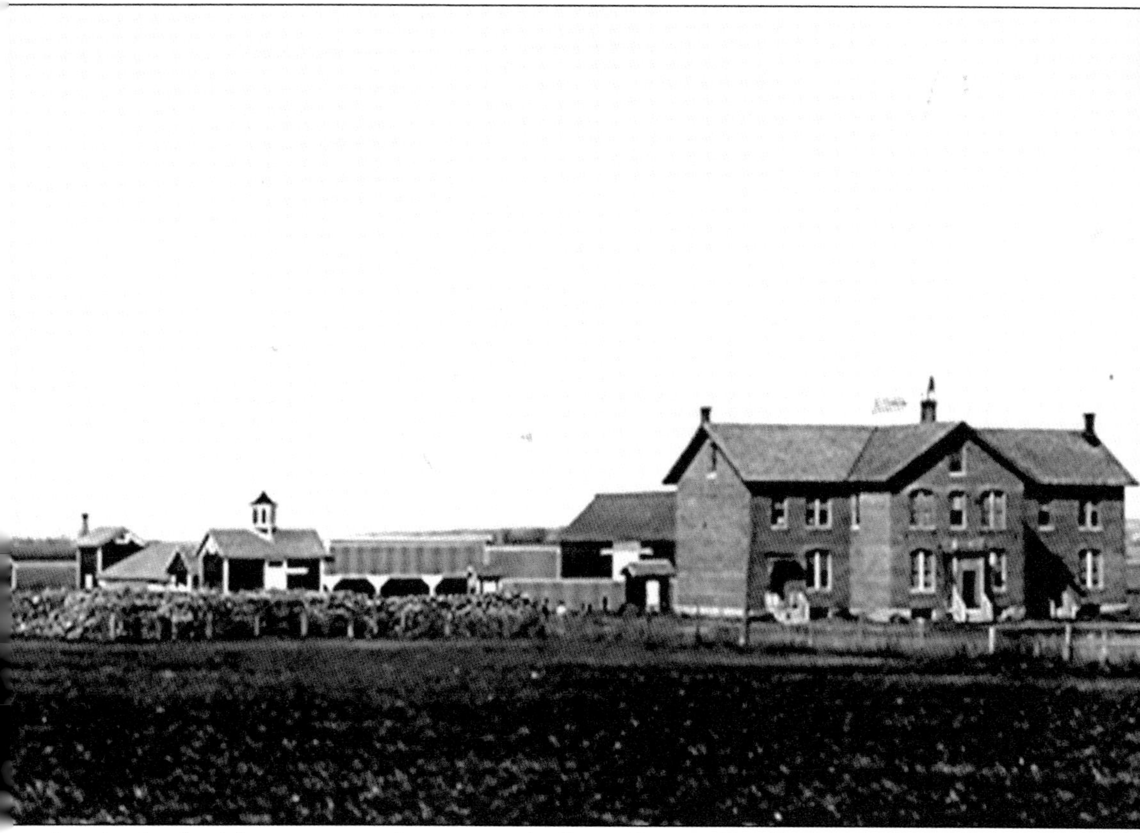

Another brick edifice represents the times at the Dunn County Poor Farm, which was adjacent to the Dunn County Asylum for the Chronic Insane. Both were located about two miles east of Menomonie in the town of Red Cedar, just east of Bullard Hill. They were both under the same management, and farming and dairying were part of the institution's operation. It is worthwhile to note that these two buildings may not be politically correct by the standards of today, but in their time they met a critical social need. (Courtesy of UWSA.)

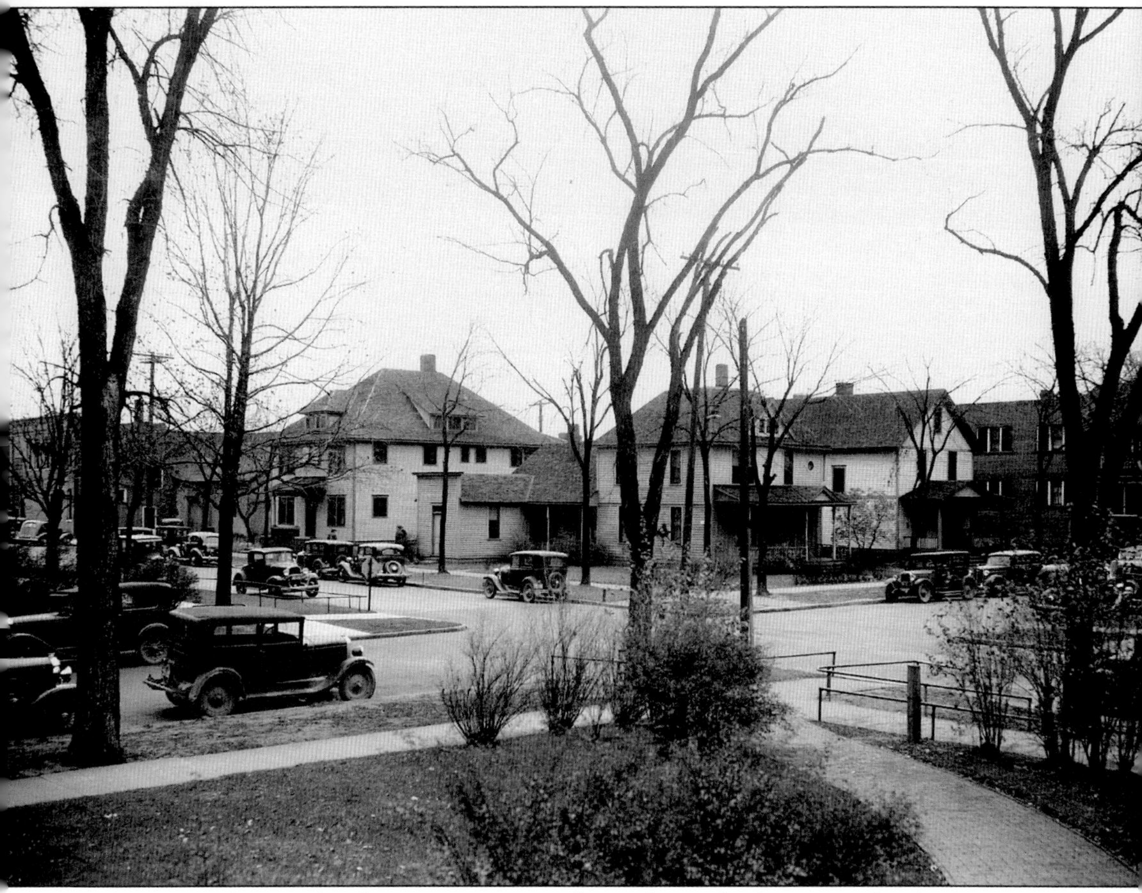

Dr. N. L. Howison lived in Menomonie and was the medical resource for the Dunn County Asylum for the Chronic Insane for 25 years. One of the prevailing philosophies was to provide "healthful work" at the institutions so that their minds "could be directed to normal channels." Dr. Howison's home is shown here. (Courtesy of UWSA.)

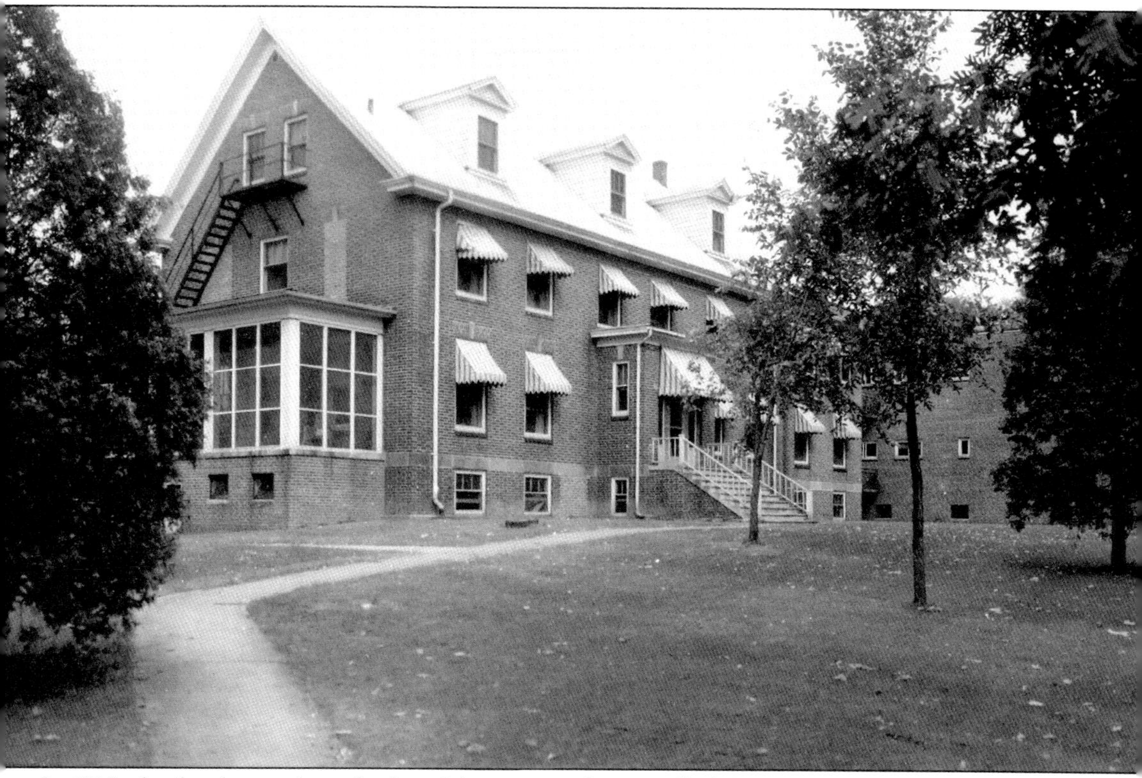

In 1915, the first hospital was built in Menomonie. It was called City Hospital of Menomonie, and for good reason. It was a city institution, and the money that supported it was raised entirely through taxes. There was no resident doctor at the time, but five registered nurses worked under a superintendent, who was also a registered nurse. The first hospital stood between Twelfth and Thirteenth Streets. City Hospital was later replaced by Memorial Hospital. In 1980, Memorial was replaced by the Myrtle Werth Medial Center, and later the Red Cedar Medical Center. (Courtesy of Sofi Doane.)

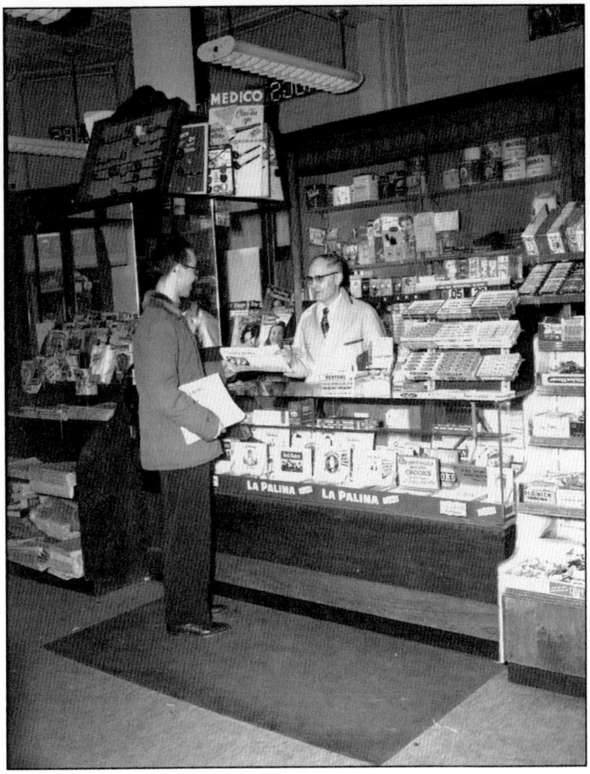

The Obermueller Store was a main source of incidentals and other important items for Menomonie residents. Here a student delivers *The Stoutonia*, the student newspaper for University of Wisconsin–Stout. Note the other magazines and cigars that grace the shelves. It may well be that many of the cigars were manufactured in Menomonie, at the Diamond Cigar Company, which was initially located in the Heller Building on Main Street, now the Lee Building. (Courtesy of UWSM.)

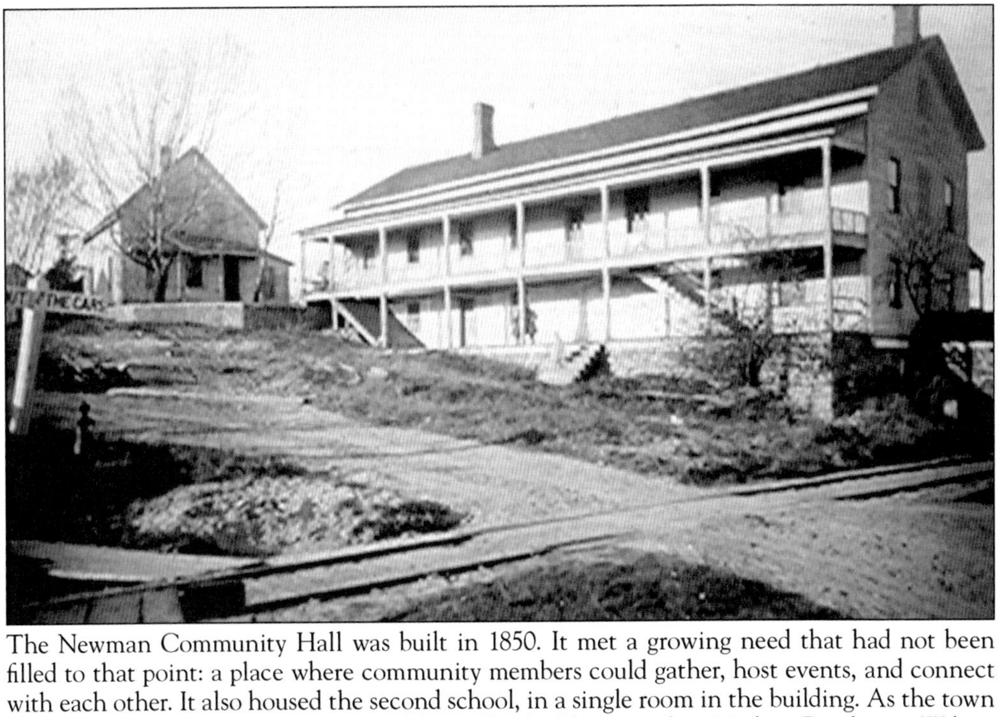

The Newman Community Hall was built in 1850. It met a growing need that had not been filled to that point: a place where community members could gather, host events, and connect with each other. It also housed the second school, in a single room in the building. As the town grew, so did the need for educating children. This building stood on Hudson Road, near Wilson Creek. Hudson Road is now called Meadow Hill Drive. (Courtesy of UWSA.)

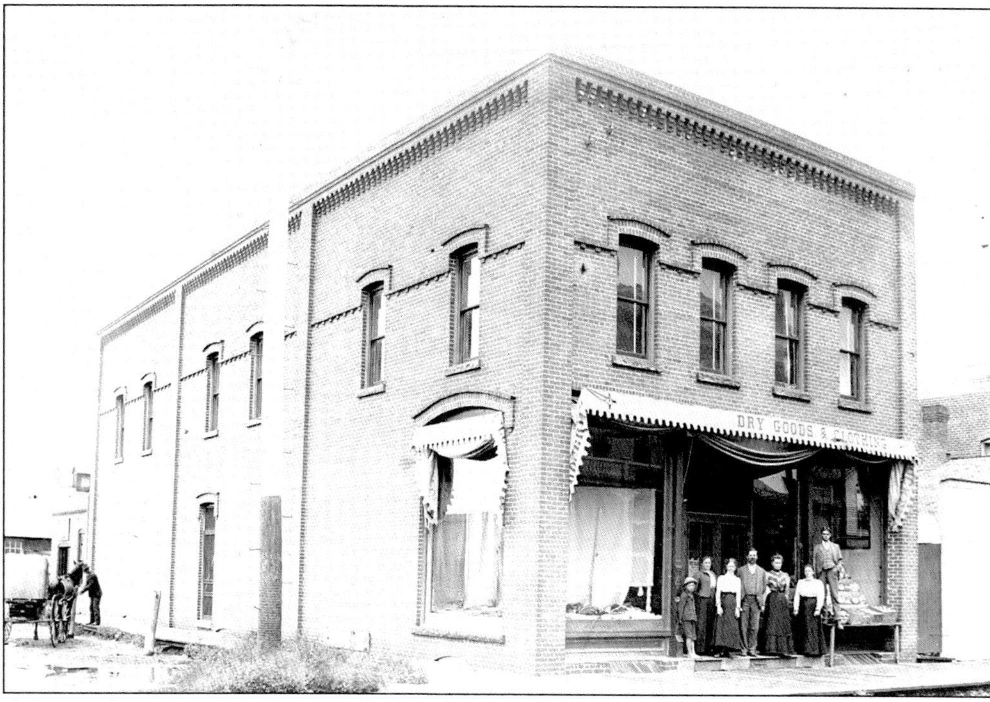

A dry goods store was worth its weight in gold during the years when clothes were handmade rather than store-bought. Here the people behind the store pose in front of their downtown building.

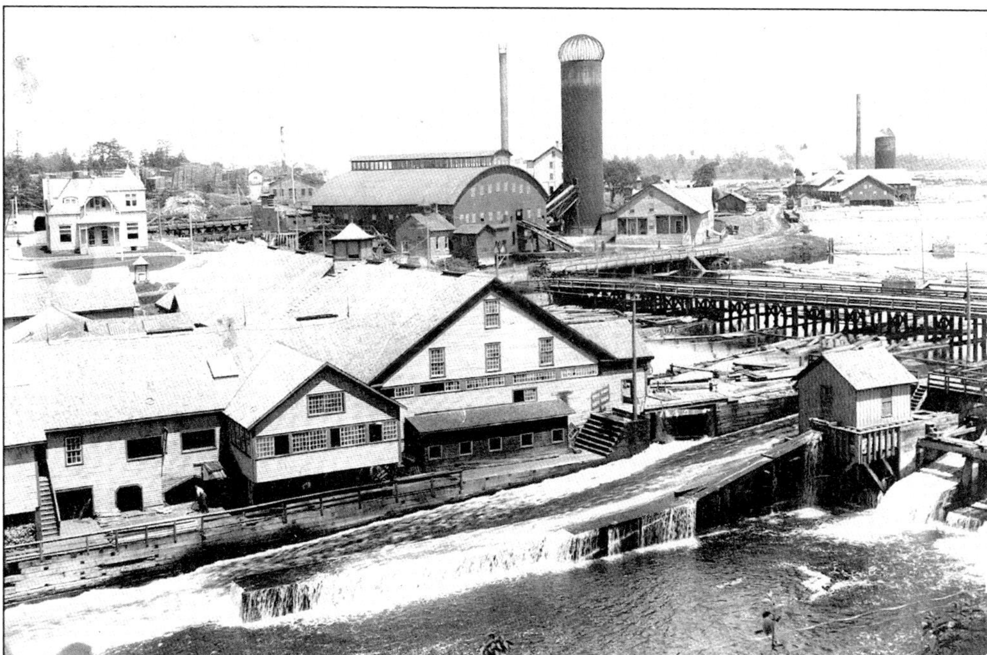

Pictured is the Knapp, Stout and Co. Company operation. The headquarters in Menomonie housed the lumber company, once known as the largest white pine lumber company in the world. (Courtesy of UWSA.)

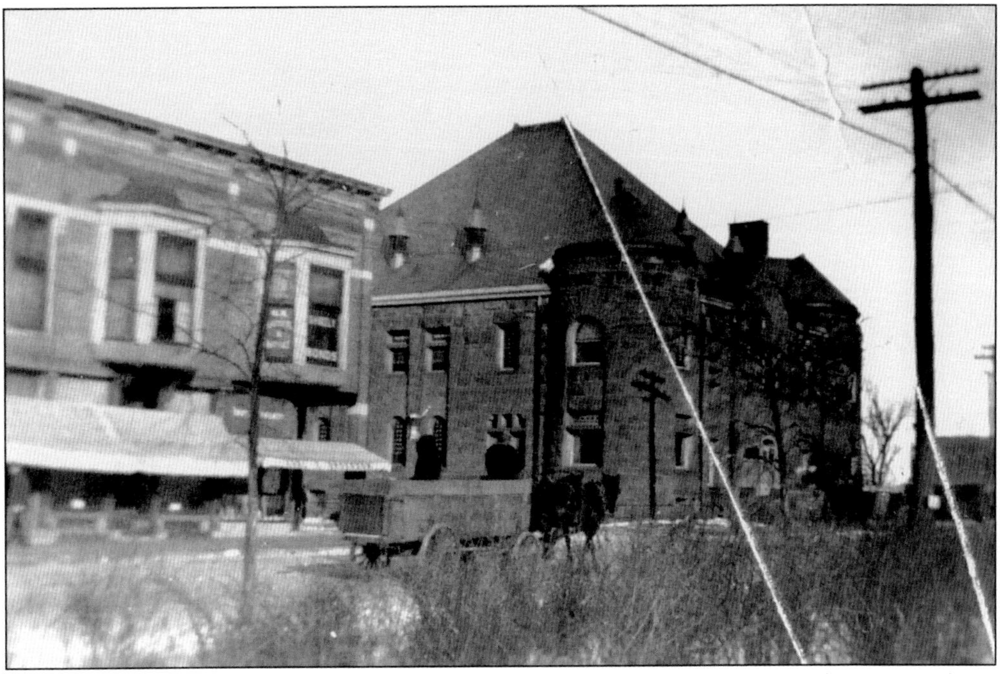

A horse-drawn wagon works its way down Main Street. The Mabel Tainter Theatre stands on the left, as much a hallmark today as it was in the late 19th century. (Courtesy of UWSA.)

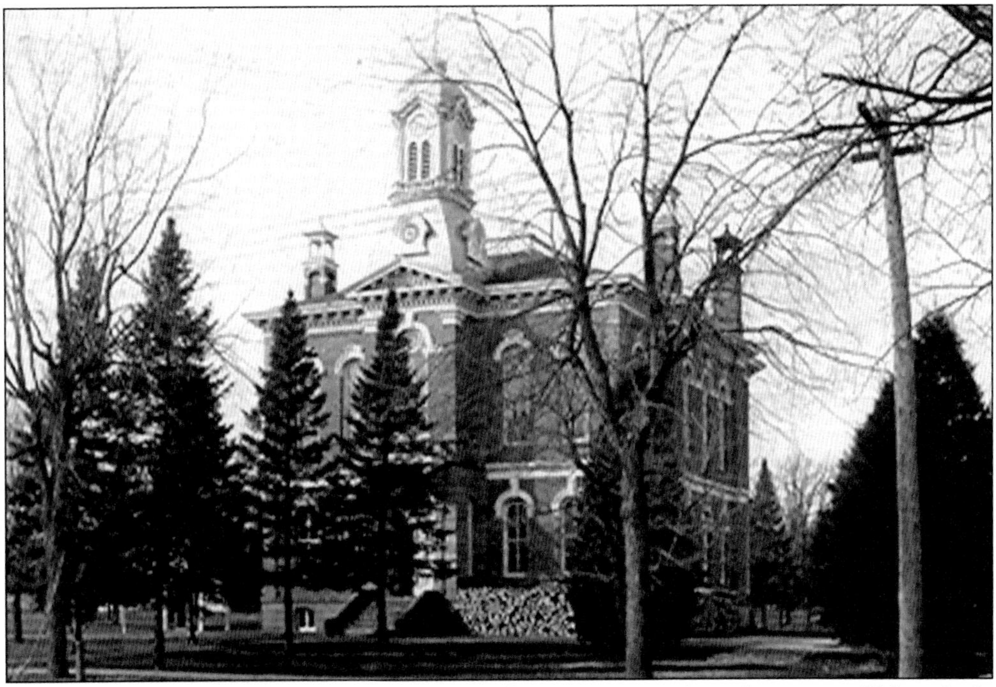

This beautiful, ornate Italianate Victorian courthouse once stood in what is now Wilson Park, just south and east of the downtown area. It was built in 1871 and was a gift of Thomas B. Wilson. (Courtesy of Sofi Doane.)

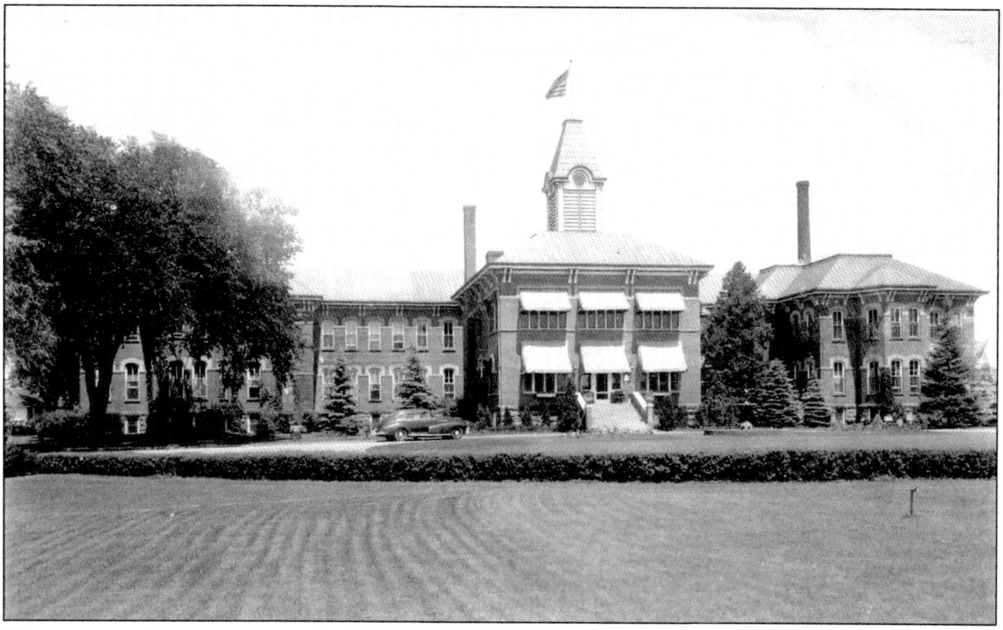

This postcard captures another important institution in Menomonie, the Dunn County Hospital. Today the institution lives on as Dunn Company Health Care Center, although the original building is gone. (Courtesy of Sofi Doane.)

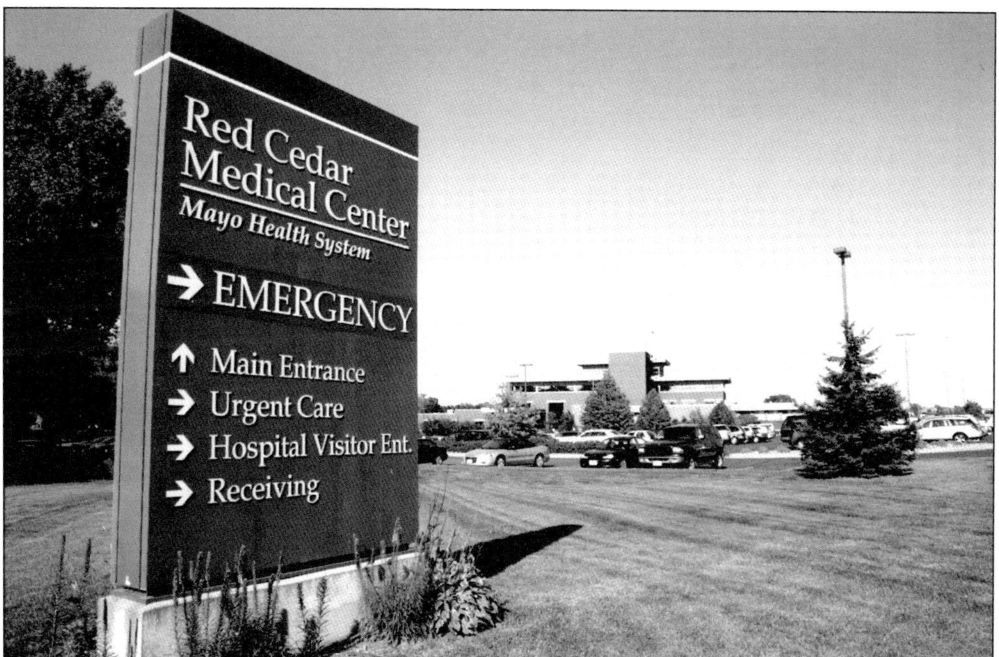

The Red Cedar Medical Center is now a part of the Mayo Health System. It offers a wide range of medical services and is highly regarded within the community. (Courtesy of Bruce Dybvik.)

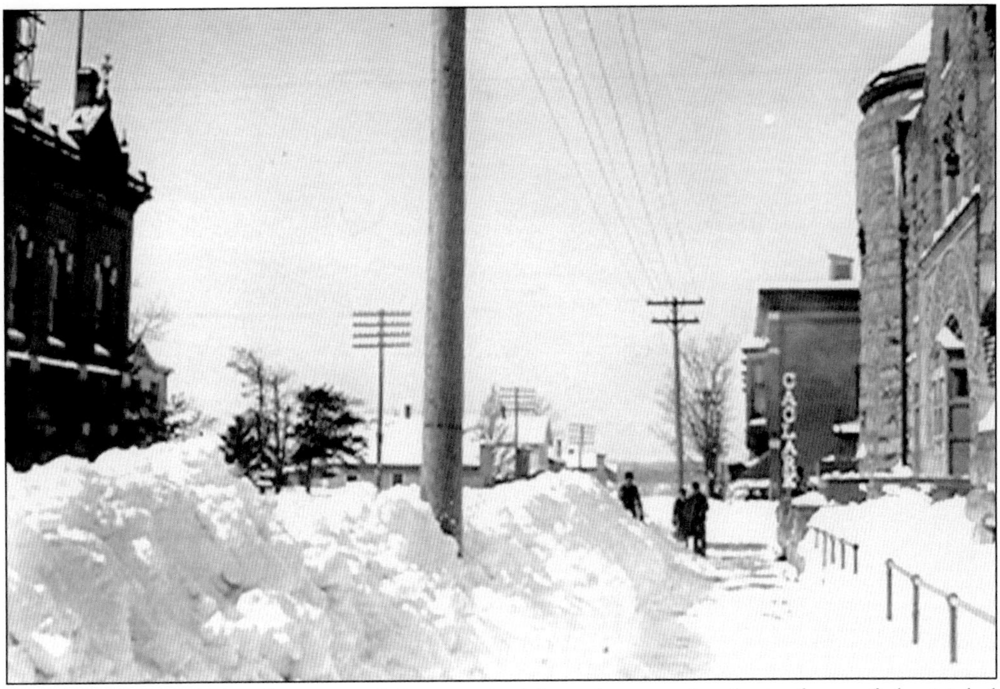

Electricity has come to downtown Menomonie. Note the snow banks in front of the Mabel Tainter Theatre. (Courtesy of UWSA.)

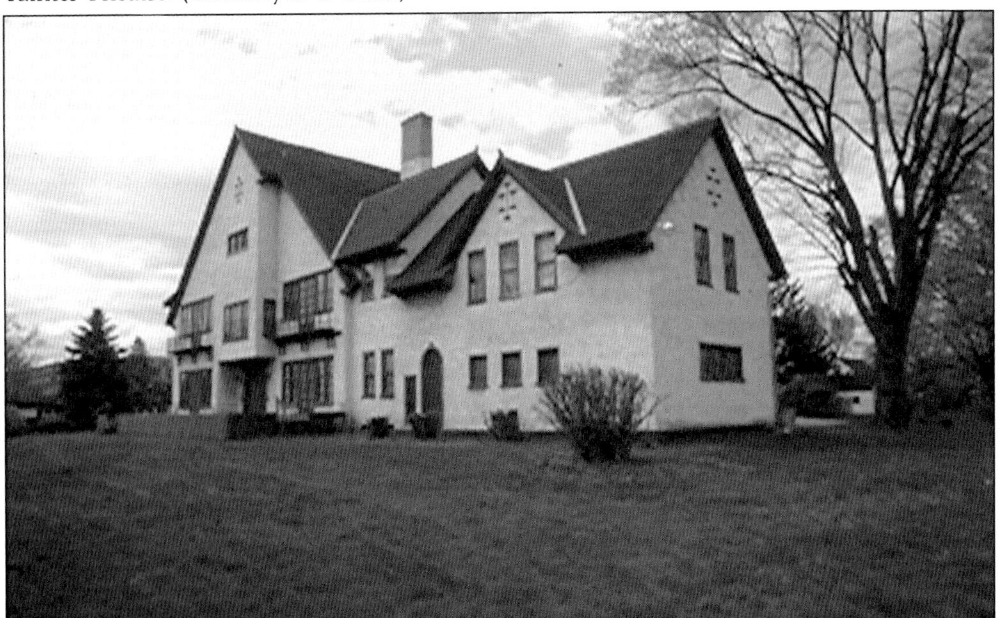

In 1976, local residents John and Jackie Dotseth, completed the restoration of the original Wilson/Stout home and opened it to the public. It continues to be an important source of information for tourists and residents wishing to walk through Menomonie history. Known as the Wilson Place Museum, it makes history come alive with its furnishings from the past and its guided tours. (Courtesy of UWSM.)

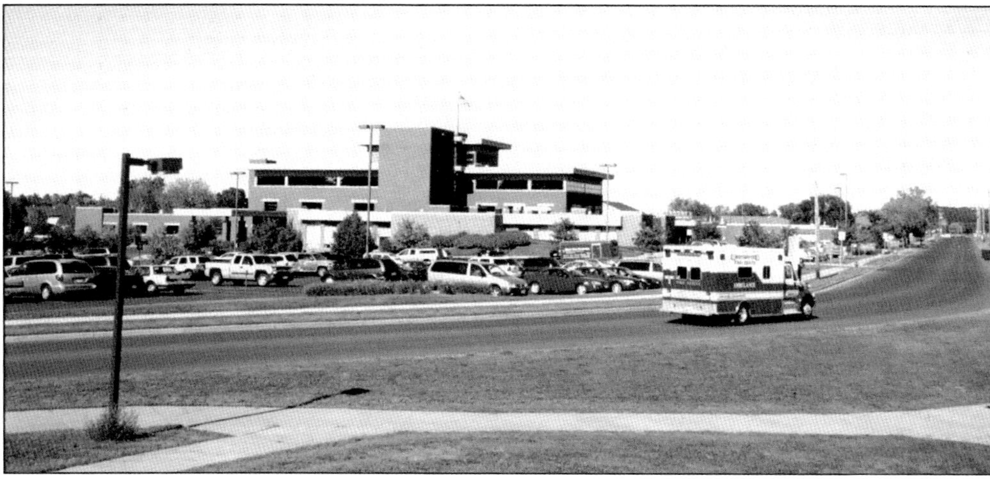

Here is a current look at the Red Cedar Medical Center, complete with ambulance. This view is from the west, just off of Highway 29, on the west side of town. (Courtesy of Bruce Dybvik.)

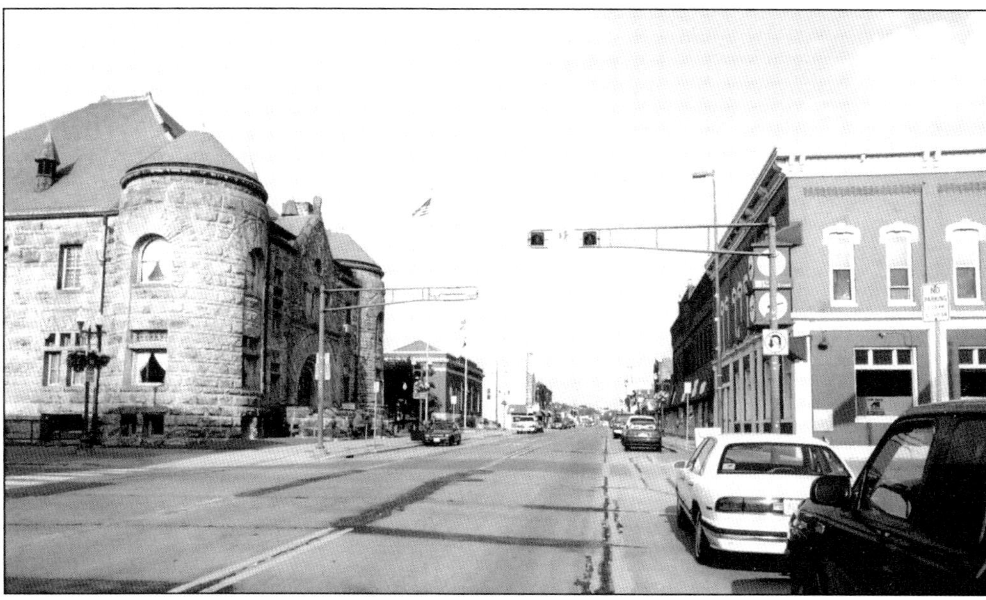

Two historic buildings face each other on Main Street in 2006, the Mabel Tainter Theatre (left) and First National Bank (right). Downtown Menomonie has seen ups and downs with the advent of malls, development north of town, and increase in retail stores in nearby Eau Claire. However a strong coalition of independent business owners and interested citizens continue to expand opportunities for the downtown, in partnership with the strong arts community in the area. (Courtesy of Bruce Dybvik.)

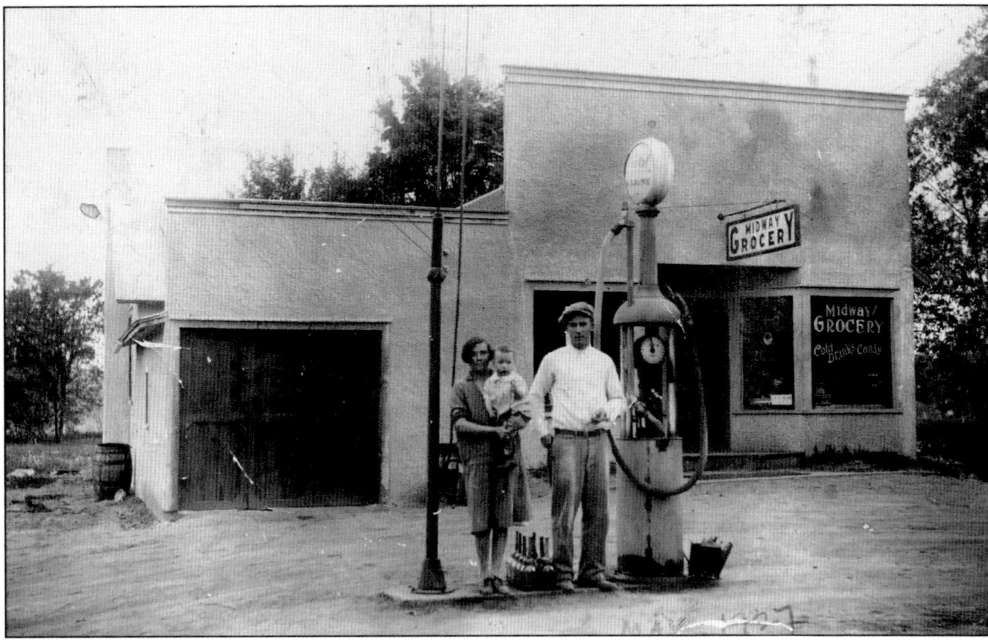

Midway Grocery was the place to buy cold drinks, candy, and many other items. Albert and Irene Oberle owned the store, and later passed it on to their daughter, Sue Oberle Lechler. It is now a popular restaurant and bar known as Dean and Sue's. (Courtesy of Sofi Doane.)

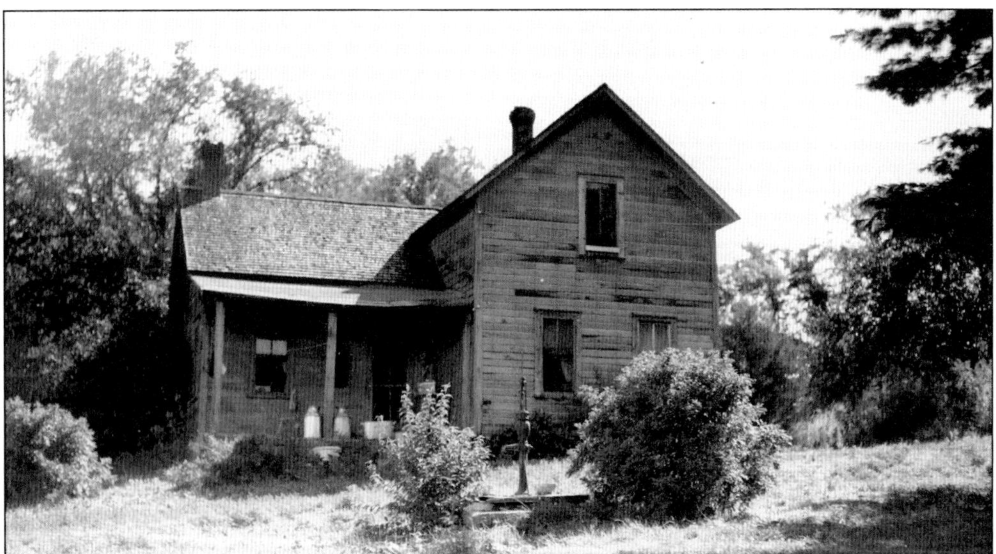

This classic rural farmhouse was located on the west side of Menomonie. Many of these homes and farms have been lost to the past, but others continue to provide comfortable housing and a connection to what went before. (Courtesy of Sofi Doane.)

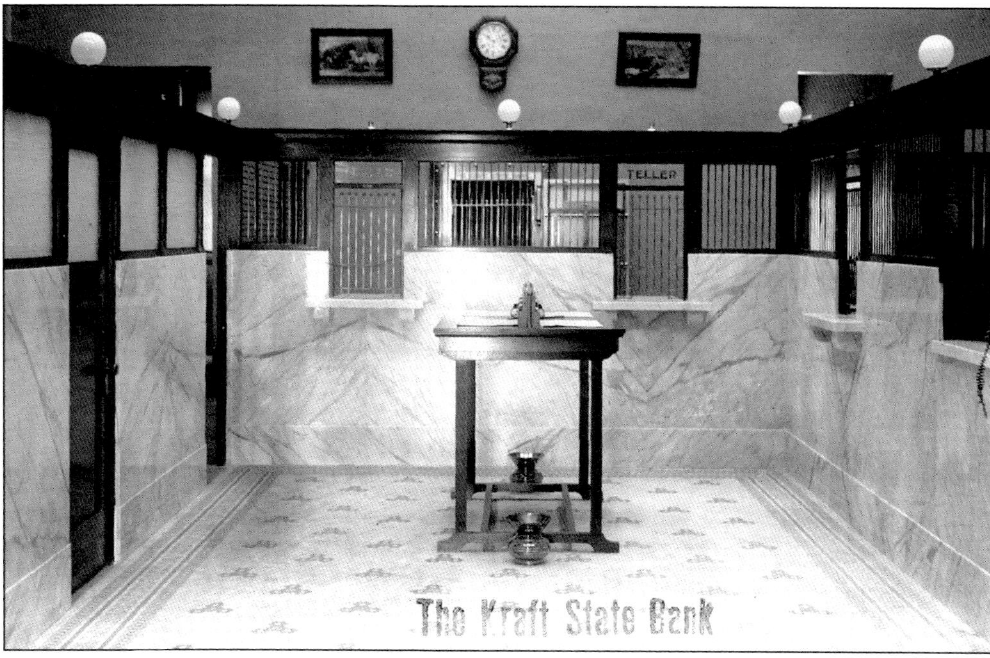

Captured in this postcard is interior of the Kraft State Bank, where, on the morning of October 20, 1931, a robbery took place that would cost bank teller James Kraft his life. Frank Webber and Charles Harmon, two of the four robbers, died of their wounds. The remaining two robbers, Francis Keating and Tommy Holden, were caught eight months later, in Missouri. It was later found that the robbers had escaped from Leavenworth Prison. (Courtesy of Sofi Doane.)

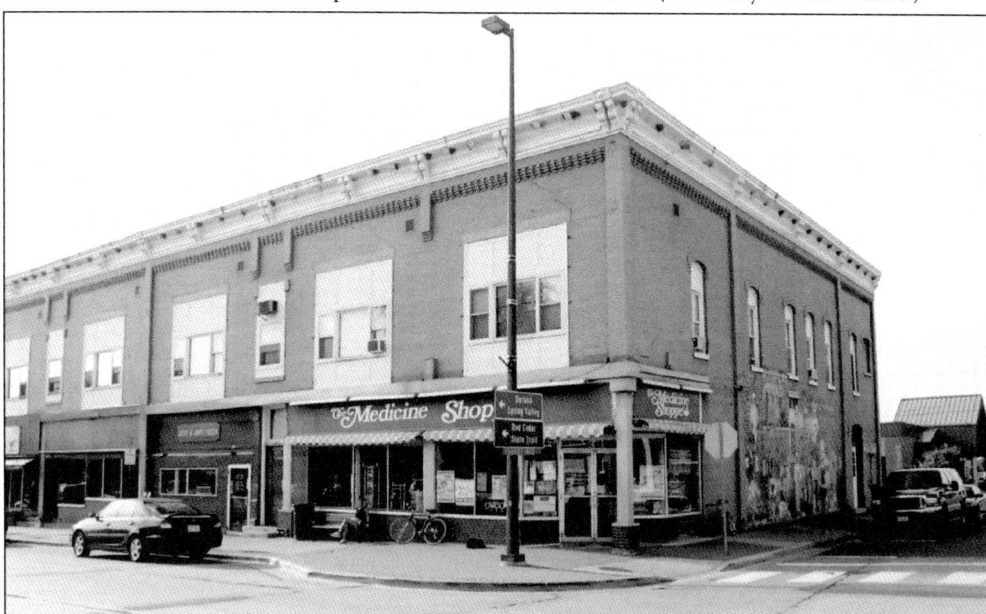

Lee Drug Store, or as it is now known, the Medicine Shop, is seen here in 2006. The fading mural can still be seen on the east side of the building, a tribute to those who spent long, arduous hours building the Mabel Tainter Theatre across the street. The Lee Building was once the Heller Building, home to the Diamond Cigar Company.

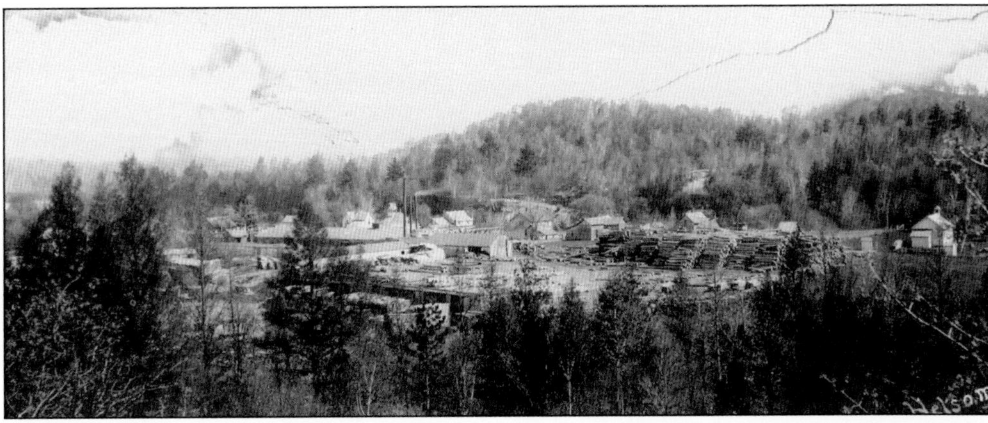

Here is a long view of the Knapp, Stout, and Co. Company lumberyards. The amount of lumber that passed down the Red Cedar River to be milled is vast, and the size of trees felled, immense.

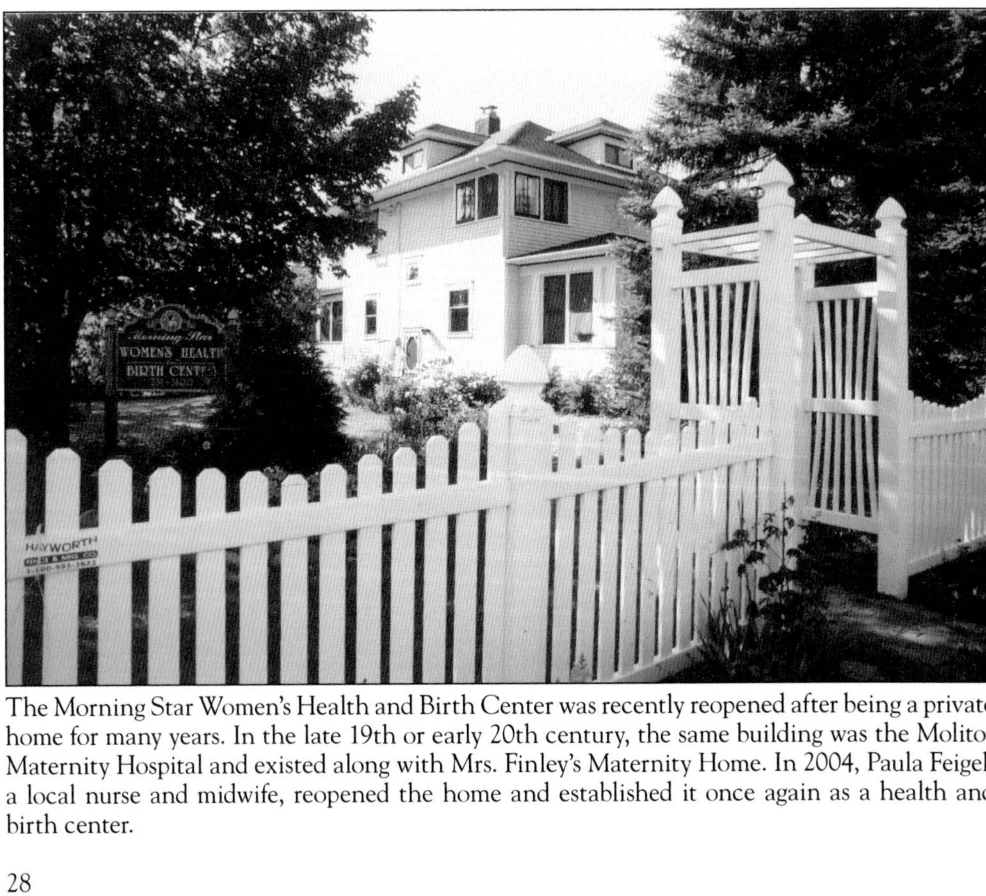

The Morning Star Women's Health and Birth Center was recently reopened after being a private home for many years. In the late 19th or early 20th century, the same building was the Molitor Maternity Hospital and existed along with Mrs. Finley's Maternity Home. In 2004, Paula Feigel, a local nurse and midwife, reopened the home and established it once again as a health and birth center.

Two

PEOPLE

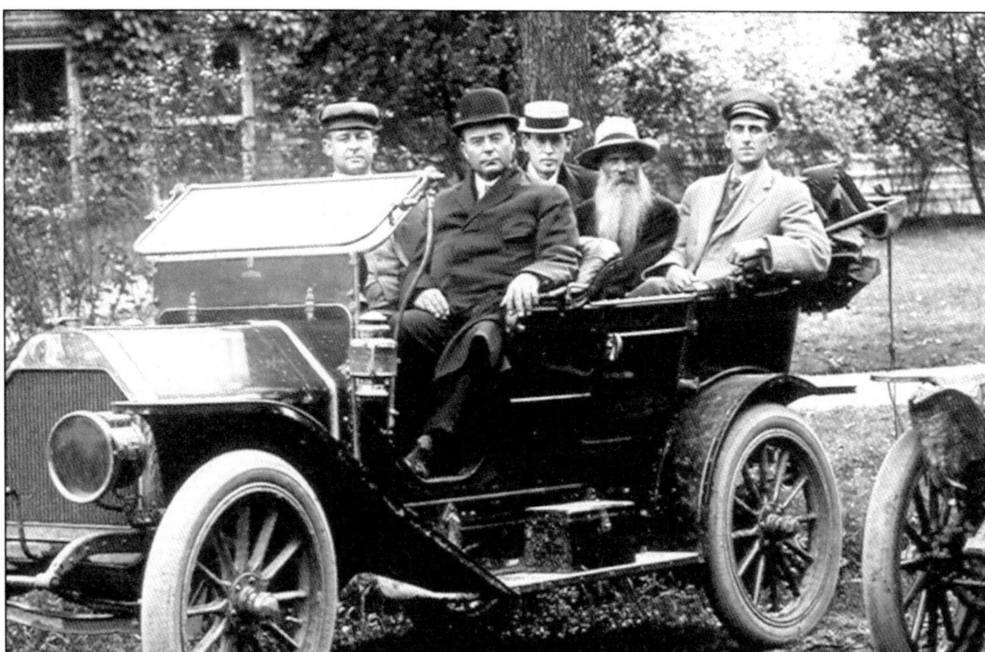

The men of Knapp, Stout, and Co. Company pose in their automobile for a group photograph. (Courtesy of UWSM.)

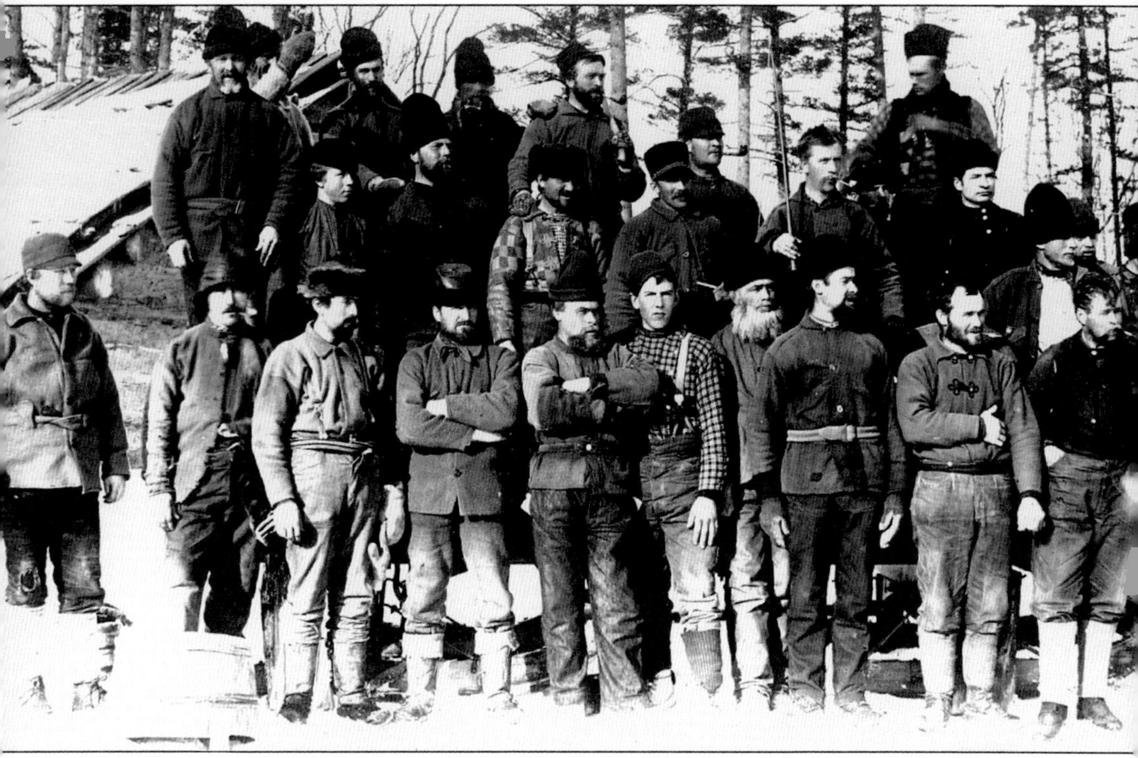

Lumbermen were a rugged bunch. Their lives were times of hard work and hard play, making many of the lumberjacks appear intimidating, especially when seen together in a group. They worked long, dangerous days, felling trees, dragging them to be floated down the river, and, the most dangerous task of all, driving them down the river to be milled. After the milling process, boards were sent even further down river via ships, to various markets along the way. (Courtesy of Mary Ramsey, UWSA.)

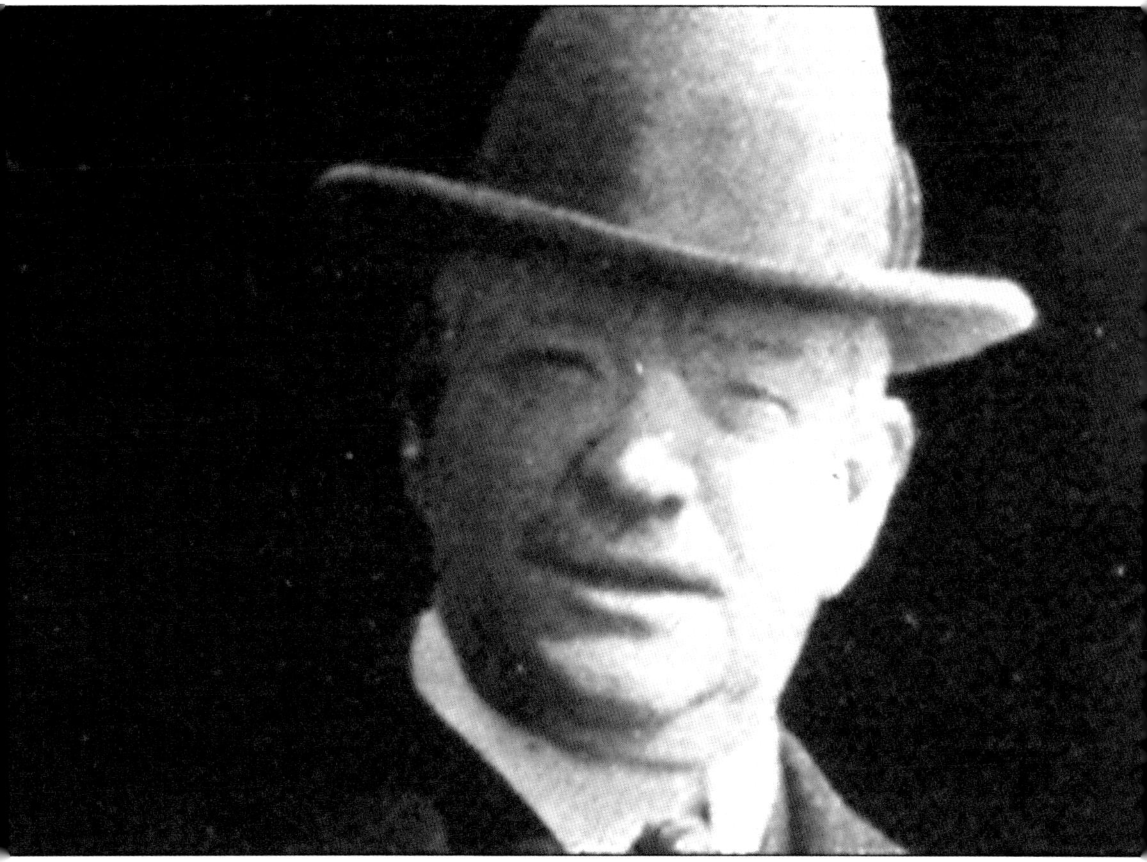

Louis Tainter was the son of Capt. Andrew Tainter, one of the four primary members of the Knapp, Stout, and Co. Company. Louis was born in Menomonie in 1862, to Andrew and Bertha Tainter. He attended public school in Menomonie, then the State Normal School in River Falls, before graduating from Eastman Business School in New York. He later returned to Menomonie where he worked in the Knapp, Stout, and Co. Company, in charge of logging operations. He was known to be an ethical, genial, and energetic man. His legacy lives on today in the beautiful limestone building now owned by the University of Wisconsin–Stout, on the corner of Broadway Street and Crescent Avenue. (Courtesy of UWSA.)

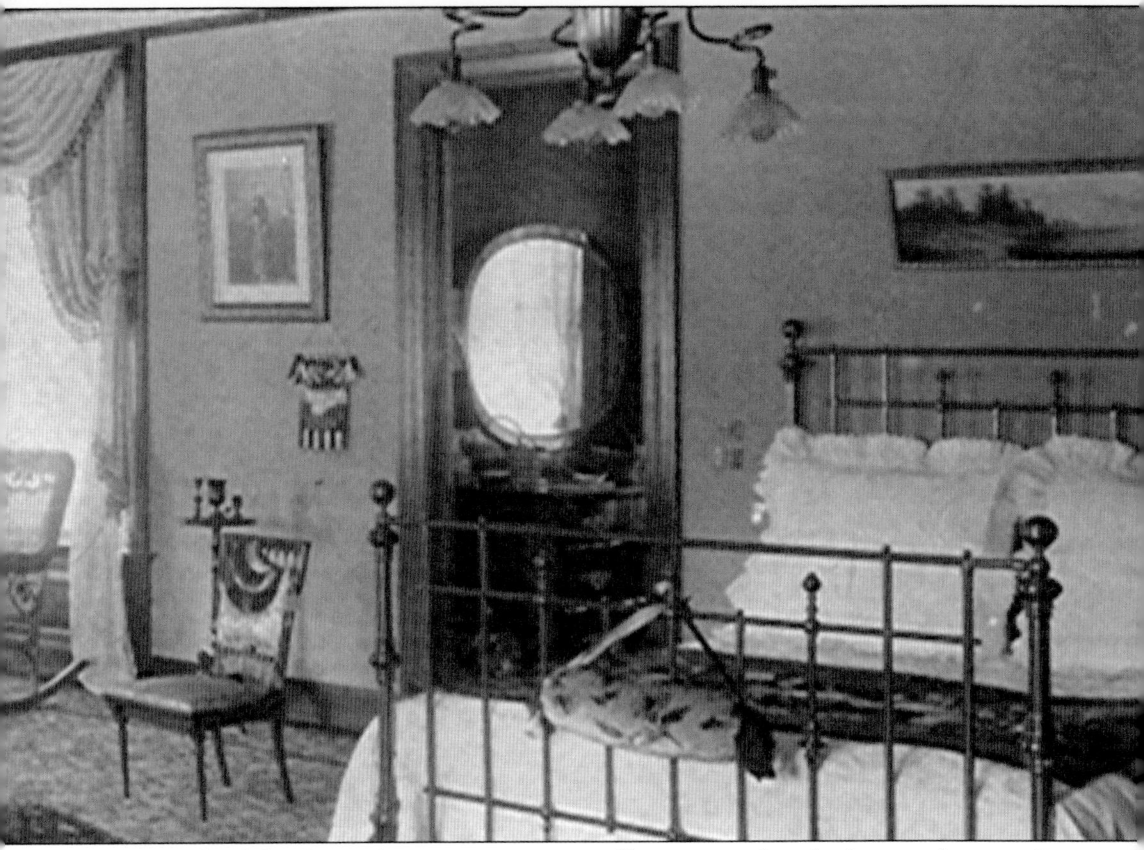

The inside of the Tainter house was an ornate affair compared to the homes of most ordinary citizens of the day. It was built with lumber from Knapp, Stout, and Co. Company, along with furnishings gathered during Andrew Tainters's many business trips across the country. It stood near the homes of the other business owners, and near the site of the lumber operation headquarters. (Courtesy of UWSM.)

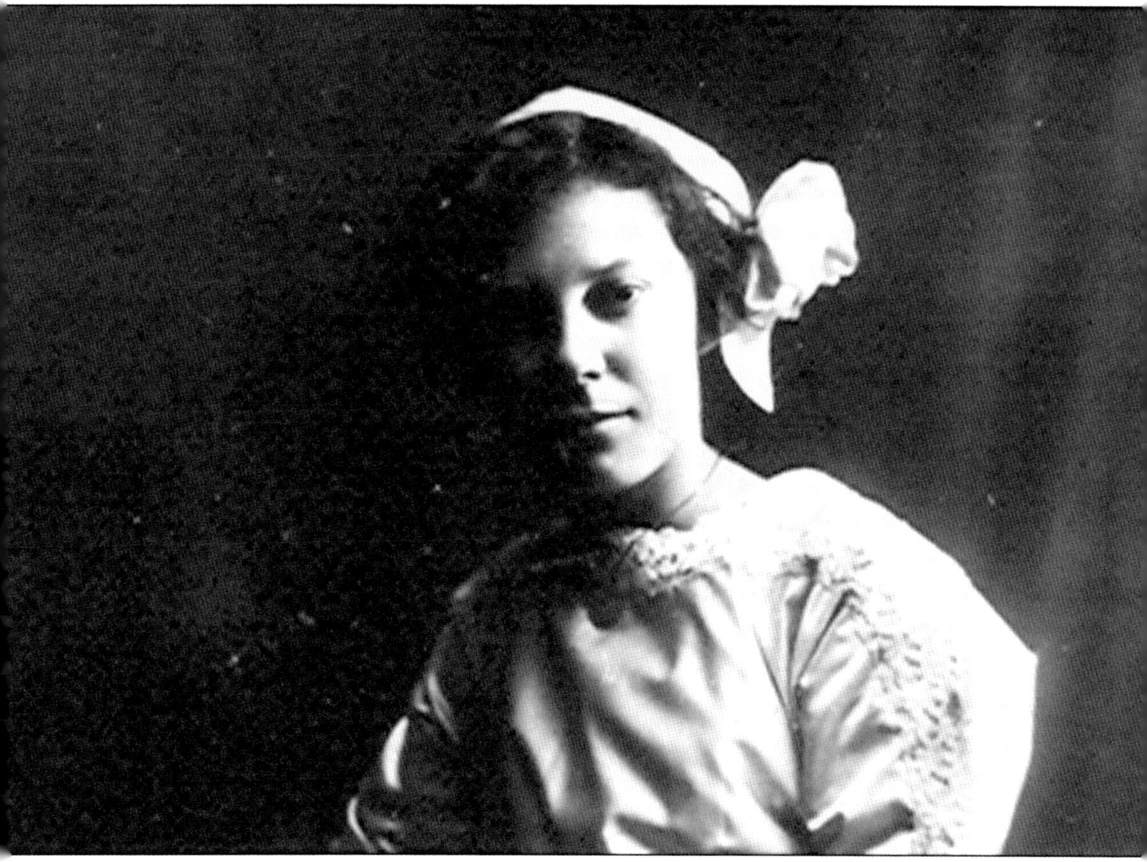

Shown here is a portrait of Bertha Tainter, wife of Capt. Andrew Tainter and mother of Mabel, for whom the Mabel Tainter Theatre was built. Bertha (Lucas) Tainter was born and educated in New York. It was said that her grandfather served with Washington at Valley Forge. She moved to the Waukesha area of Wisconsin, after marrying William Lesure, in 1845. He died shortly afterwards, and in 1855 she moved to Menomonie with her parents. It was here that she met and eventually married Capt. Andrew Tainter. They had four children, Louis, Mabel, Ruth, and Fannie. Bertha was known to be an educated, interesting, and caring woman, who took great interest in current events. She died in St. Paul, Minnesota, in 1916. (Courtesy of UWSA.)

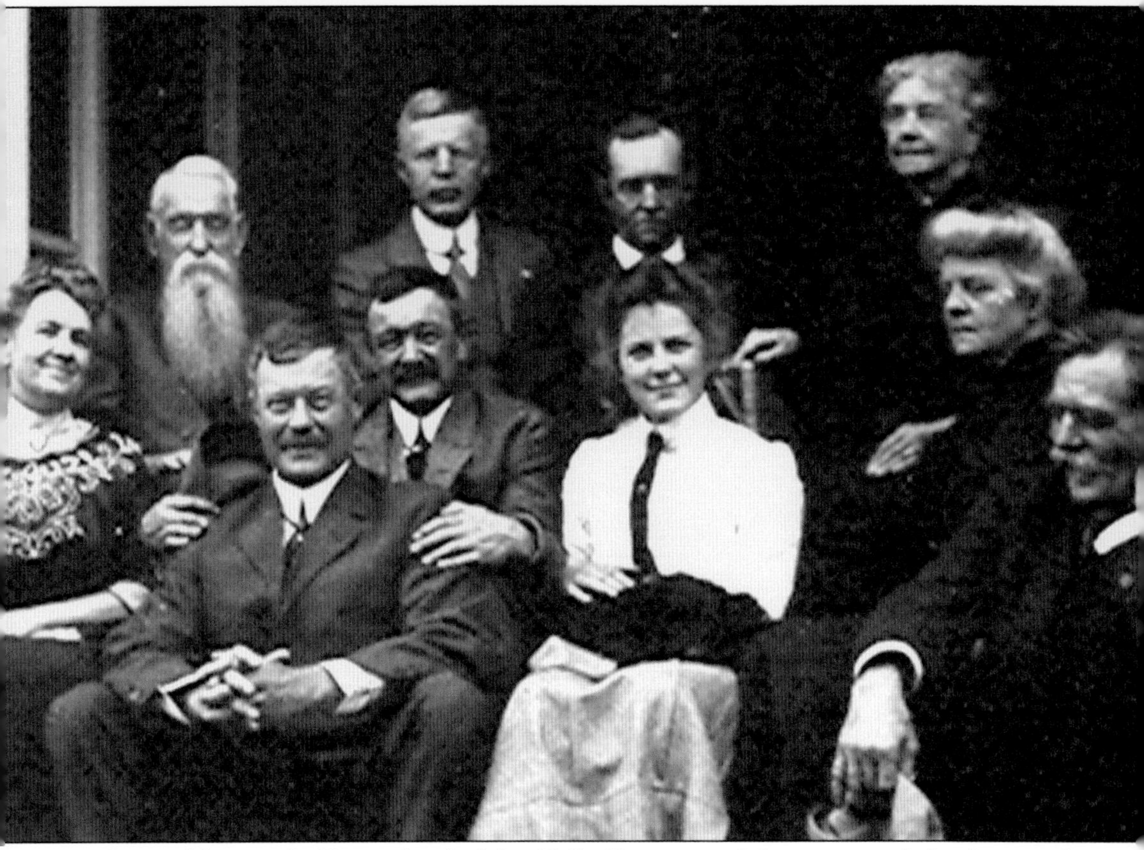

Pictured here is the Knapp family. John Holly Knapp presided over not only his business but his family as well. His was an interesting heritage, having grown up in New York state and playing as a child with a neighbor, Nashauskuk, son of Native American chief Black Hawk. He became familiar with the Sauk language and was considered to be an excellent orator. He came to Menomonie in 1846, bringing with him his considerable skills and education. He was afflicted with an unknown illness much of his life, which caused him to search far and wide for cures. Despite this difficulty, he was president of Knapp, Stout, and Co. Company for years, as well as a dedicated family man and respected member of the Menomonie community. (Courtesy of UWSA.)

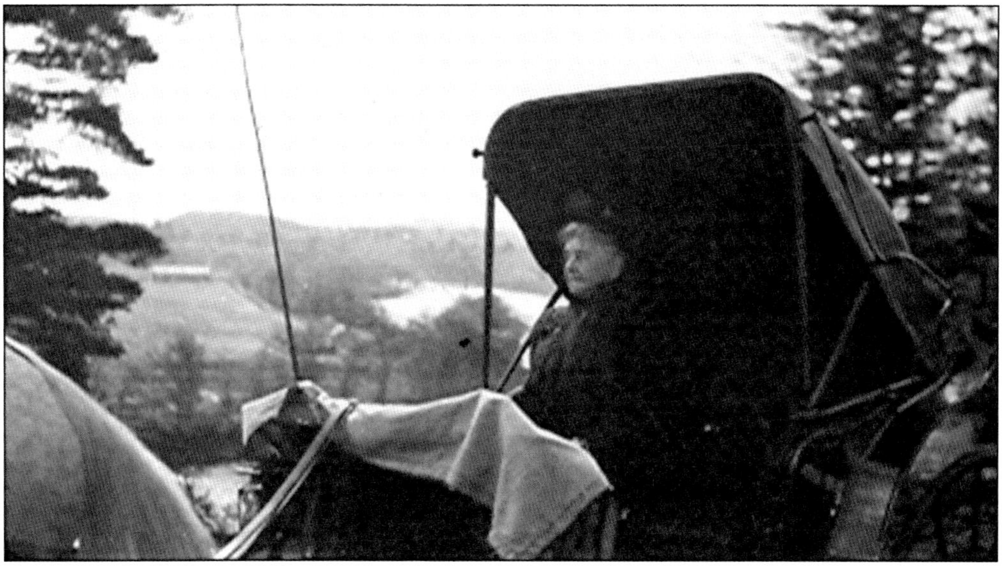

Caroline (Field) Knapp takes a buggy ride through the beautiful rolling hills of Dunn County on her 81st birthday. Daughter of the prominent New York family, Theodore and Elmira Field, Caroline married John Holly Knapp Jr. in 1849. She was a graduate of Mount Holyoke, in Massachusetts, and had met John Knapp while visiting the west. The two had one son, Henry Eno Knapp, before she died in 1854. (Courtesy of UWSA.)

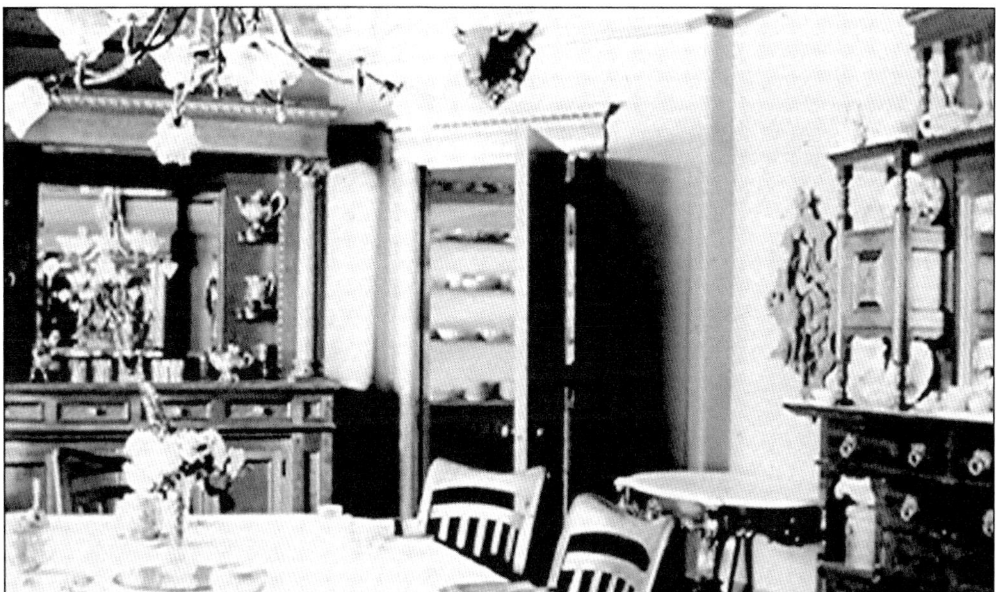

Here is a view of the Knapp dining room. Note the ornate furniture with the animal head trophy above the door in the corner. Although John Holly Knapp owned and comanaged part of Knapp, Stout, and Company, he maintained his home in Fort Madison, Iowa, until 1863. He then moved his family, by riverboat, to Menomonie where he built a luxurious (for the times) home near the site of the headquarters of lumber operations. Knapp was on the road much of the time, selling lumber or negotiating deals, so his family occupied the home more than he did for many years. (Courtesy of UWSA.)

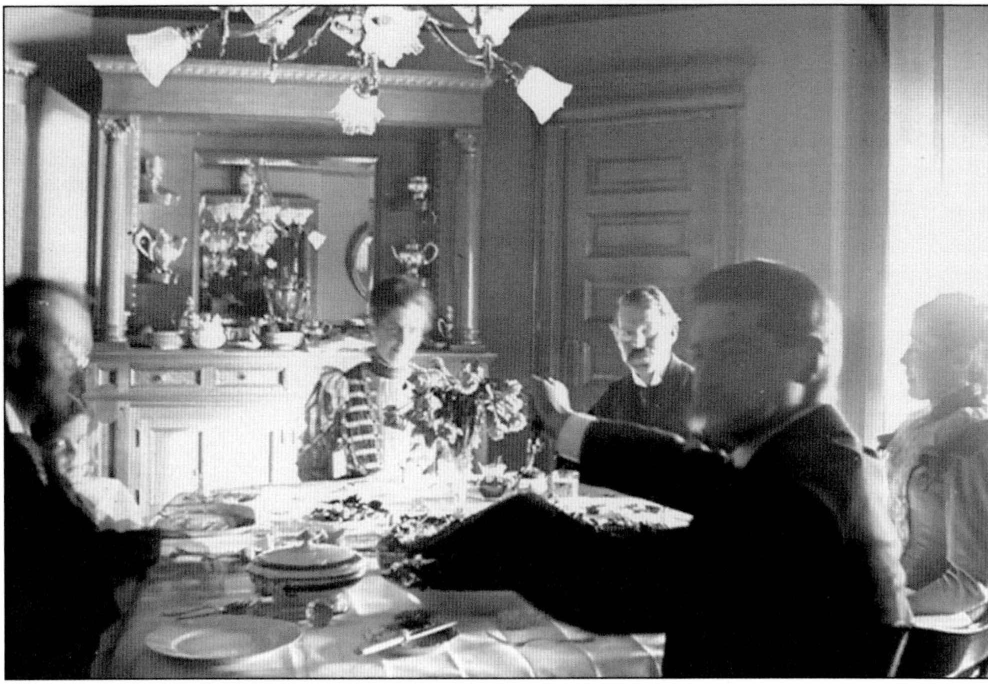

The Knapp family enjoys a meal together in their dining room. The animal head, in the previous photograph (page 35), appears to be removed for this picture. (Courtesy of UWSA.)

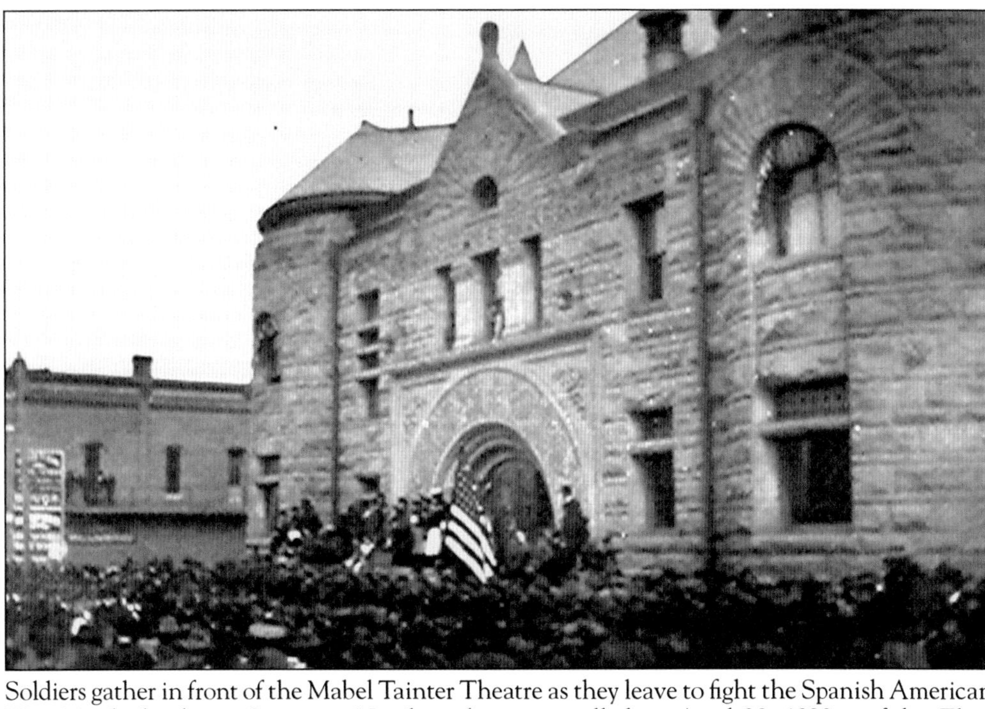

Soldiers gather in front of the Mabel Tainter Theatre as they leave to fight the Spanish American War. No doubt this is Company H, when they were called on April 28, 1898, to fight. They fought one battle in Puerto Rico in August of 1898. There were no casualties in the company, but reports were that illness was rampant. (Courtesy of UWSM.)

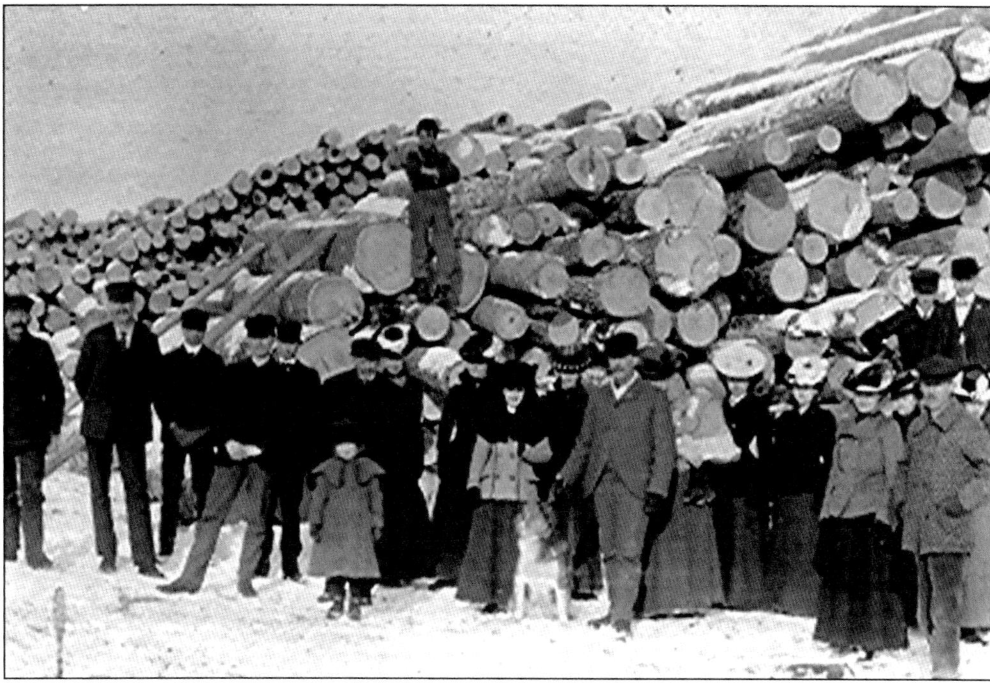

Photographs such as this one provide a look both at the amount and size of lumber that moved through the Knapp, Stout, and Co. Company process. It also serves as evidence to the importance of lumbering in the region. Knapp, Stout, and Co. Company was once the largest lumbering operation in the world. (Courtesy of UWSA.)

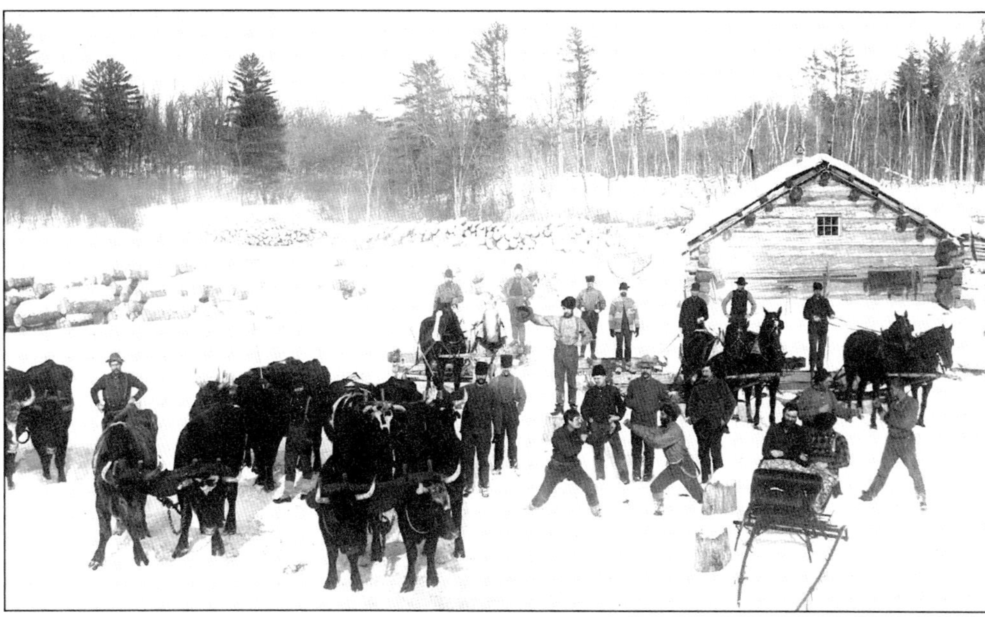

Lumbermen were a volatile, energetic bunch, and fights often broke out, whether to settle a grudge or just to practice the fine art of fisticuffs for future use. (Courtesy of UWSA.)

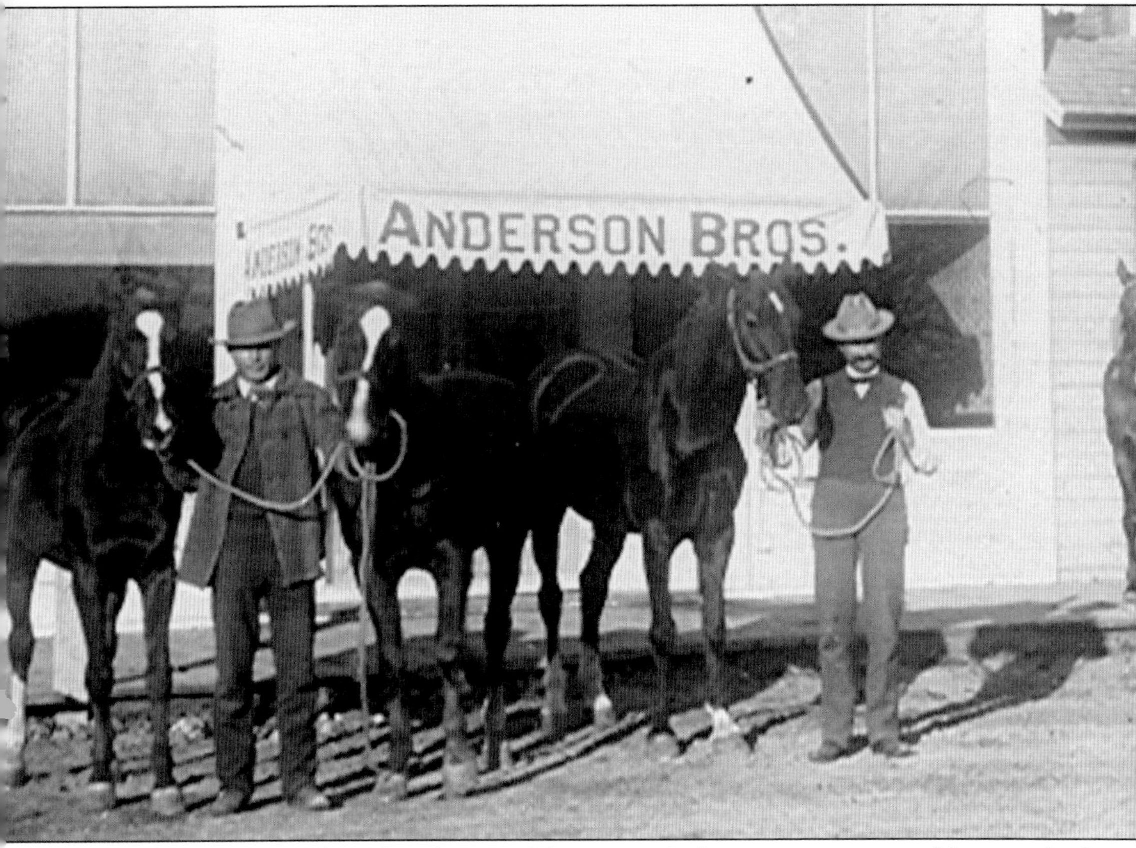

Lumbering was not the only industry in Menomonie. Industries grew up around liveries—brick making, piano making, cigar making, and many other related small businesses supported the residents. Liveries were important to transportation before cars came onto the scene. Capt. Andrew Tainter also brought well-known horse people to town with his highly innovative Oaklawn Farm and racetrack. (Courtesy of UWSA.)

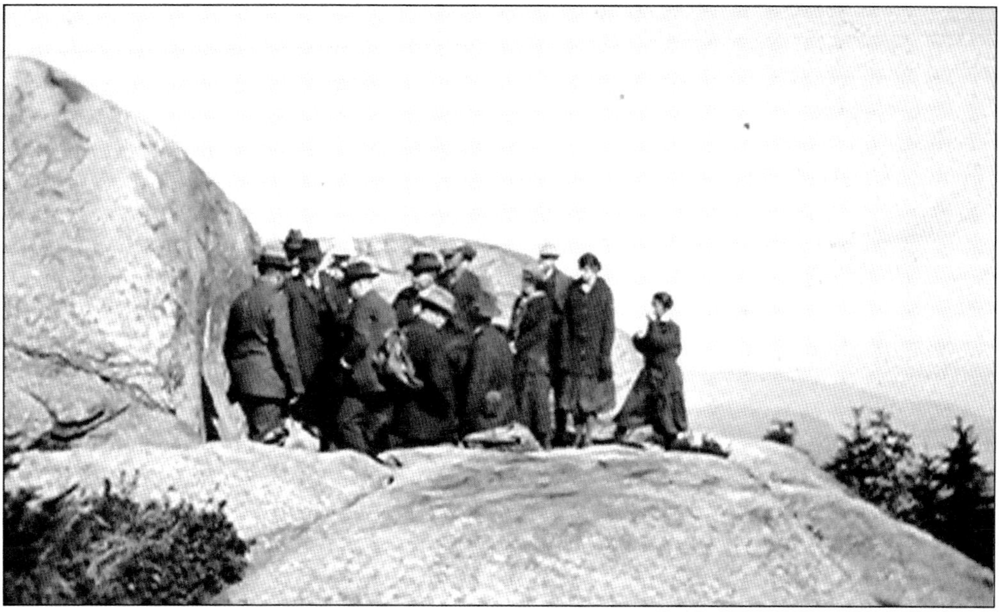

Louis Smith Tainter, son of Capt. Andrew Tainter, was born in Menomonie in 1862. He lived there for many years, but later in life moved first to California, then Massachusetts. He died in 1920 in Boston, and his will dictated that he be "cremated and buried in an indestructible container in a suitable excavation hollowed out of solid rock on Whiteface Mountain in New Hampshire." This photograph shows that his wishes were carried out on the part of those who cared deeply for this genial, friendly, and educated man. (Courtesy of UWSA.)

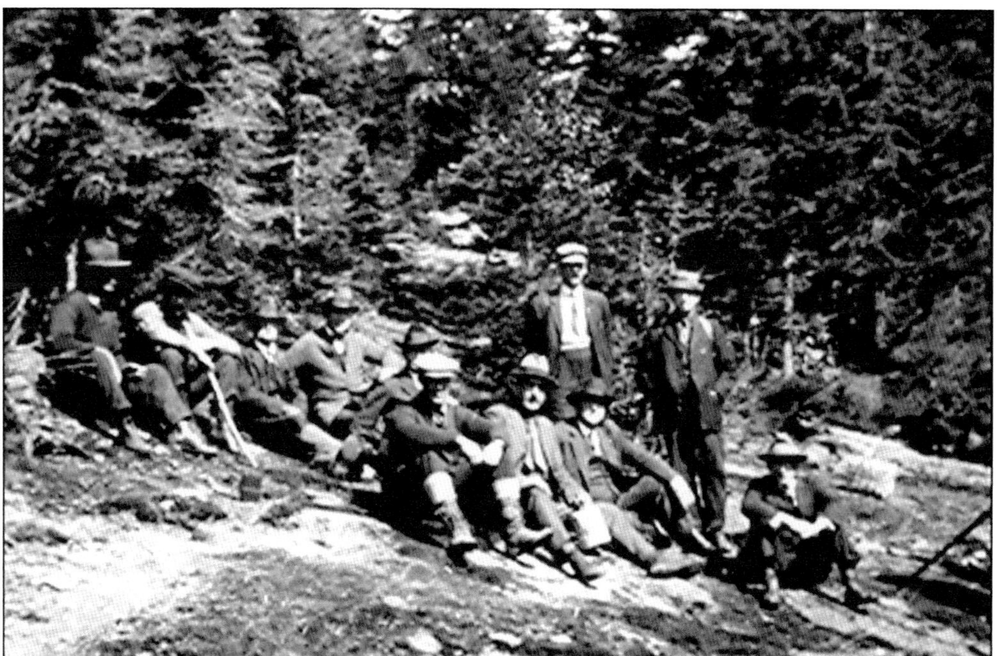

The burial party that carried out the wishes of Louis Smith Tainter is shown taking a break after their very difficult task. The location is Whiteface Mountain in New Hampshire. (Courtesy of UWSA.)

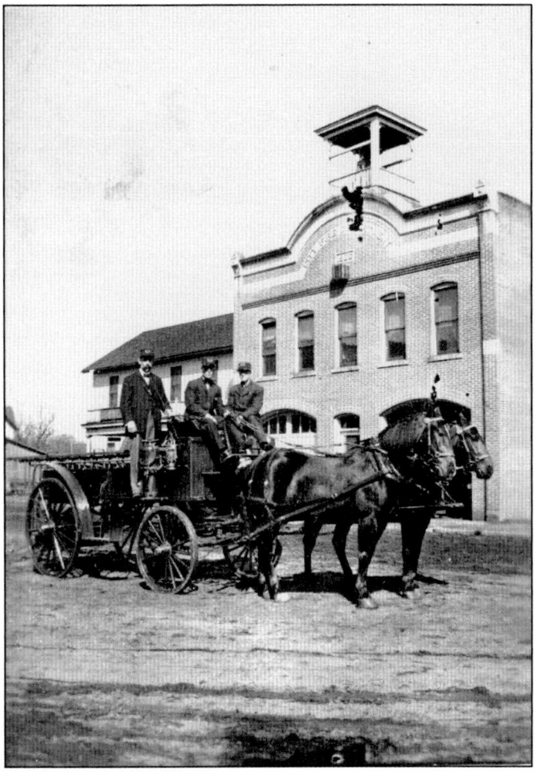

From the 1890s to the 1950s, the city hall, police station, and fire station were all adjoining facilities. There were several major fires in Menomonie during the 1800s and early 1900s, including the Stori Concert Hall, buildings in the 300 block of Main Street, and the first Stout Manual Training and Domestic Science and General School. The opening of the new fire station in 1906 was a cause for community celebration. (Courtesy of UWSA.)

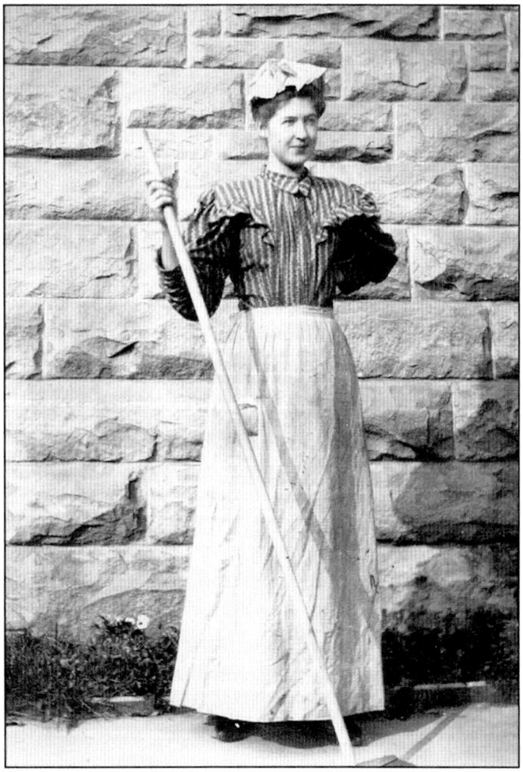

It is not clear whether this woman is caretaking the Mabel Tainter Theatre grounds, or readying herself for a theatrical production. She stands in front of the building that still stands today, looking the same as when it was built in the late 1880s. However, a renovation project is scheduled to begin in 2007, to add handicapped accessible doors, restrooms, and an updated entry from the backside of the building. (Courtesy of UWSA.)

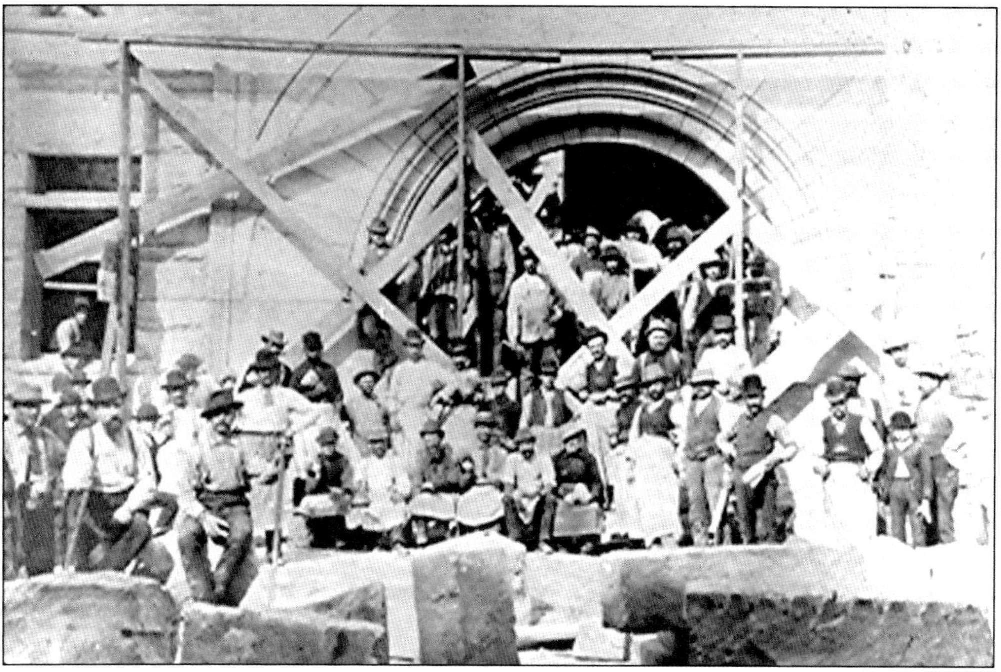

Here is an example of the number of stonemasons and other construction workers who built the Mabel Tainter Theatre. Note the scaffolding around the arched doorway. Today a mural on the Lee Drug building across the street commemorates these dedicated and skilled craftsmen. (Courtesy of UWSA.)

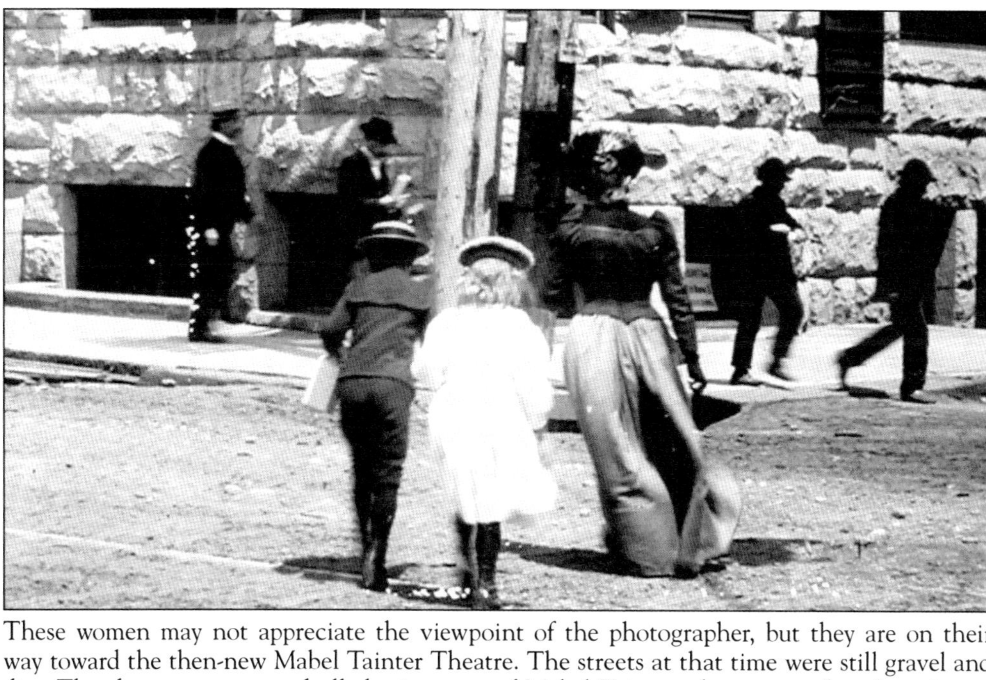

These women may not appreciate the viewpoint of the photographer, but they are on their way toward the then-new Mabel Tainter Theatre. The streets at that time were still gravel and dirt. The theater represented all the interests of Mabel Tainter, the woman for whom it was dedicated. It offered a reading room, assembly hall, free library, and meeting place for the Grand Army of the Republic and the Unitarian Congregation. (Courtesy of UWSA.)

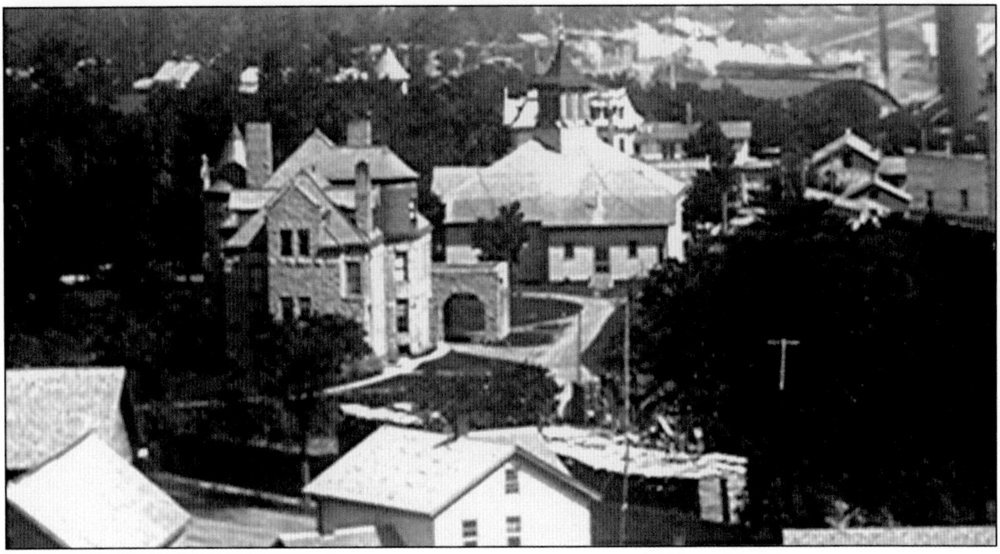

Here is the Louis Smith Tainter house as it looked when built in the late 1890s, on the corner of what is now Crescent Avenue and Broadway Street. This incredible limestone building is well preserved and is home to the University of Wisconsin–Stout Alumni offices and the Stout Foundation. (Courtesy of UWSA.)

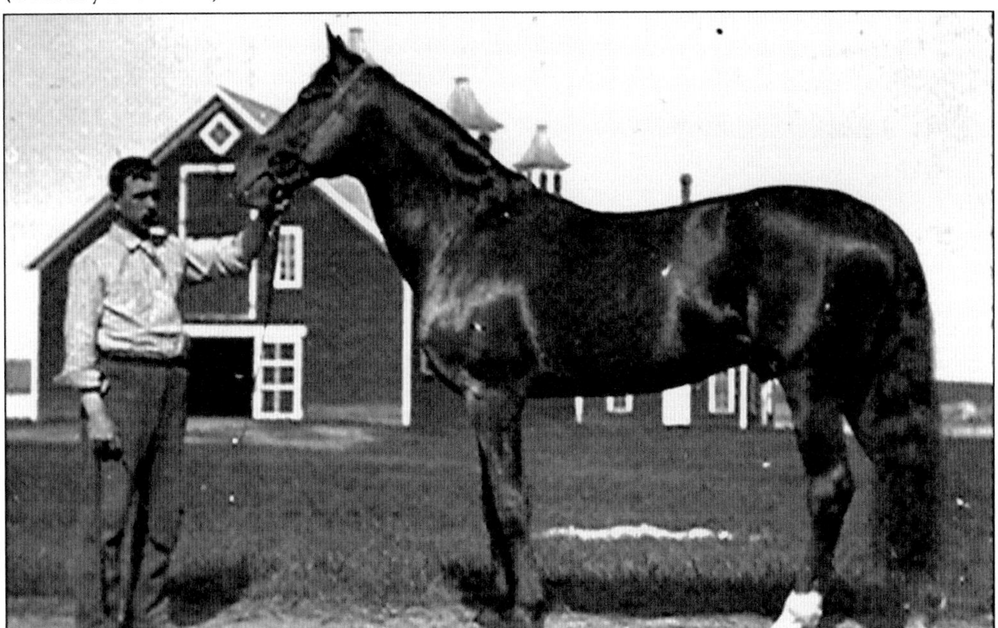

Oaklawn Stock Farm was the home of Capt. Andrew Tainter, primary stockholder in the Knapp, Stout, and Co. Company. He began the stock farm in 1889 and developed an impressive number of racehorses over the years. He also developed many innovative farm operations, including a racetrack where Menomonie citizens enjoyed spending Sunday afternoons. Captain Tainter also raised highly respected breeds of sheep, cattle, and hogs. The farm stood on ground that is now the Stout Technology Park. The original home is a beautiful bed-and-breakfast known as Oaklawn Bed and Breakfast, operated by Maggie Foote, long-time Menomonie resident and active community member. (Courtesy of UWSA.)

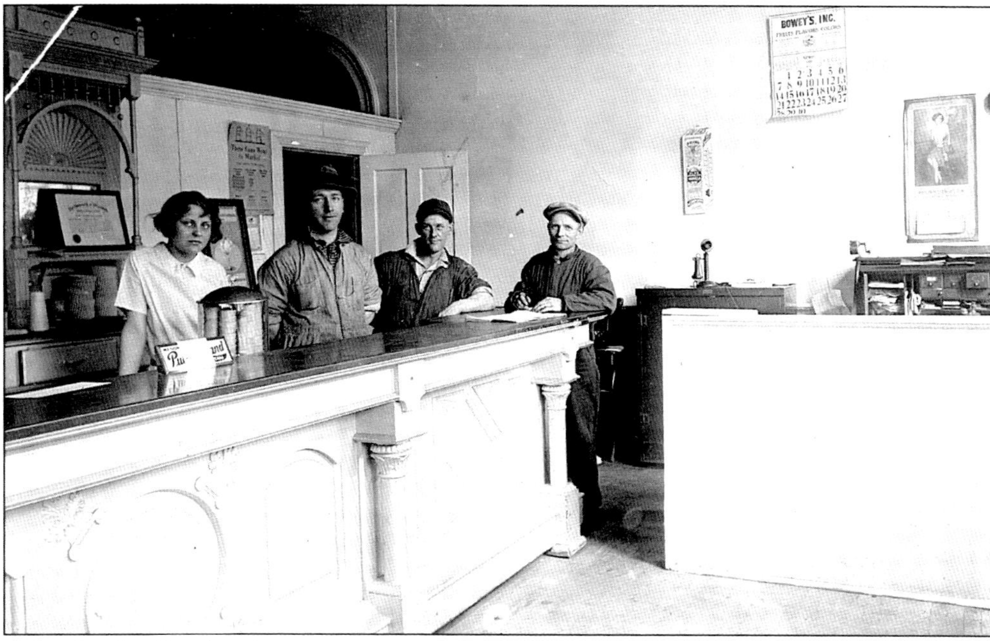

A local café offered a place to connect with neighbors and grab a good lunch while in town. (Courtesy of Milton Bowe, UWSA.)

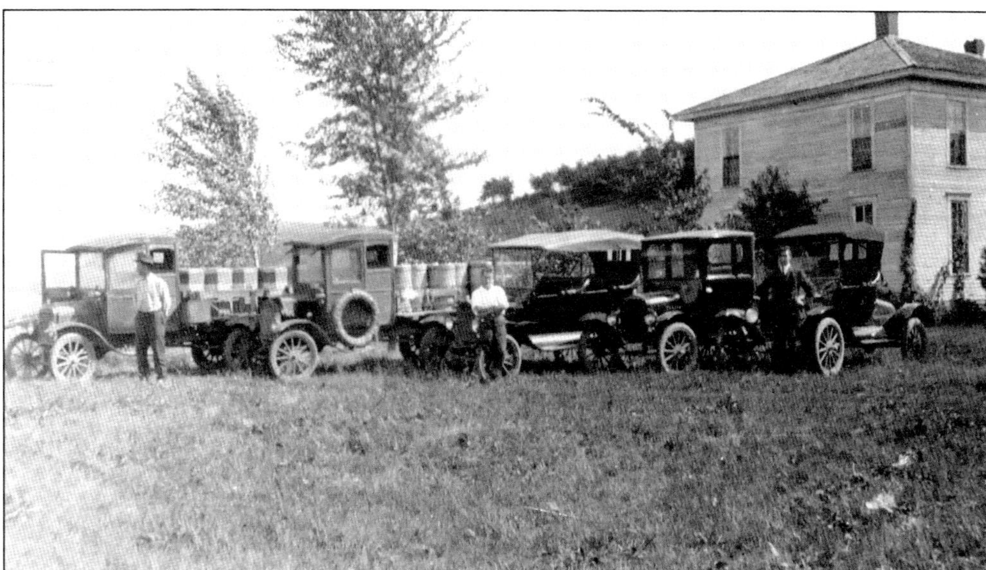

Men gather in front of a traditional foursquare farmhouse, the Homestead property, with their trucks in 1920. The foursquare farmhouse is considered even today to be one of the most popular, practical, and most efficient designs for housing. (Courtesy of UWSA.)

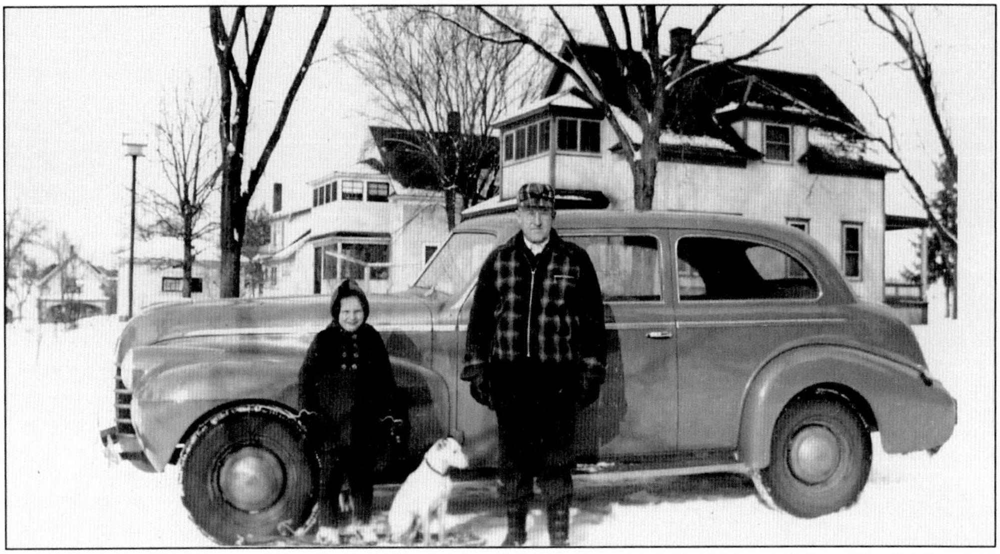

Alta Vasey Morgan stands in front of 1214 Sixth Avenue around 1939, with her dog Mike and Paul Vasey, her father. Morgan likes to recall the time she and her brother Winston "Pinky" Vasey went sliding, and the only one making it to the bottom of the hills was Mike, the dog. Morgan lives in Menomonie today, and continues her community involvement in a number of valuable areas. (Courtesy of Alta Morgan.)

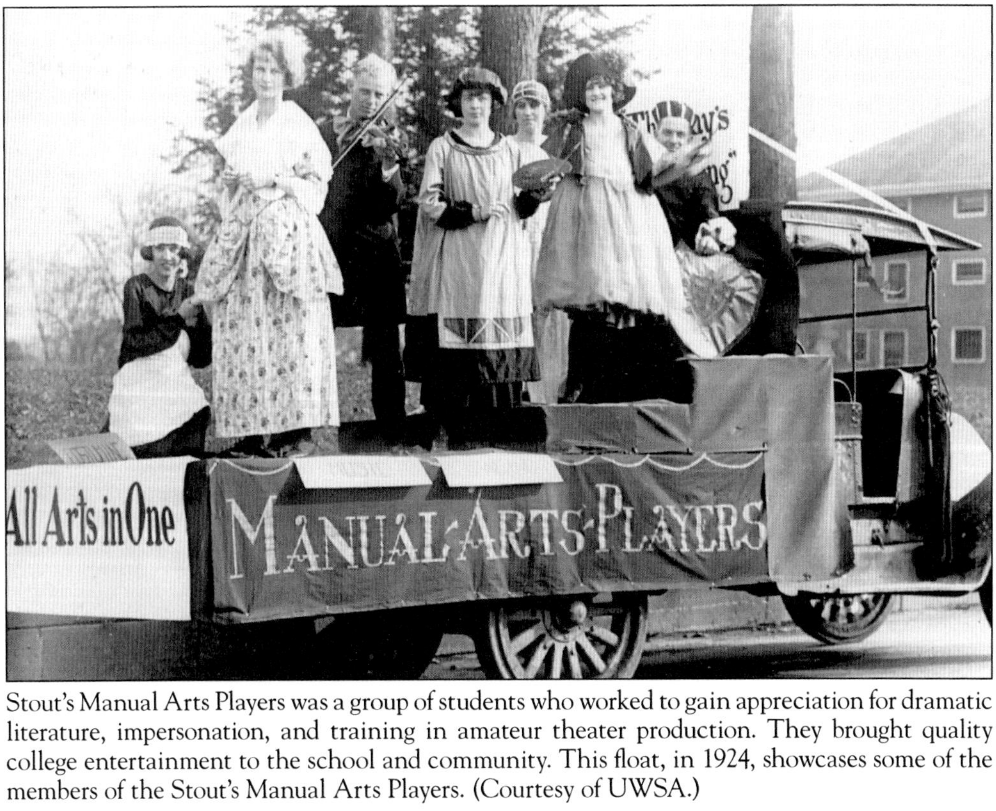

Stout's Manual Arts Players was a group of students who worked to gain appreciation for dramatic literature, impersonation, and training in amateur theater production. They brought quality college entertainment to the school and community. This float, in 1924, showcases some of the members of the Stout's Manual Arts Players. (Courtesy of UWSA.)

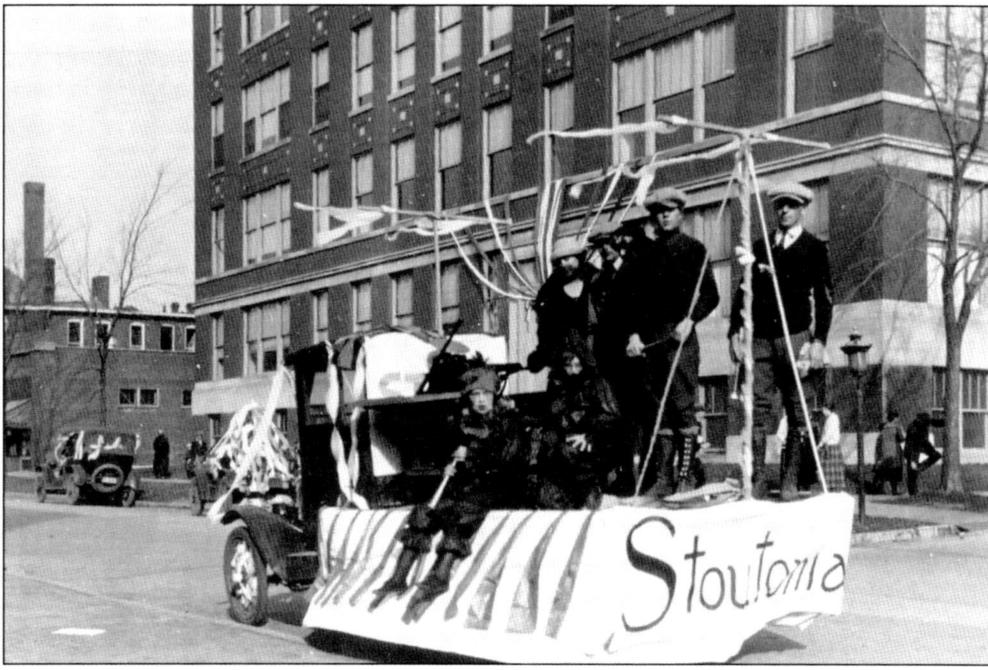

The Stoutonia float is pictured here in the homecoming parade, around 1939. *The Stoutonia* is the student newspaper of the University of Wisconsin–Stout. In 1935, it was published weekly and had over 30 staff members, whose job was to "concentrate efforts toward . . . high journalistic and typographical character." (Courtesy of UWSM.)

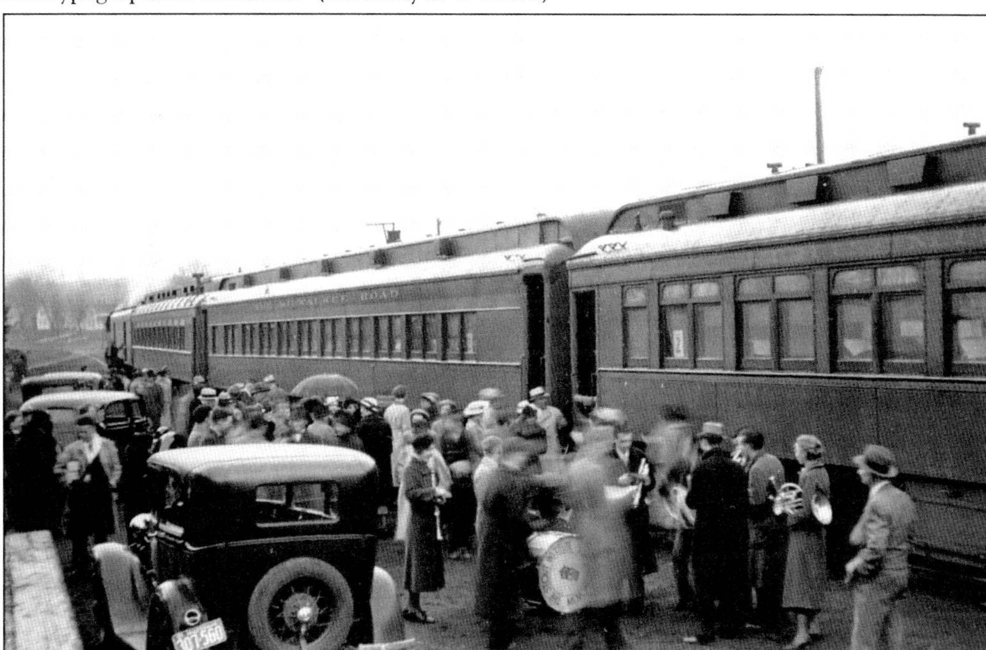

The Stout band gives a rousing send-off at the Milwaukee Road railroad station. Railroads were important not only to the logging industry, but also to the other industries cropping up in the Menomonie area. (Courtesy of UWSM.)

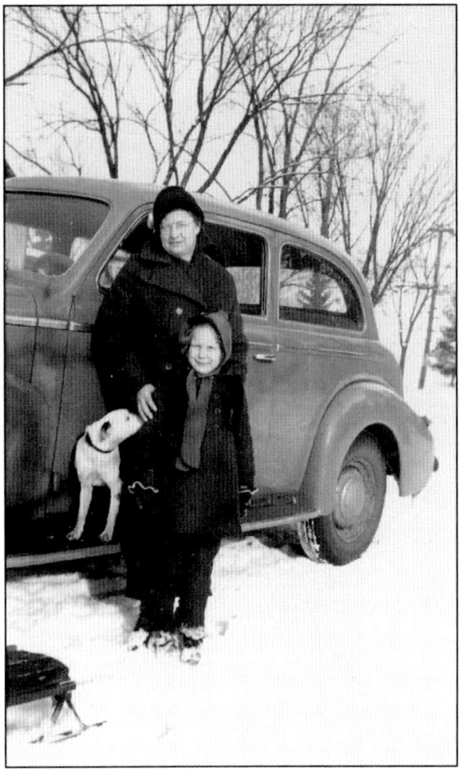

Alta Vasey Morgan, her loyal dog Mike, and her mother are pictured in 1939, near the family car on Sixth Avenue. The Vaseys, a well-known and respected Menomonie family, would later move to a home in Park Circle, where Alta continues to live today. (Courtesy of Alta Vasey Morgan.)

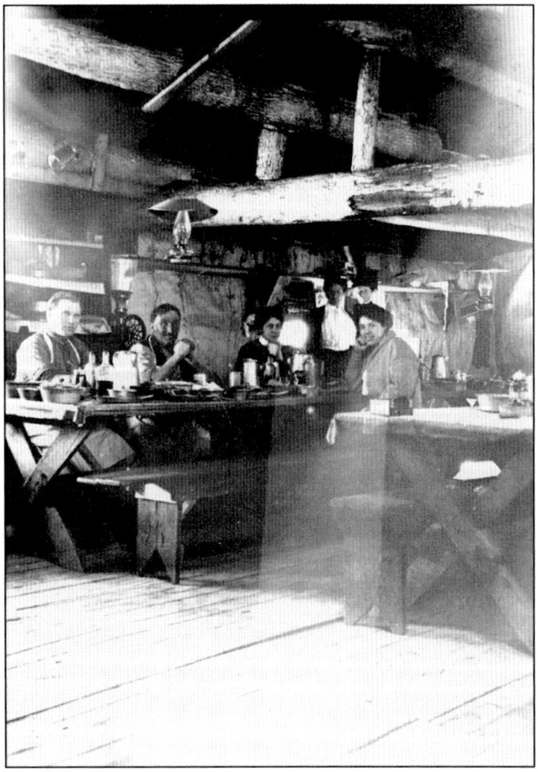

Ed Weus and John Minnie, Stout Manual School students, visit the Weston Lumber camp, west of town, in 1912. (Courtesy of UWSA.)

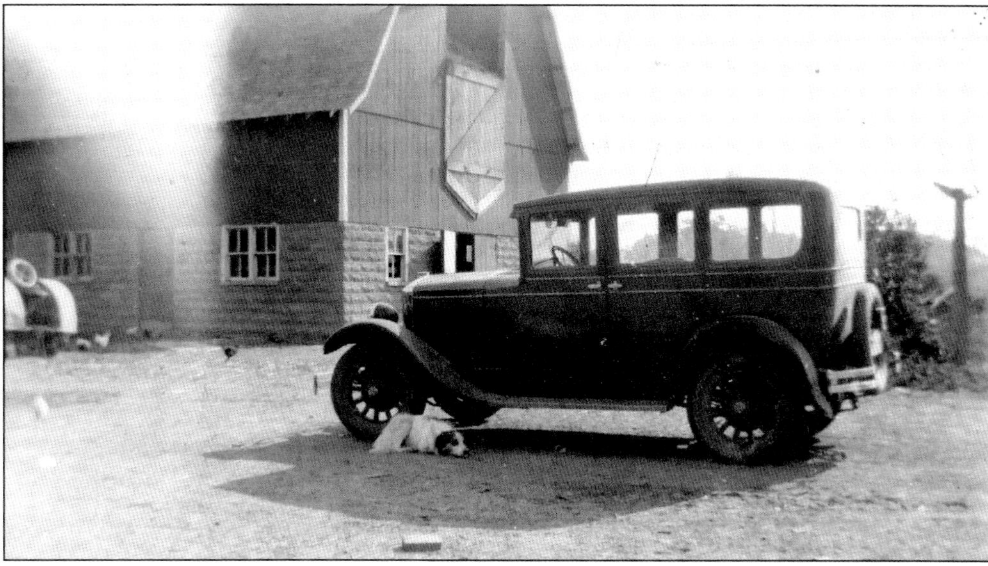

"Grandpa's car," seen here in 1946, is most likely 1936 vintage, but still a proud example of what value families placed on their vehicles. (Courtesy of Sofi Doane,)

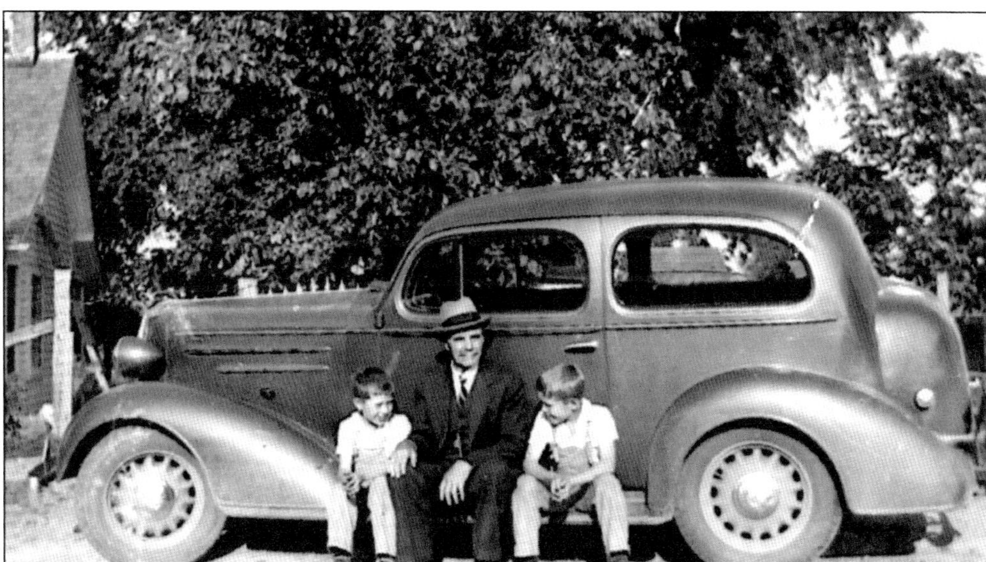

"Dad's car" was another proud, all-important family vehicle. Running boards were great places to sit in 1940. The boy on the left is Don Clements, the names of the other two are unknown. (Courtesy of Sofi Doane.)

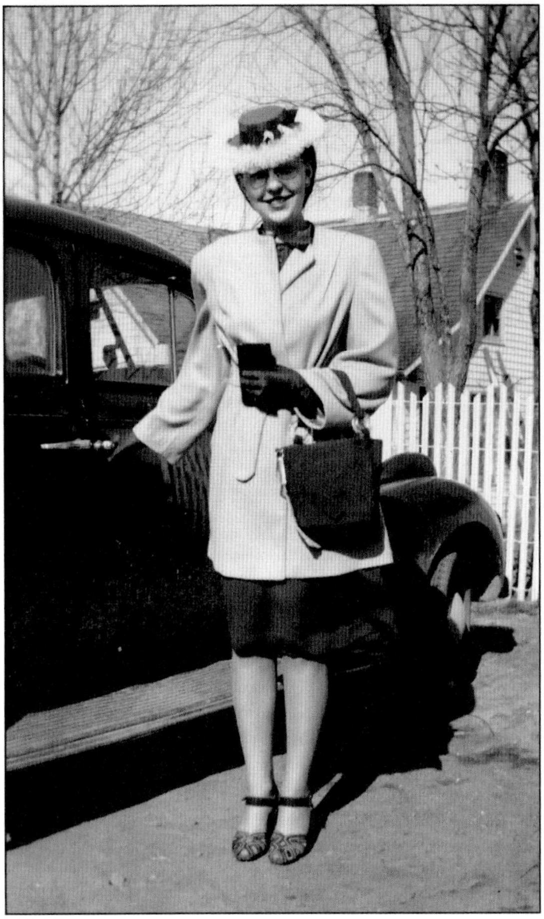

Here Joan Clements Buss poses in front of her car. (Courtesy of Sofi Doane.)

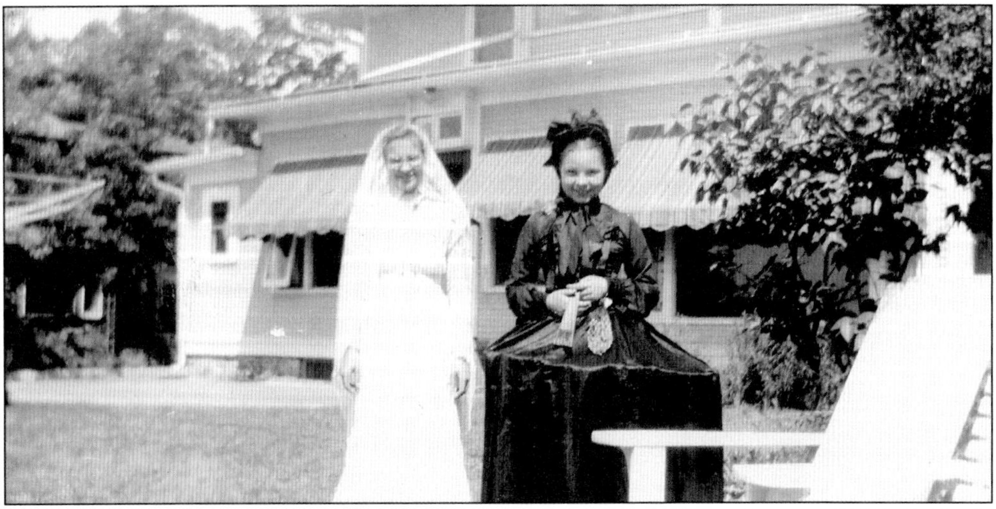

Alta Vasey Morgan and Nora Averi stand in the backyard of the Vasey home at 323 Park Circle Drive in Menomonie. Morgan's great grandfather George LaPointe founded O. and N. Lumber in Menomonie in 1915. Under this name, he came to own a chain of 35 lumberyards around the Dunn County area. (Courtesy of Alta Vasey Morgan.)

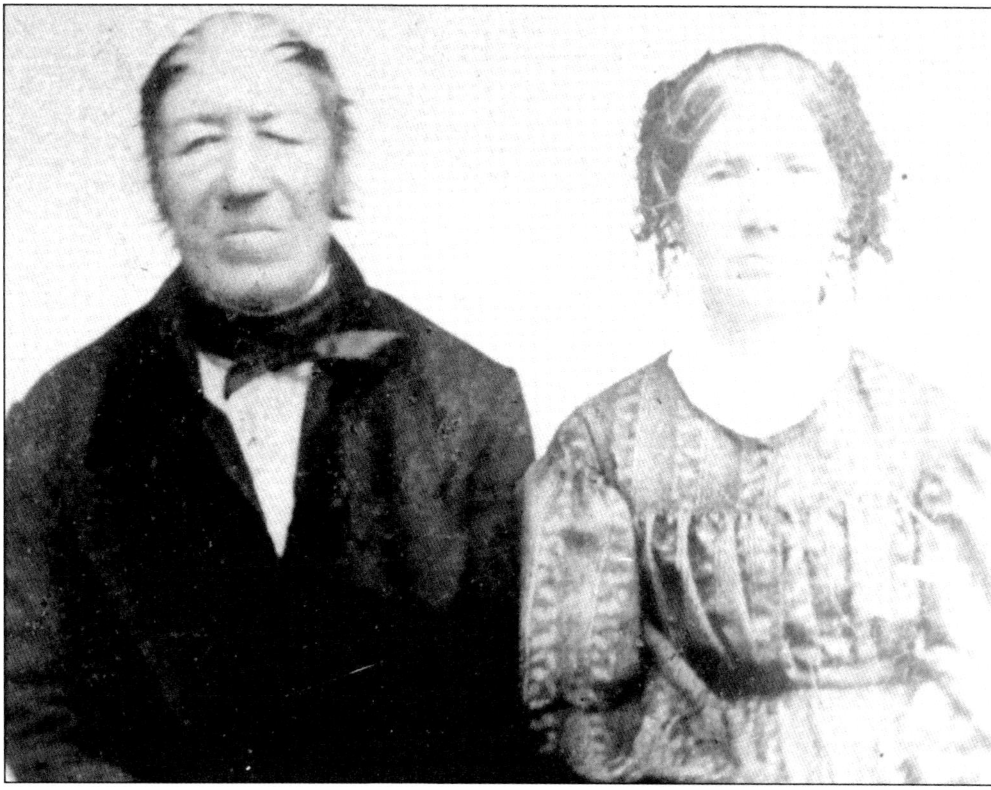

This is a portrait of William Vasey, born in December 1782 in Yorkshire, England, and Jane Frankish, born in April of 1791.

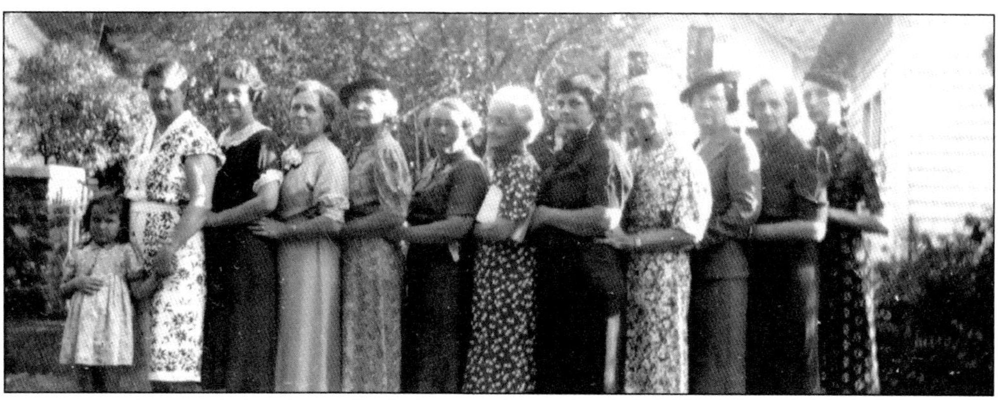

The Menomonie Vasey ladies are seen here in this photograph taken behind the home located at 1214 Sixth Avenue. Pictured from left to right are Alta Vasey, her mother, Lonavern, Lillian McDonald, and Maude McCloud. The remaining women are unidentified. (Courtesy of Alta Vasey Morgan.)

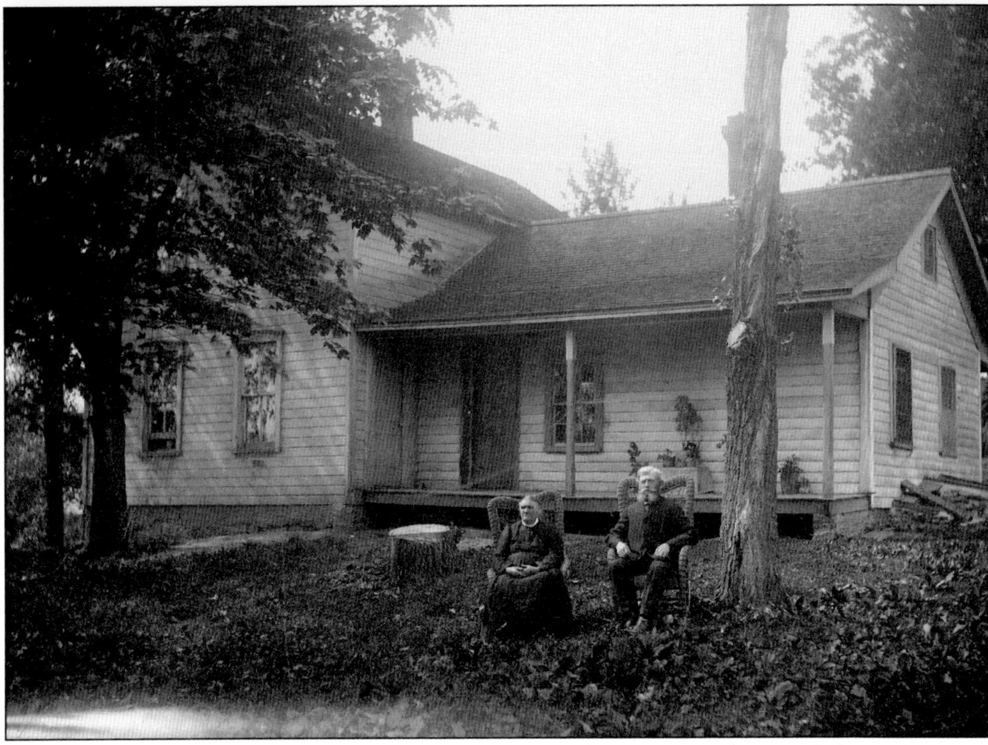

August and Louise Haase are seen here. Both August and Louise were born in Polvon, Germany. They were married in Germany and came to the United States in 1873, where they lived for 10 years in Menomonie before moving to a farm in the town of Menomonie where they lived for the next 36 years. They had 13 children. (Courtesy of Joyce Newton.)

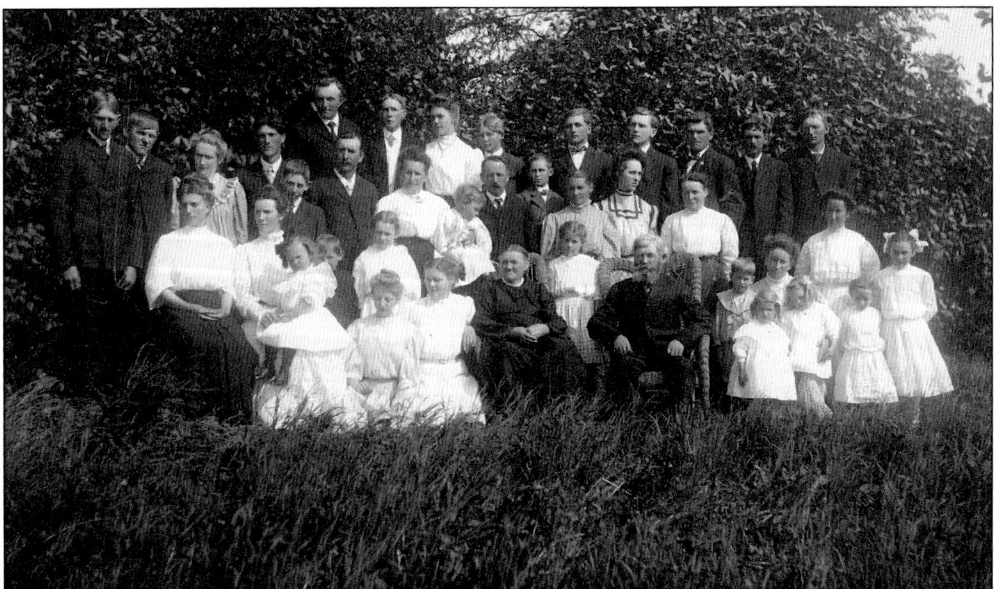

August and Louise Haase pose with their family in this image. (Courtesy of Joyce Newton.)

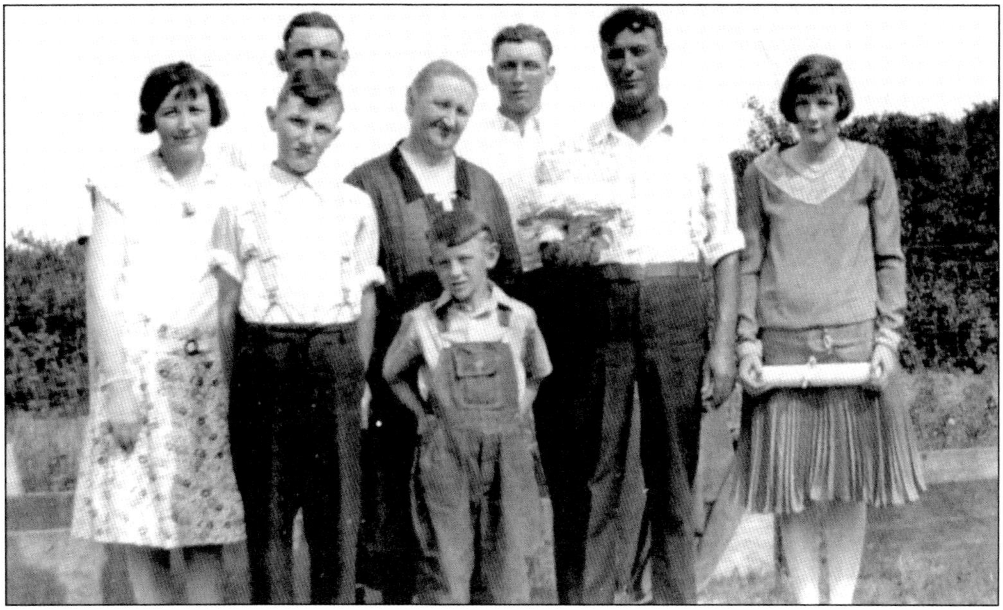

Hetcil and Amelia Holden are pictured with their family. Hetcil Holden was born in the town of Lucas, west of Menomonie, in 1886. Amelia was born to August and Louise Haase in 1884, also in the town of Lucas. They eventually married and farmed for the rest of their lives in the towns of Lucas and Menomonie. They had six children. Pictured around 1933 are, from left to right (first row) Arthur "Jack"; (second row) Gertrude, Otto standing behind Russell, Amelia, Roy, Hetcil, and Ruth. (Courtesy of Joyce Newton.)

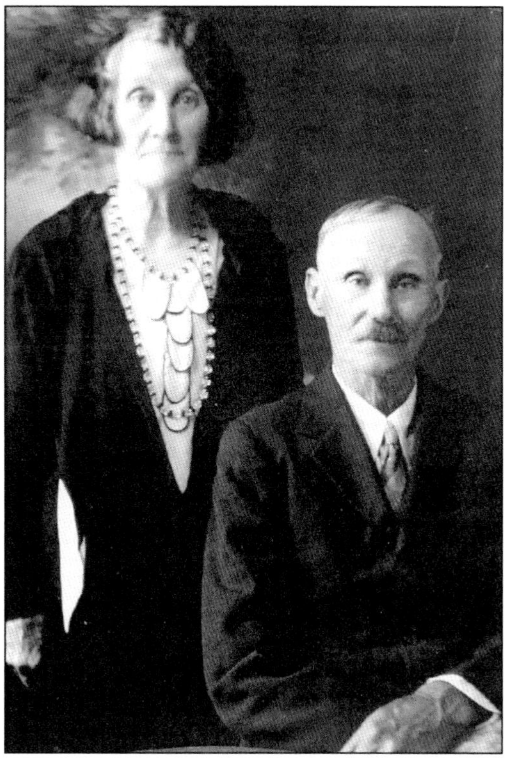

James "J. T." and Alice Holden lived in Centerton, Arkansas, for many years before moving and marrying in Menomonie on June 20, 1880. They were to have 13 children; sadly 3 of them died as babies. Hetcil Holden, in the previous photograph, was one of their children who remained in the Menomonie area. (Courtesy of Joyce Newton.)

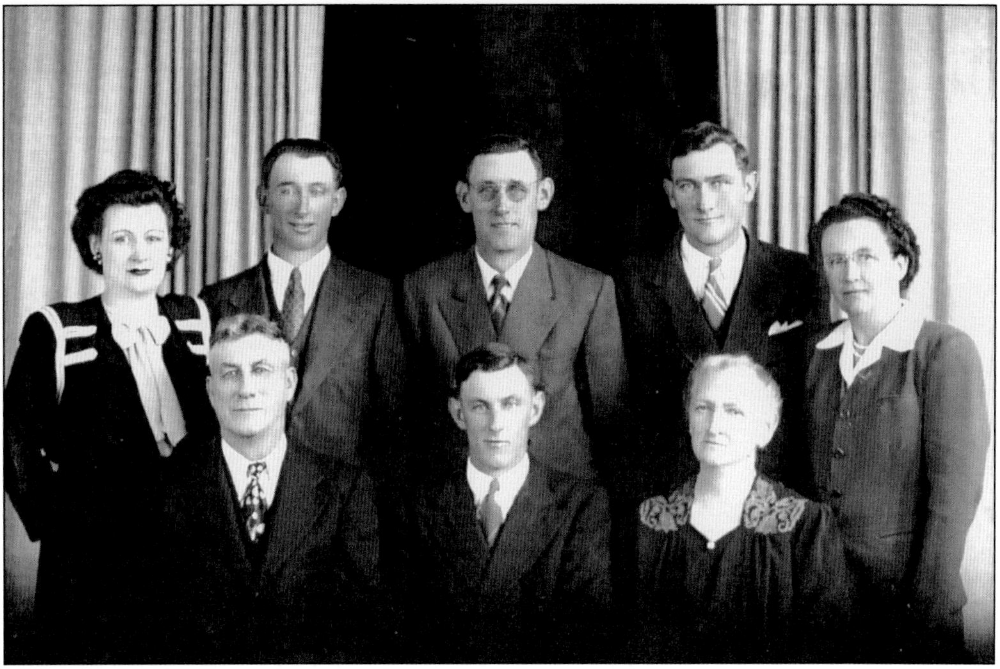

The Holden family is seen in later years, around 1941. From left to right are (first row) Hetcil, Jack, and Amelia; (second row) Ruth, Roy, Otto, Russell, and Gertrude. (Courtesy of Joyce Newton.)

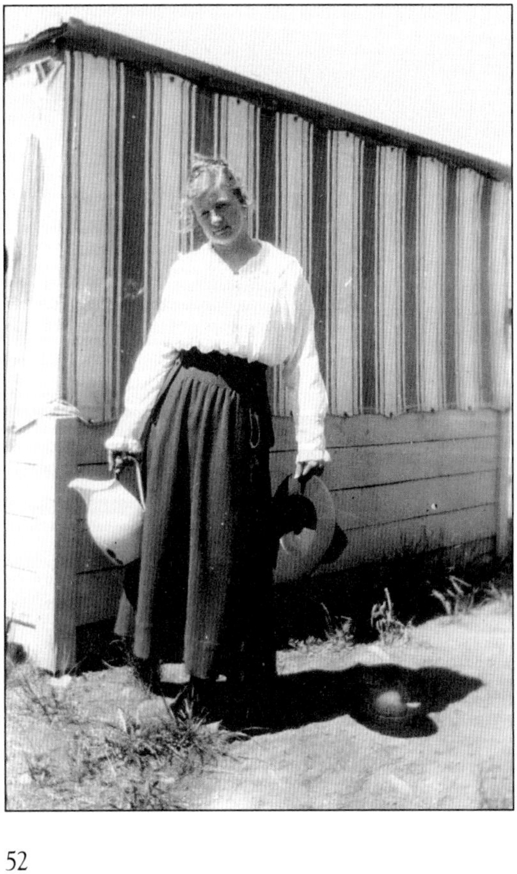

Lona (Harshman) Vasey is pictured here on her honeymoon, July 4, 1917, in the town of Dunn. Vasey's parents, Charles and Jessie Harshman, were pioneer residents of the town of Spring Brook. (Courtesy of Alta Vasey Morgan.)

Here, Fred Clements and Irene Oberle celebrate the wedding of their children. Fred's son Don married Irene's daughter Jerene. The photograph was used in 2006 as a cover for the Oberle family reunion. (Courtesy of Sofi Doane.)

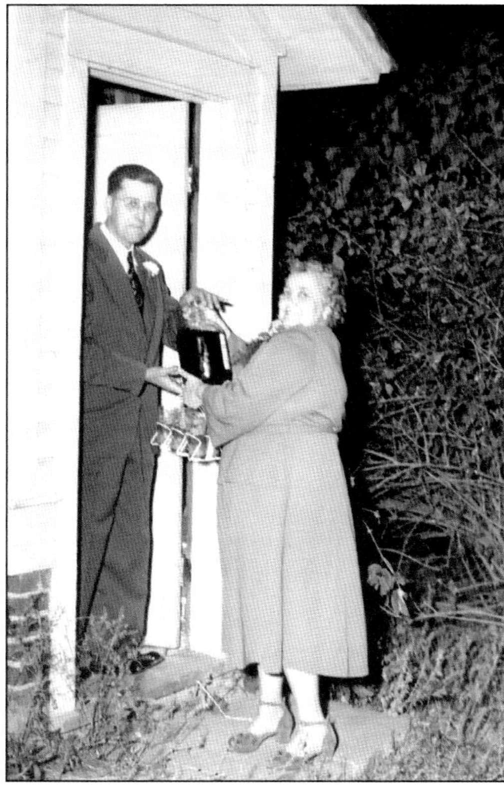

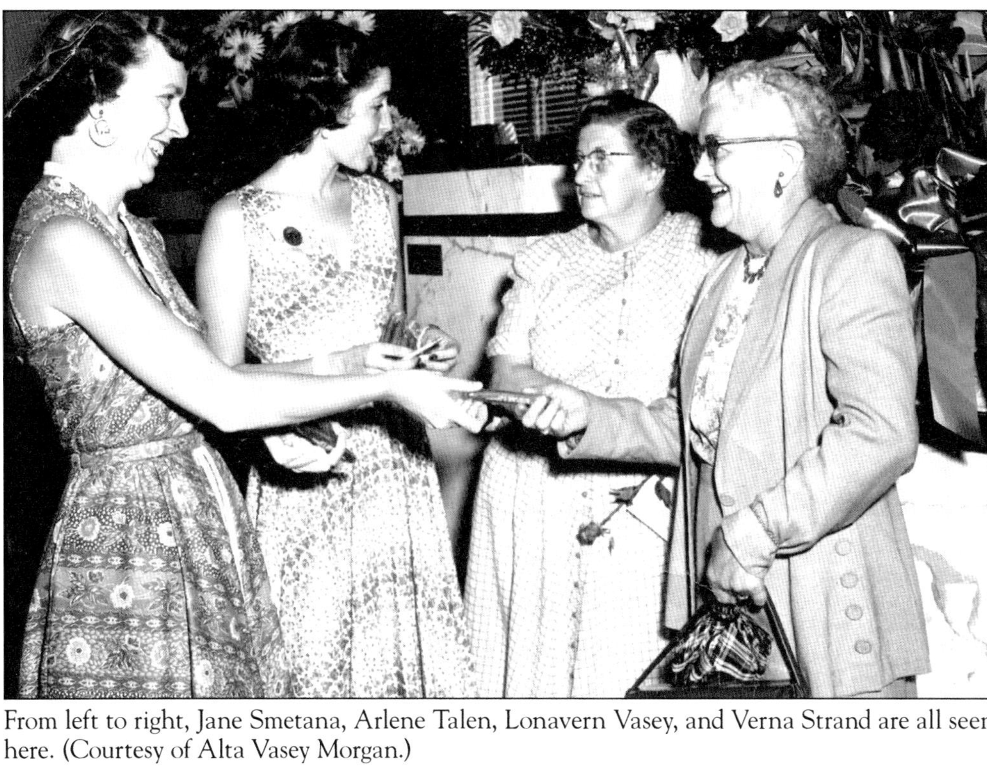

From left to right, Jane Smetana, Arlene Talen, Lonavern Vasey, and Verna Strand are all seen here. (Courtesy of Alta Vasey Morgan.)

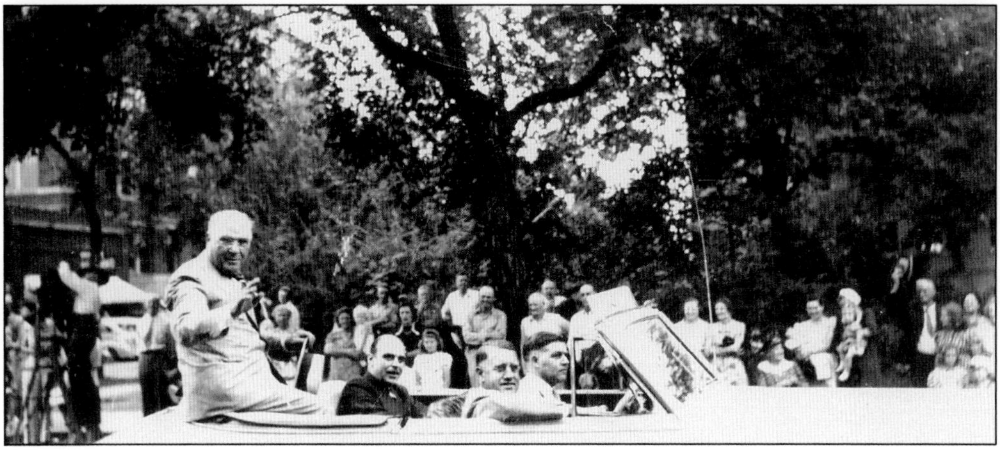

Paul Vasey rides in the car with United States senator Cordell Hull in a centennial parade in Menomonie. Senator Hull was a Democrat who served in Pres. Franklin D. Roosevelt's cabinet. He died in 1955. (Courtesy of Alta Vasey Morgan.)

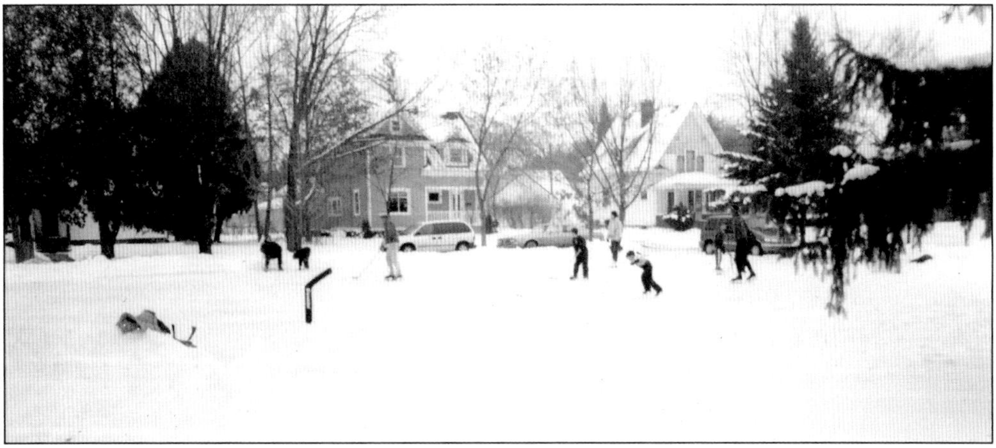

Ice-skating was always popular at the rink in Park Circle Drive. (Courtesy of Alta Vasey Morgan.)

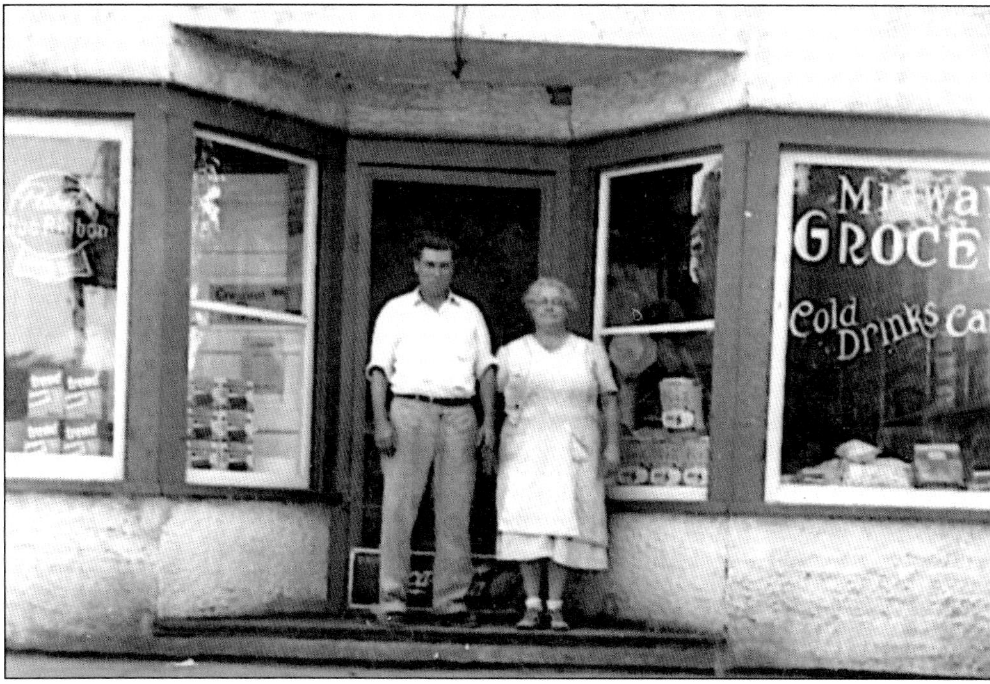

Seen here is the Midway Grocery. Albert and Irene Oberle owned this store for many years. It is now the site of Dean and Sue's, a popular bar and restaurant for locals and students alike. (Courtesy of Sofi Doane.)

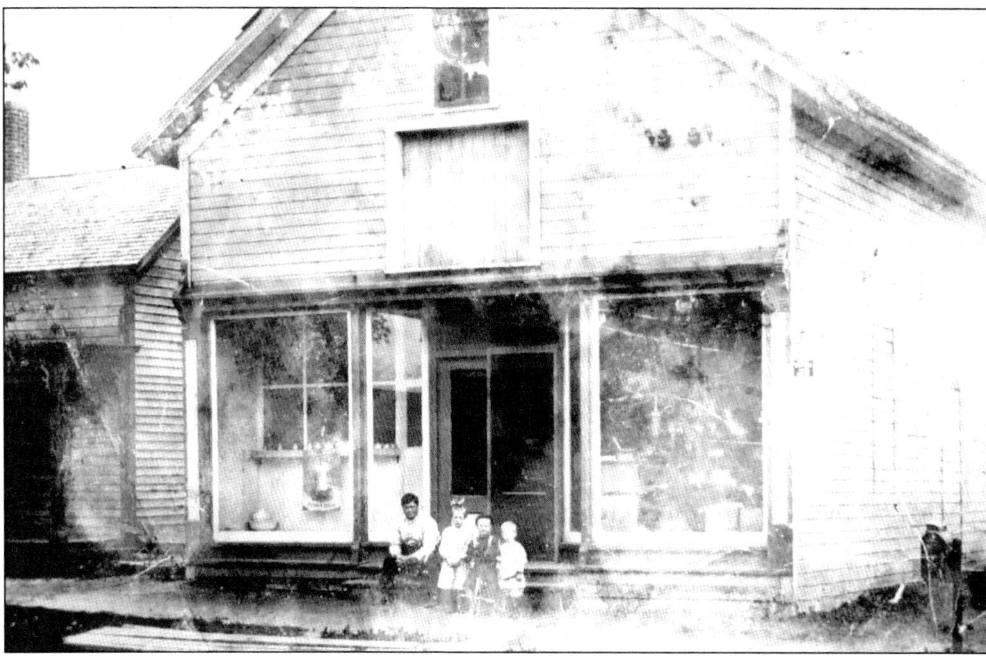

This small grocery, pictured here in 1916, was owned by Patrick James Galvin. He sits in front of the building with two unidentified children. The store opened about June 1, 1907, and burned on February 6, 1926; it was later rebuilt. It was located on the southeast corner of Thirteenth and Sixth Avenues. (Courtesy of Mary Galvin Shows.)

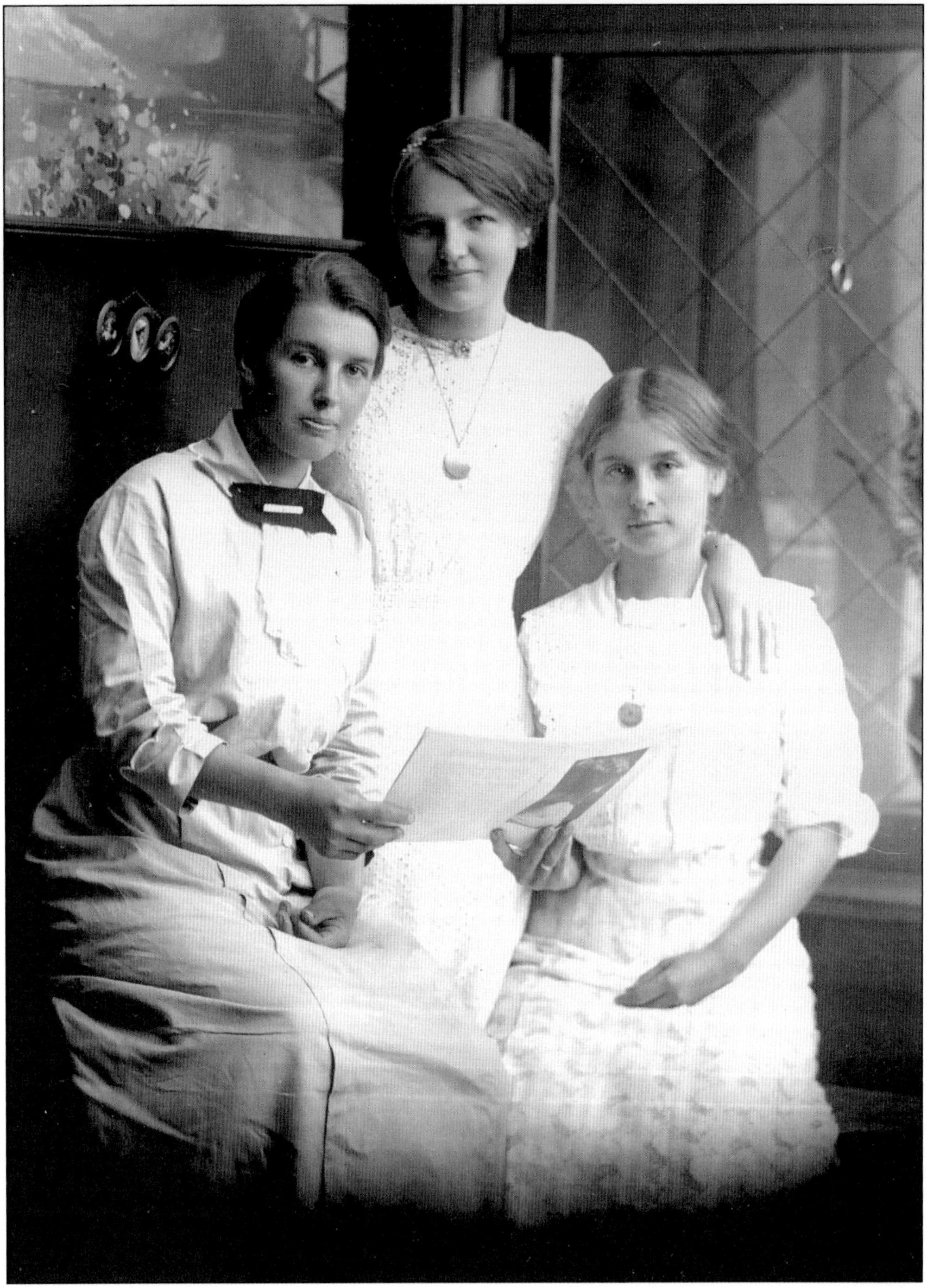

Edna Mattison, Mabel Doane, and Mabel Harshman pose for a Christmas photograph in the Belair Studio in Menomonie. The studio was owned and operated by George Belair, a local photographer who studied with Robert Helsom, and later did a portrait of James H. Stout. (Courtesy of Gary Hinrichs.)

Three

Resources and Recreation

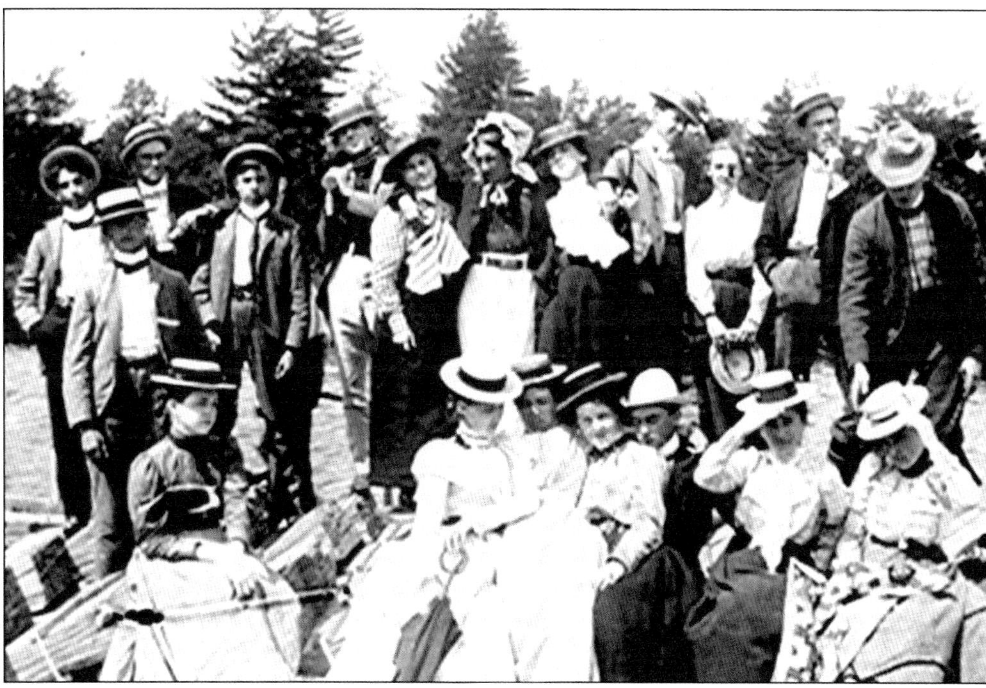

A rafting party was often the way to spend a weekend afternoon. People gathered on the river to float to Downsville or Dunnville, and then would return back to Menomonie by train. (Courtesy of UWSM.)

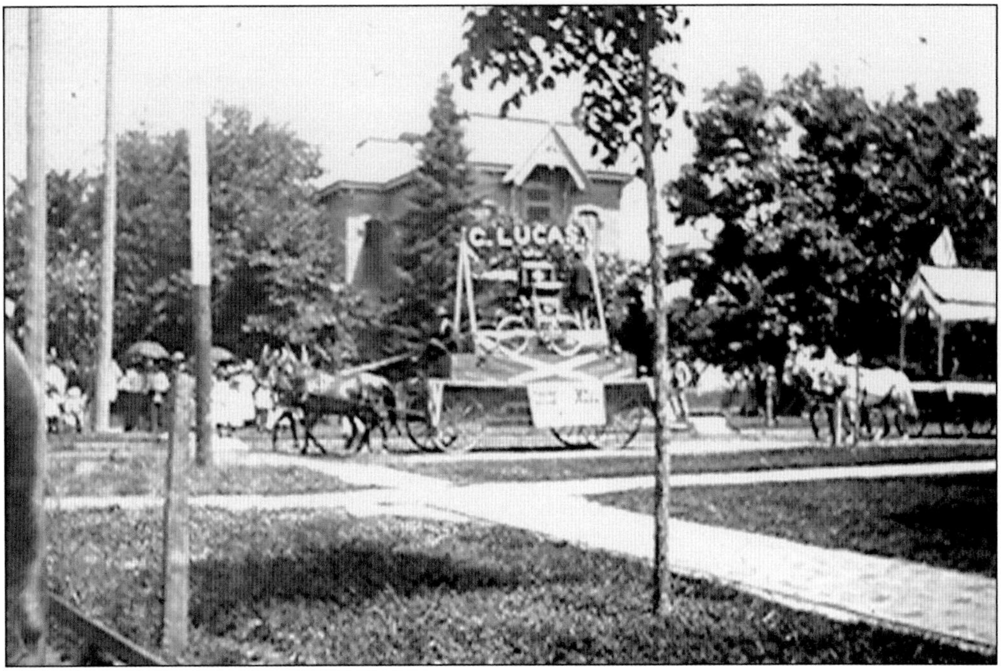

A Fourth of July parade passes by downtown Menomonie buildings. Note the C. Lucas above the horse drawn carriage. (Courtesy of UWSA.)

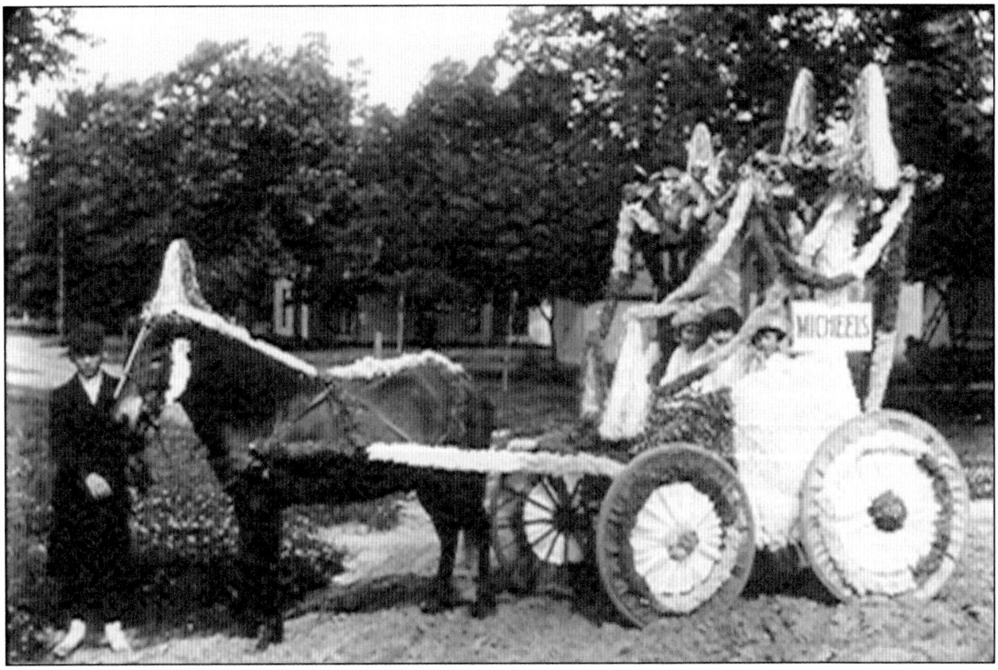

Herman Micheels was a prominent Menomonie businessman who owned a successful clothing store in town. He and his family came from Germany and settled in Menomonie in 1880. His father, August, had been a tailor in Germany and was able to take up this trade in his new country. Herman later developed his own expertise in the area of retail clothing. (Courtesy of UWSA.)

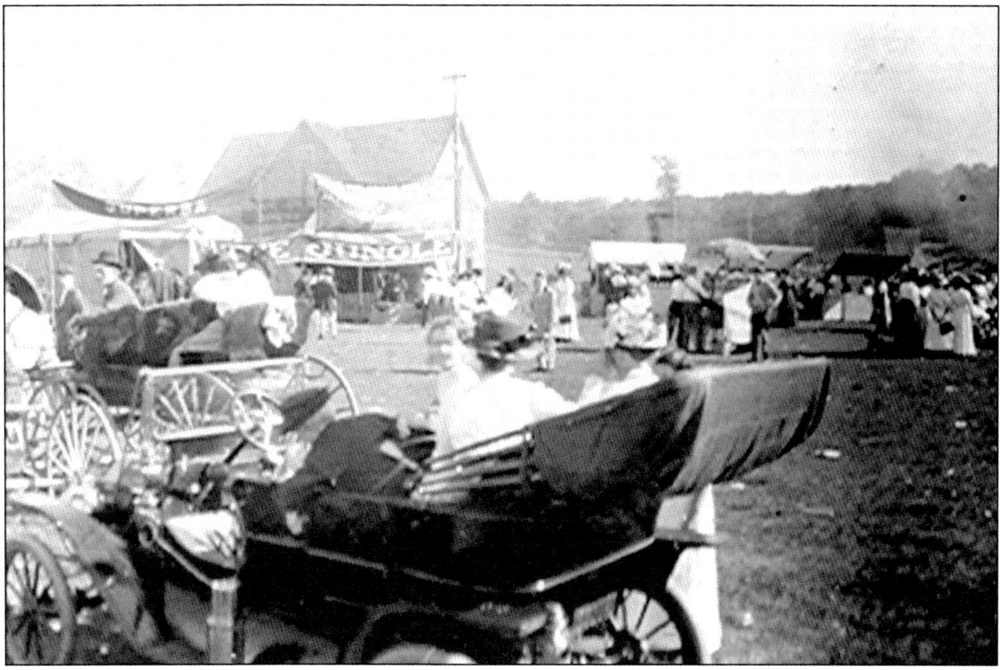

The fair in Menomonie is still important today. Held at the Dunn County Recreation site, it attracts people from miles around, just as it likely did when this photograph was taken in the 1800s. (Courtesy of UWSA.)

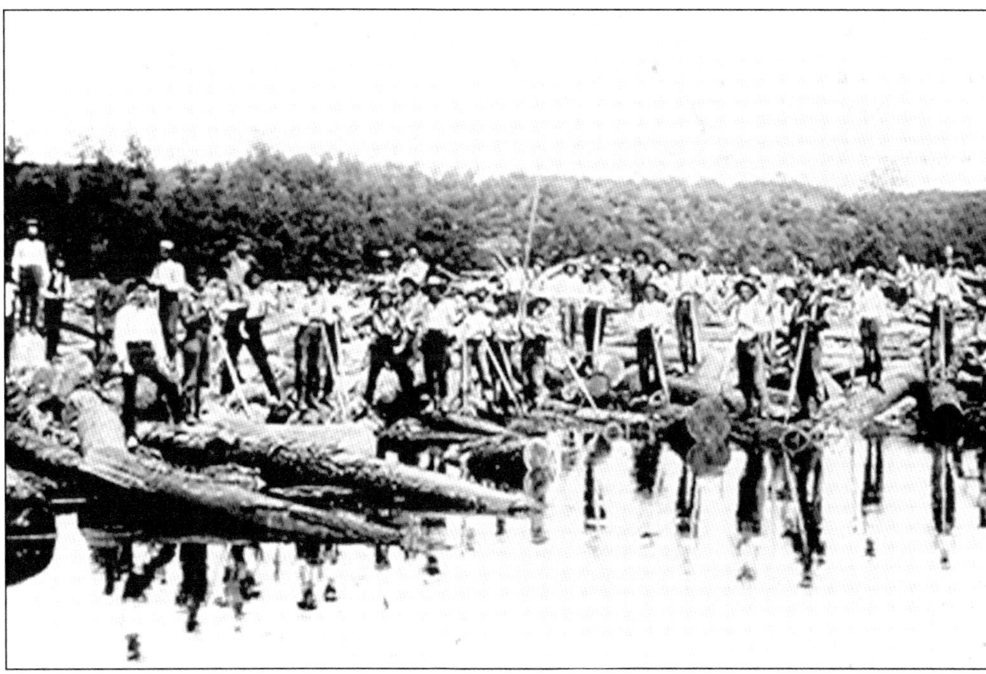

Riding the logs downriver was considered to be the most dangerous of all assignments for lumbermen. Skills in the art of maneuvering, rolling, jumping, and balancing were critical. (Courtesy of UWSA.)

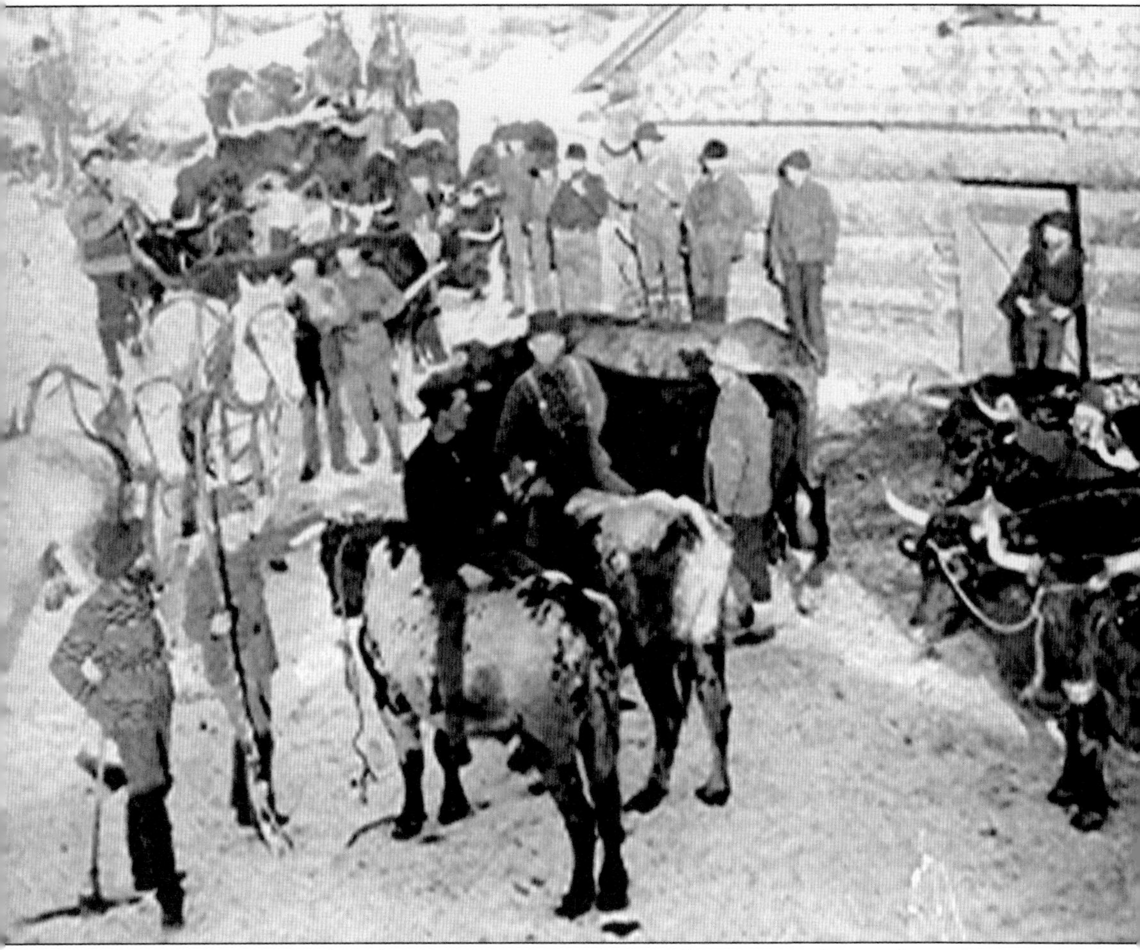

The Menomonie stockyards were an important part of the economy during the early part of the 20th century in this rural area. The Govin farm, east of town, was the location for many of the field stock exchanges. (Courtesy of UWSA.)

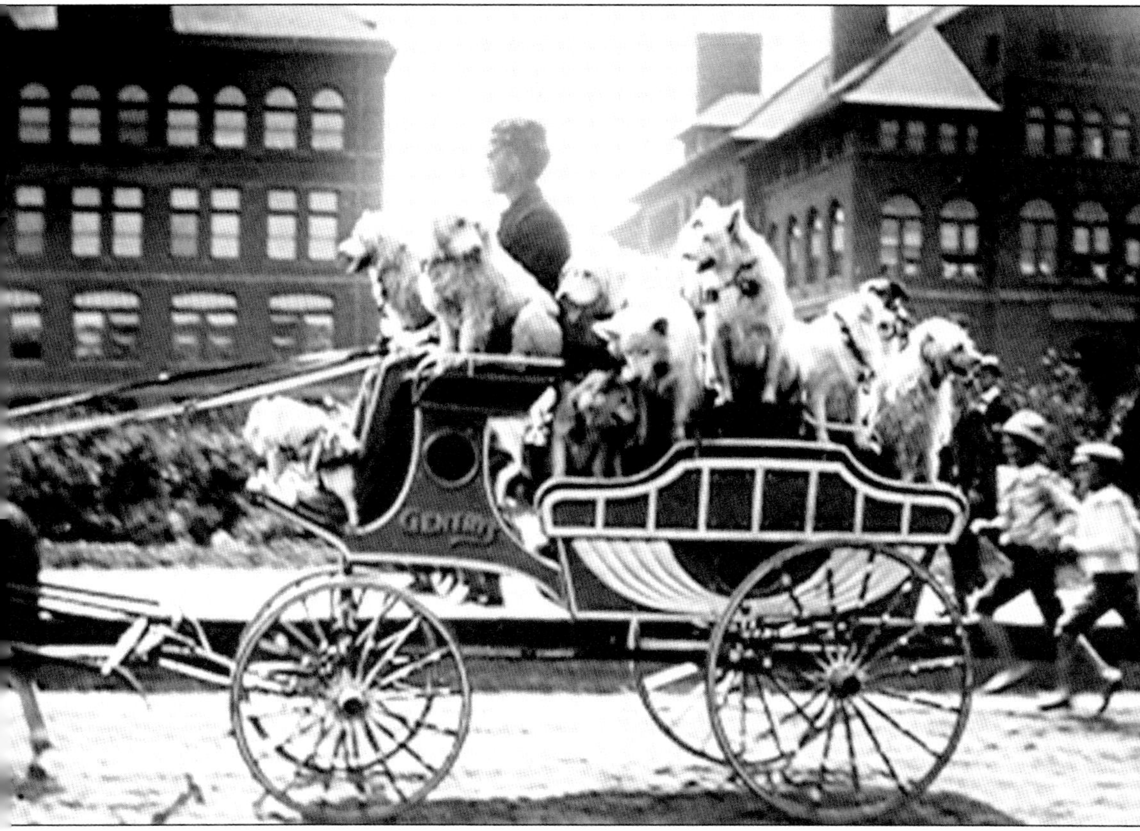

In this image, the Gentry Circus comes to town. The brick buildings of the Stout School of Manual Training and Domestic Science School, and the old Menomonie High School can be seen in the background. Both buildings are now gone. (Courtesy of UWSA.)

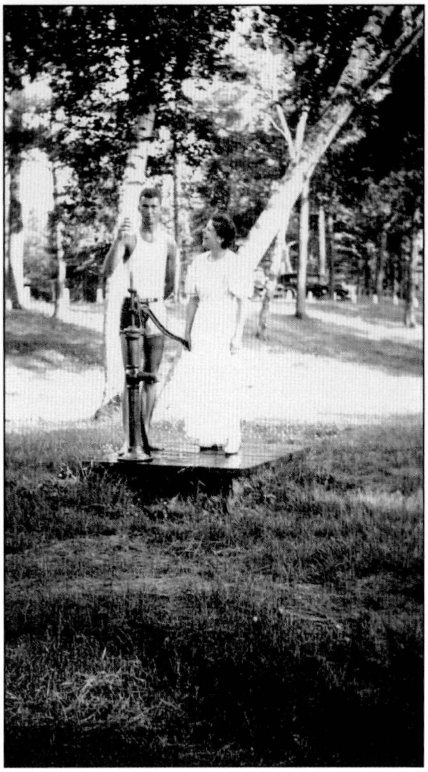

Harold Sack and Amelia (Mickey) Smilanich, Stout Institute students, enjoy a cool drink of water at Wakanda Park around the 1930s. Wakanda Park is now a multiuse park, including a water park, picnic areas, baseball fields, paths, and Frisbee golf course. (Courtesy of UWSA.)

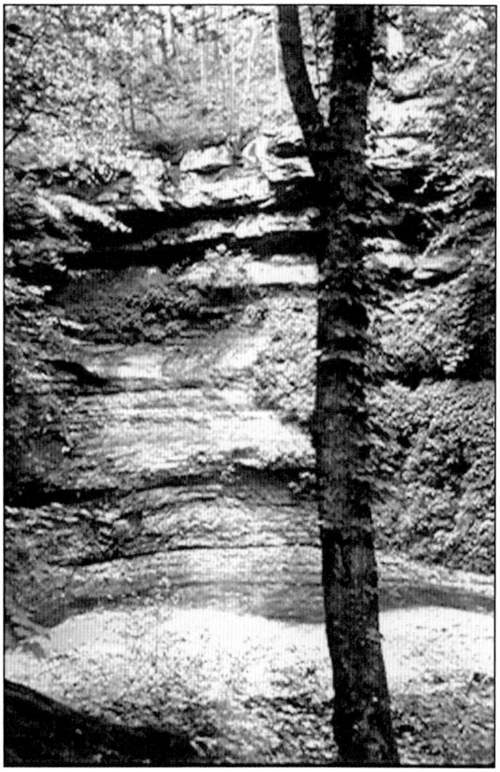

Shown here is the Devil's Punchbowl in 1914. This beautiful natural space has been nurturing people for years with its unique limestone, sandstone, and vegetation. It is located in the Paradise Valley area, west of town, near the Red Cedar Trail. These rocks date from the Late Cambrian Period, which was about 500 million years ago. (Courtesy of UWSA.)

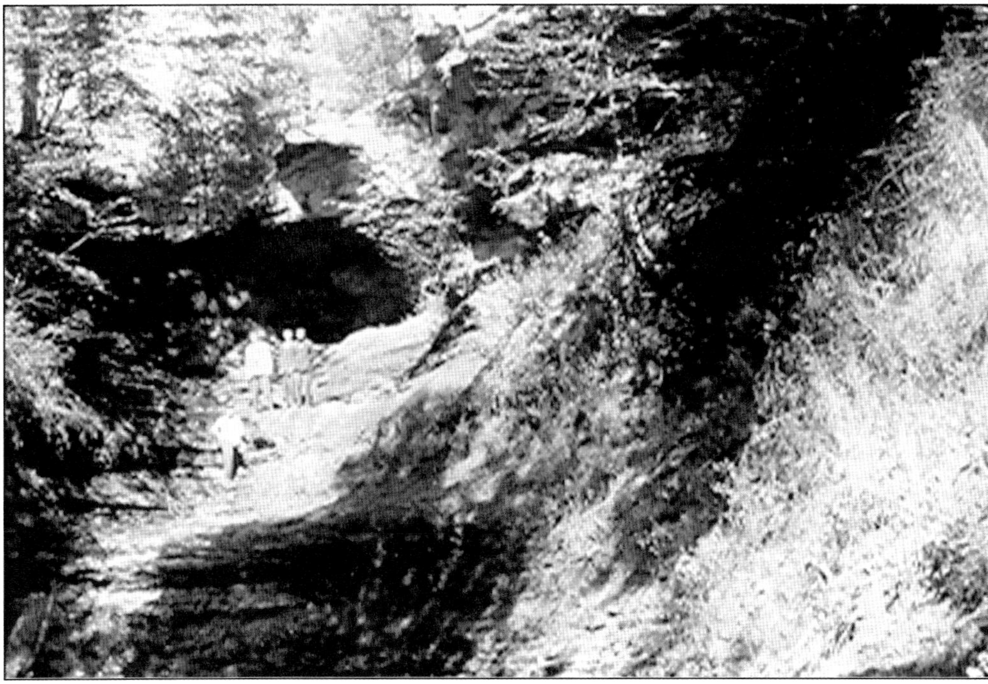

Here is another view of people exploring Devil's Punchbowl, where people continue to use this site for picnics and climbing. (Courtesy of UWSA.)

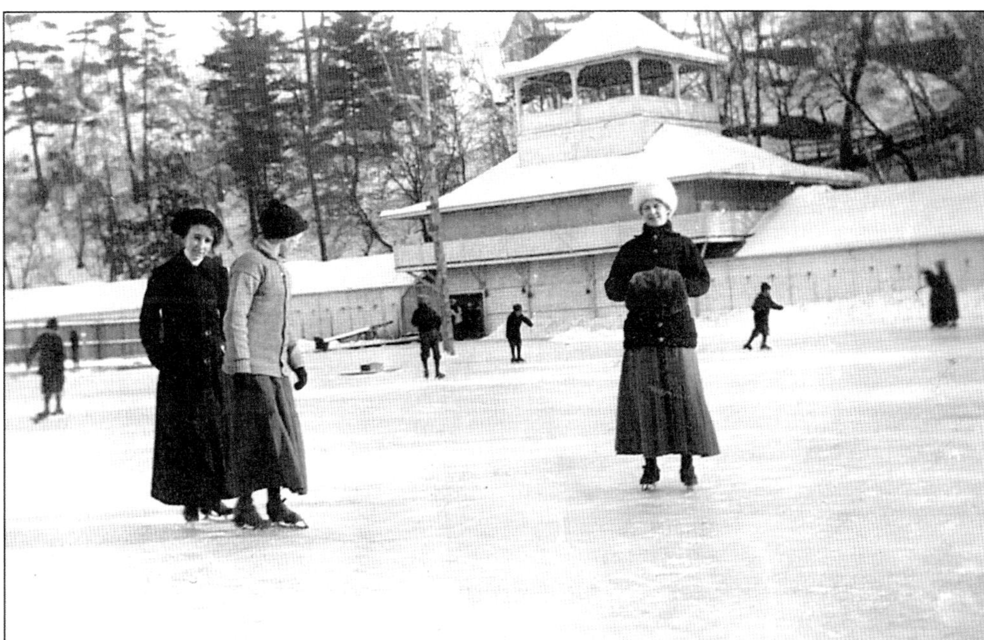

Ice-skating on the lake is always fun. The building in the background was called White's Boathouse and was located on Lake Menomin from 1910 to 1957. (Courtesy of UWSA.)

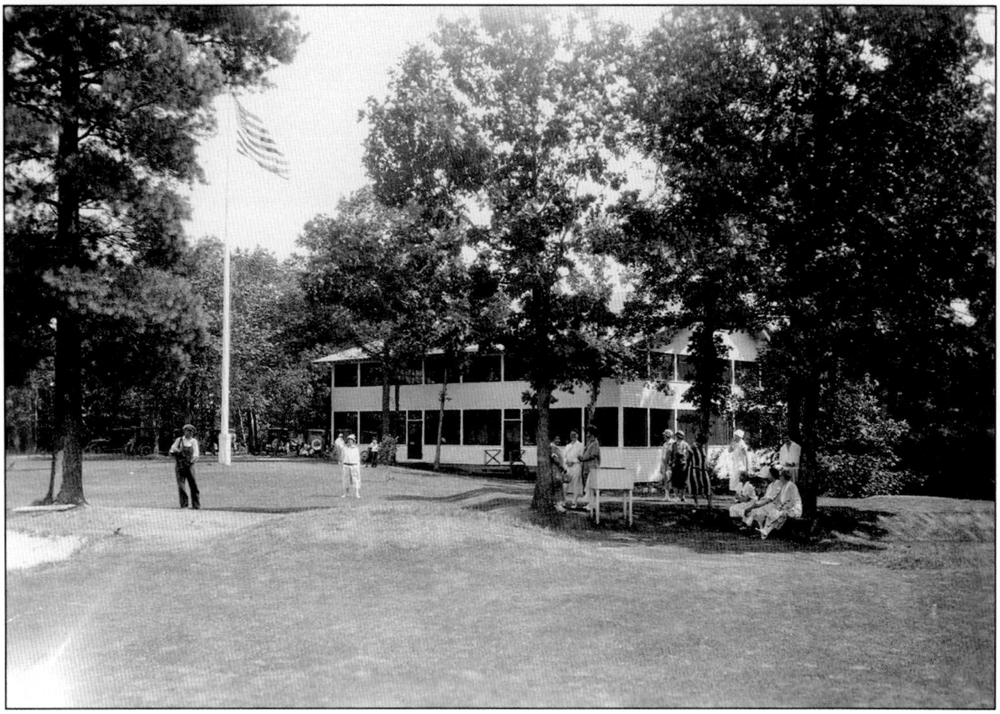

Pictured here is the Menomonie Country Club in 1929, proof that the area included opportunities for play as well as work. (Courtesy of UWSA.)

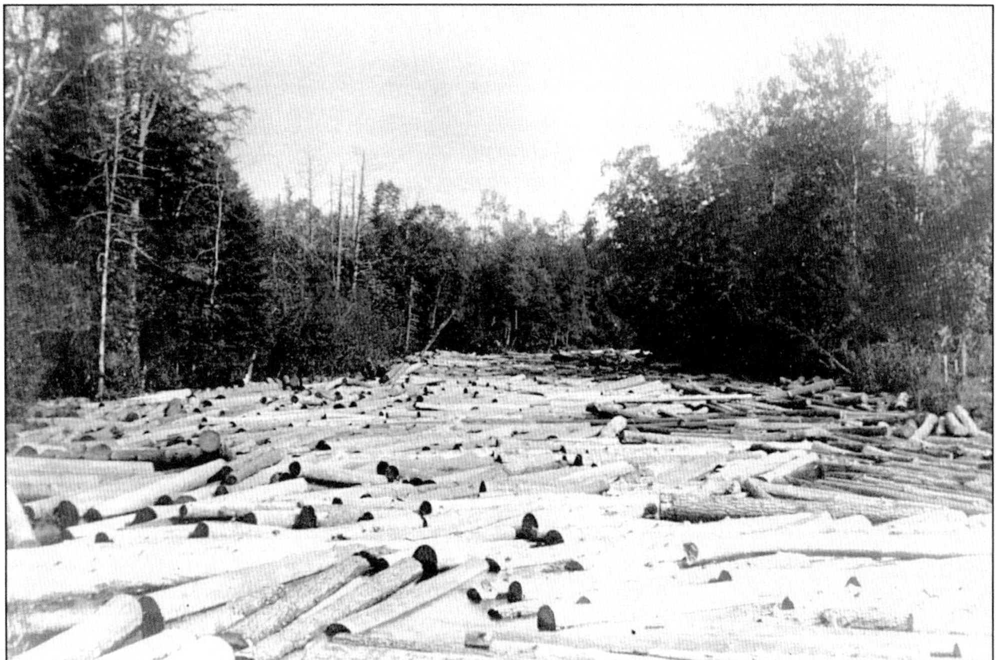

The amount of logs that traveled the river on a daily basis, from land in northern Wisconsin to the mills in Menomonie, is difficult to imagine today. The river was a critical element to the success of the lumber era. (Courtesy of UWSA.)

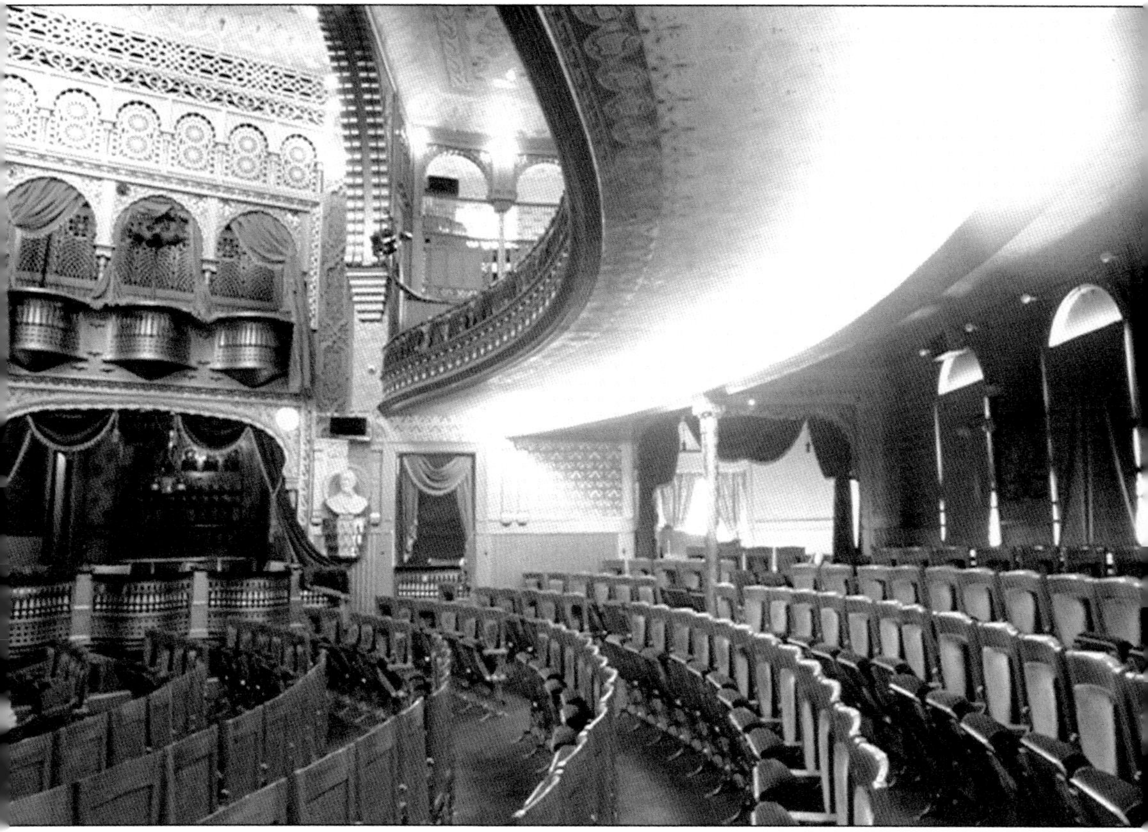

The Mabel Tainter Memorial Theatre interior looks much the same today as when it was built in 1890. There are three sizes of chairs in the theater, to accommodate different sizes of people. The stage and surrounding seating continues to make this a desired location for performers. (Courtesy of UWSA.)

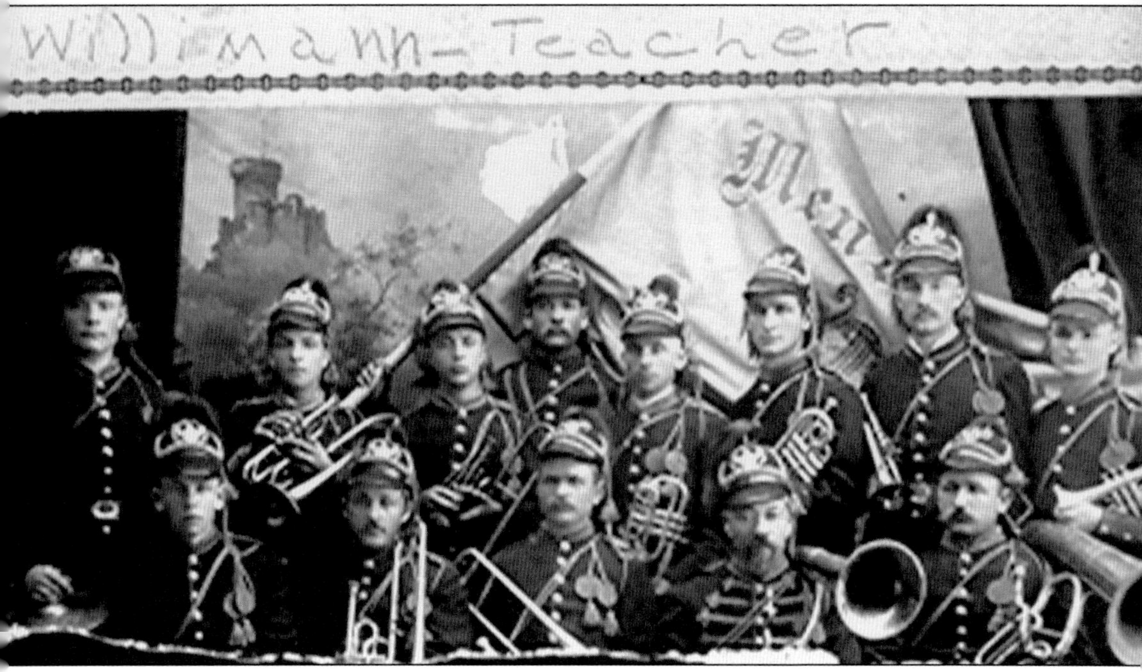

The Ludington Guard was formed in 1877 as a cavalry unit. Some of the soldiers later formed a band, to play music when in parades. They called themselves the Ludington Guard Band, and today the band still exists, playing concerts once a week during the summer months in the band shell in Wilson Park. (Courtesy of UWSA.)

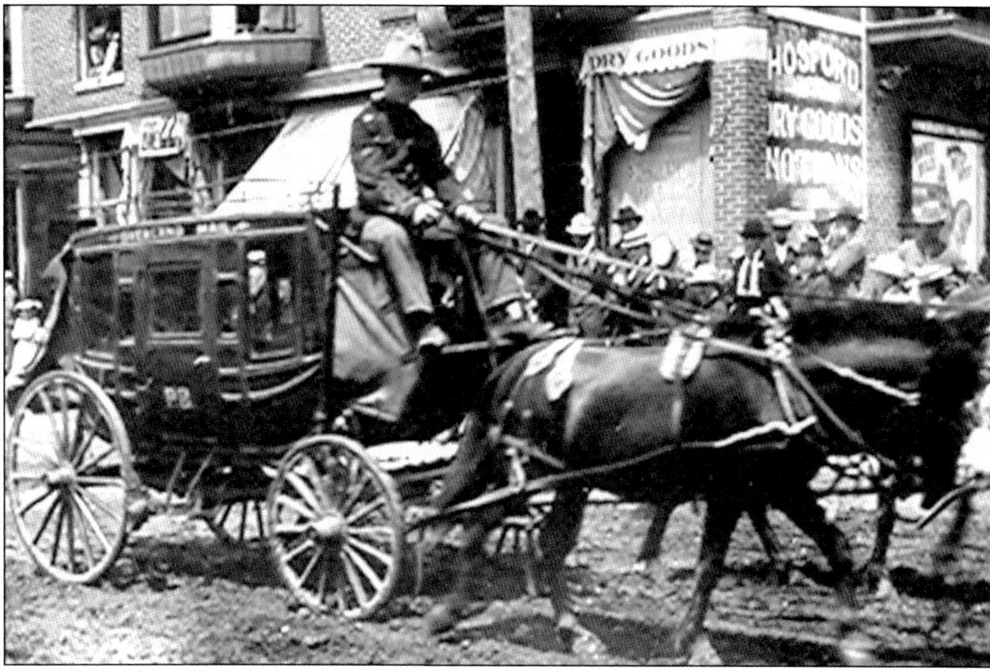

The Wild West Show parade marches down the street. The building in the background looks to be the Heller/Lee Building, based on the bay windows on the second story. (Courtesy of UWSA.)

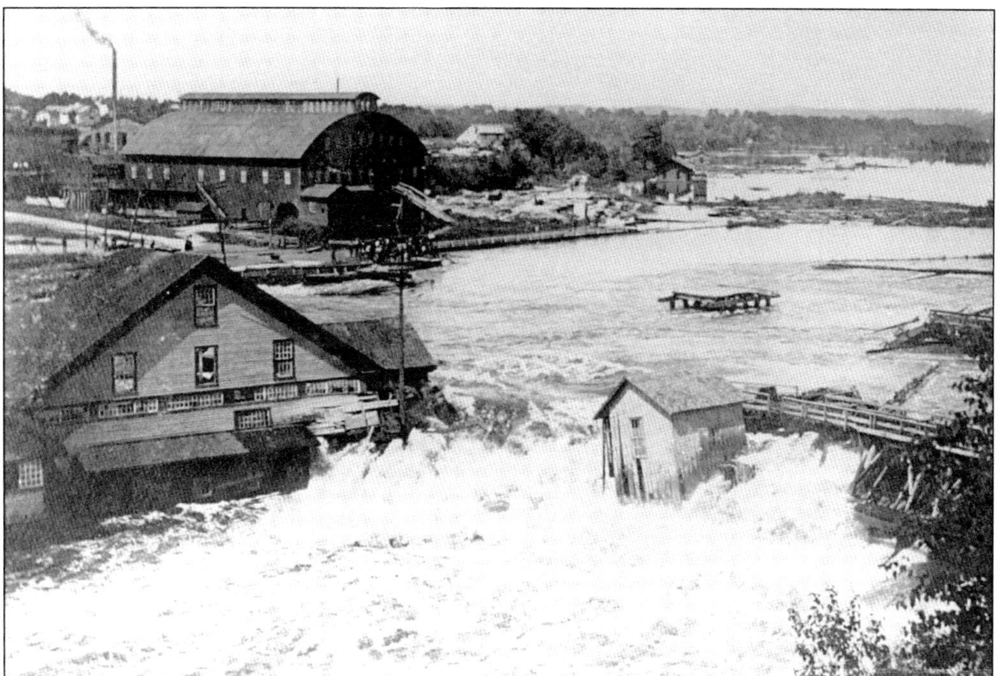

Flooding was always a danger, especially during spring months. In June 1880, a flood took out the dam on Wilson Creek. The Knapp, Stout, and Co. Company offices can be seen here in close proximity to rising floodwater. (Courtesy of UWSA.)

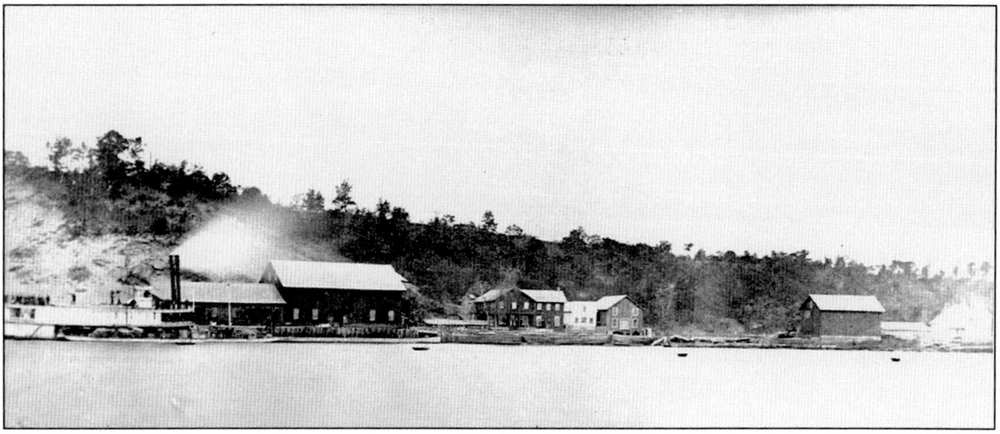

Rumsey's Landing is seen here, on the west bank of the Chippewa River, about two miles below what is Meridean today. This was a river port in the 1840s, and a major shipping point for wheat produced from the Rusk Prairie area. Before Eau Claire was a village, Rumsey's Landing was a thriving place where steamers and other good-sized boats would arrive and depart. This picture was taken about 1865. (Courtesy of UWSA.)

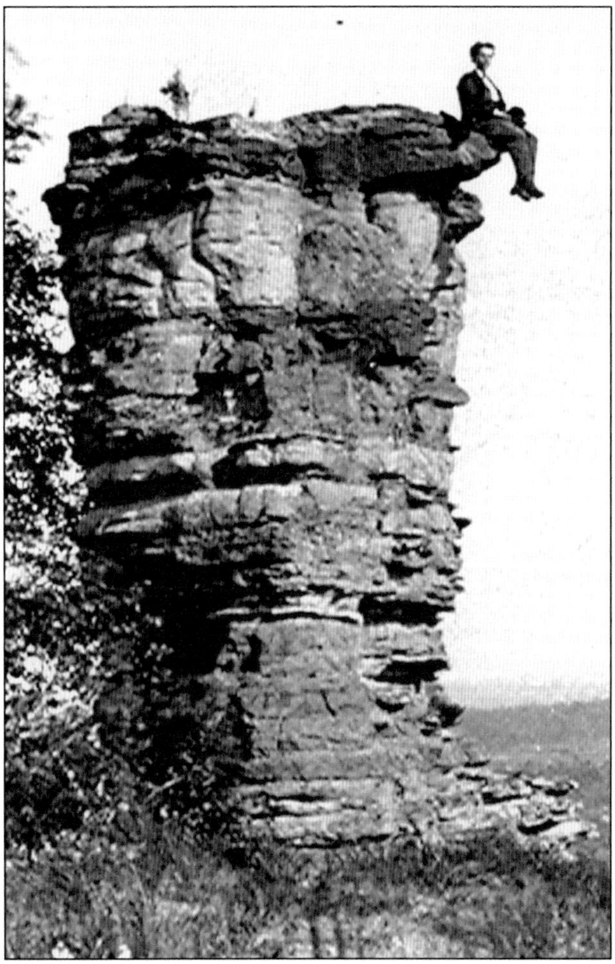

Chimney Rock, an unusual rock formation, now sits on private property, north of Menomonie, but is no less a point of interest. It has been the destination of visitors for over 100 years. (Courtesy of UWSA.)

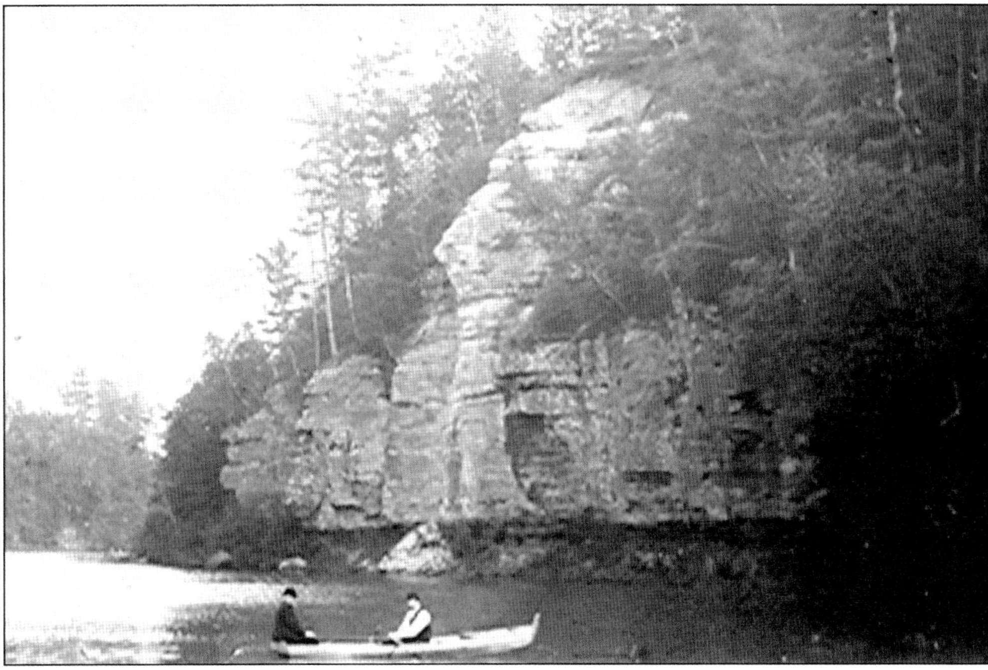

Wilson Creek was a pastoral setting for boat rides and scenery. The limestone cliffs rise far above the creek, giving the experience an almost inspirational feel. (Courtesy of UWSA.)

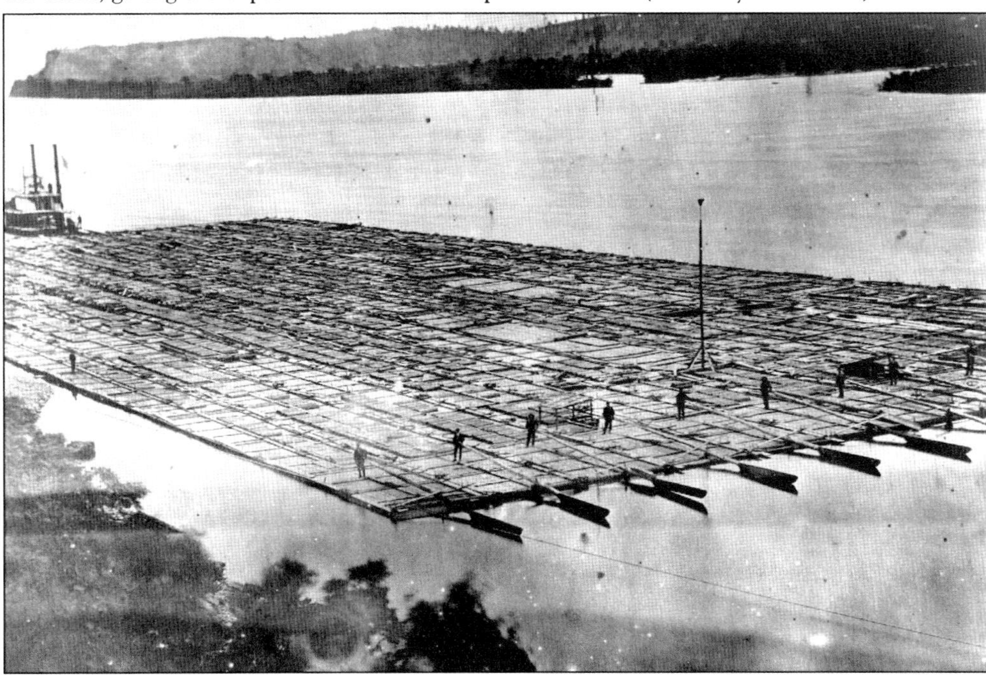

Towed by the steamer *Annie Girdon*, this raft of logs travels down the river to be milled. Although the focus in the history of Menomonie is on lumber, there was also a considerable fleet of ships and steamers that traveled the river. The *Annie Girdon* was built in 1866 in Iowa, and was owned by the Knapp, Stout, and Co. Company. It would travel the Red Cedar and Chippewa Rivers. (Courtesy of UWSA.)

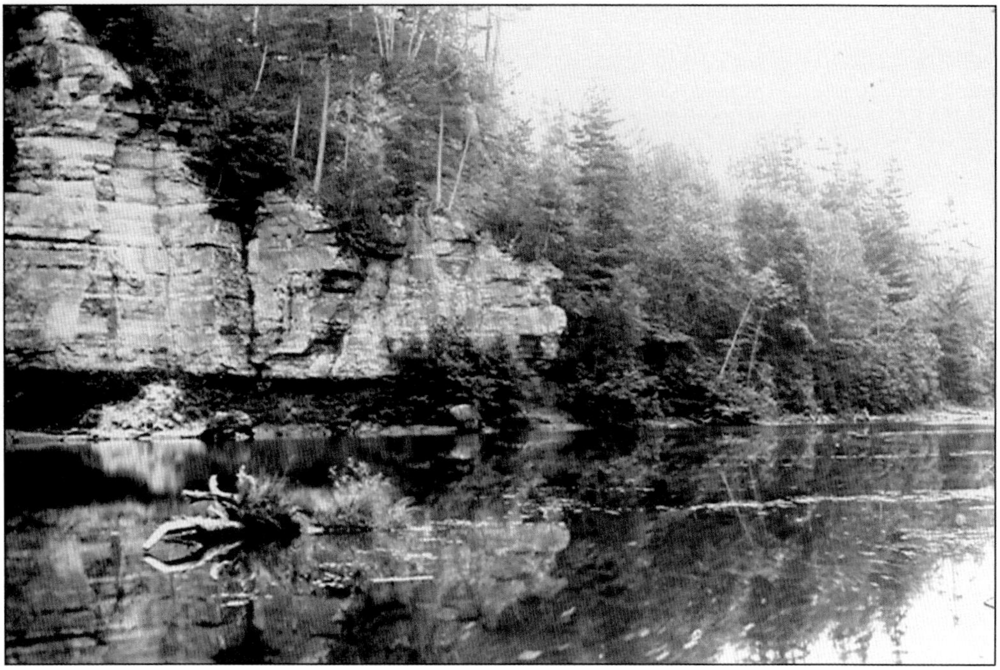

Here is another view of Wilson Creek. It is no longer possible to boat or canoe down the creek and enjoy a backdrop such as this. (Courtesy of UWSA.)

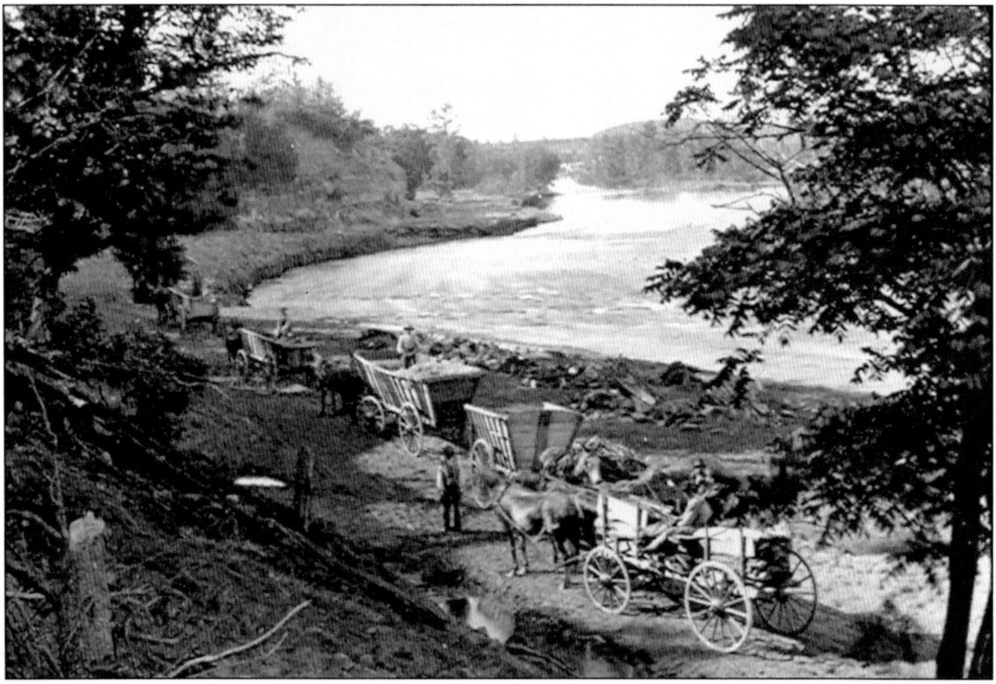

Horses were used in a variety of ways before the advent of the engine. Here they carry logs and rocks alongside the river in rustic wagons. (Courtesy of UWSA.)

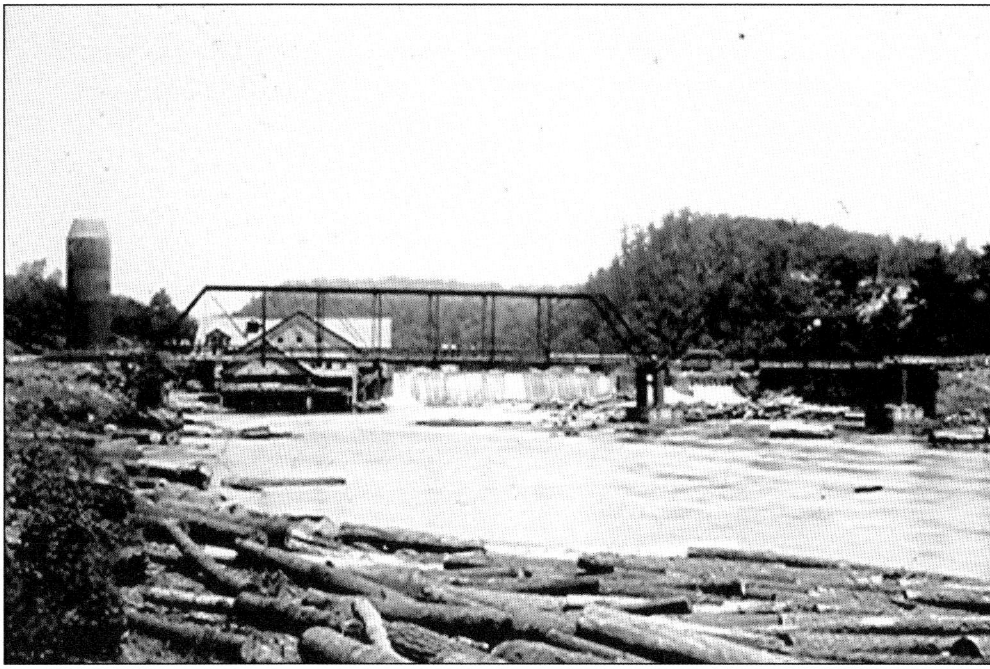

The dam at Cedar Falls is located a few miles north of Menomonie. Cedar Falls was once a site for one of the many mills run by the lumber company. (Courtesy of UWSM.)

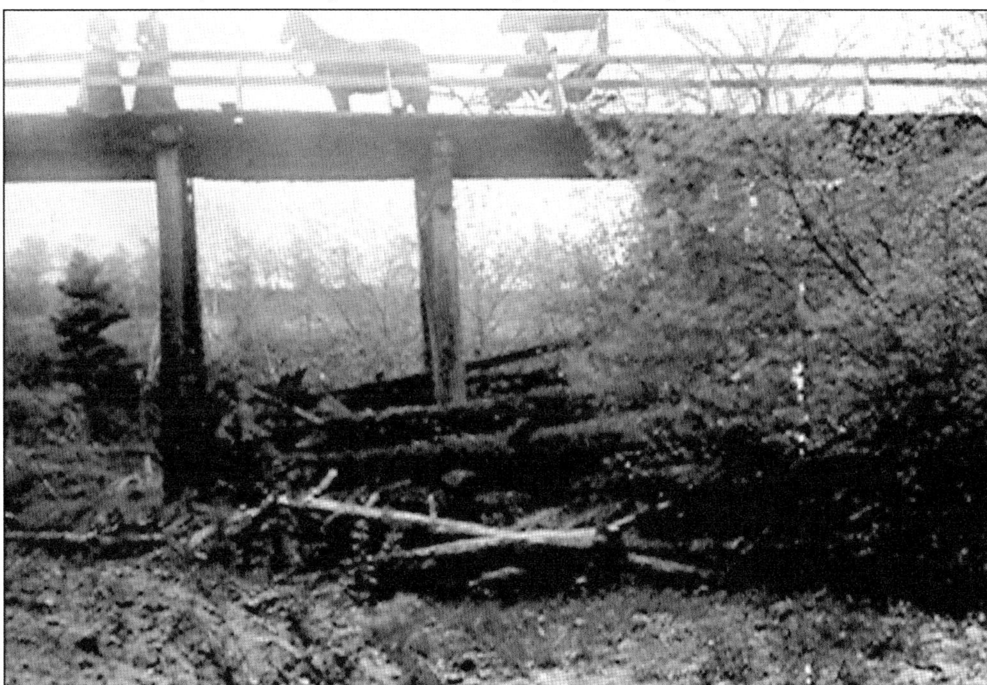

Paradise Valley, on the west end of town, is still a very desirable place to explore, either by car or bicycle. This bridge carried horse-drawn carriages from one side of the river to the other. Now, the Red Cedar Trail runs alongside the river, and along Paradise Valley Road part of the way. (Courtesy of UWSA.)

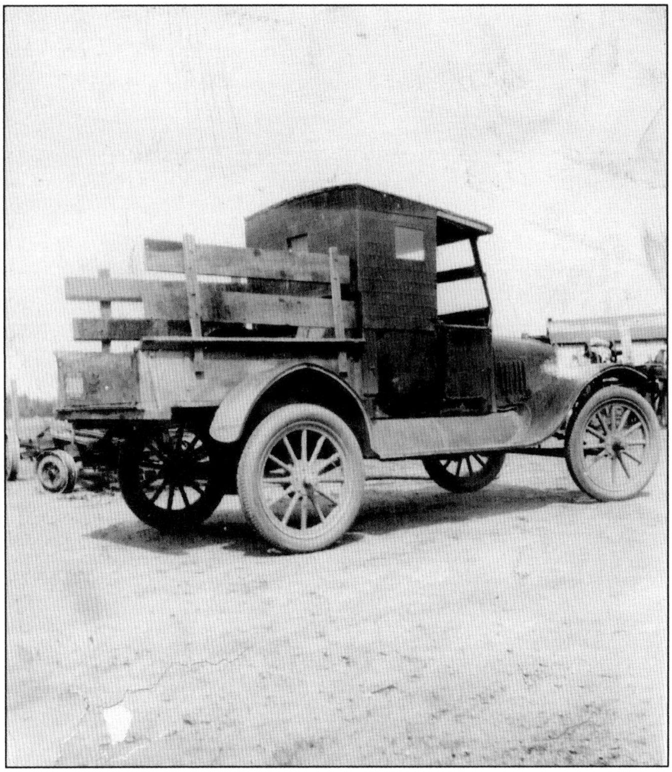

An old pickup truck could make life easier on the farm, no matter what its style. (Courtesy of UWSA)

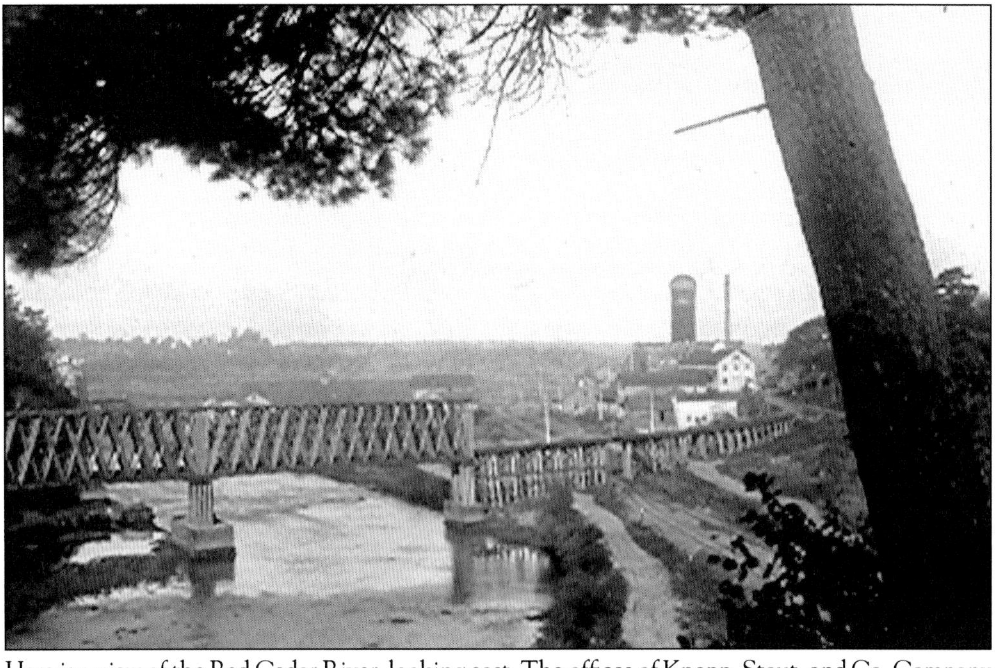

Here is a view of the Red Cedar River, looking east. The offices of Knapp, Stout, and Co. Company can be seen in the background. Menomonie's downtown area was to the right and behind the offices. Note the railroad bridge; it still stands, although a new walking trail may be planned for it in the future. (Courtesy of UWSA.)

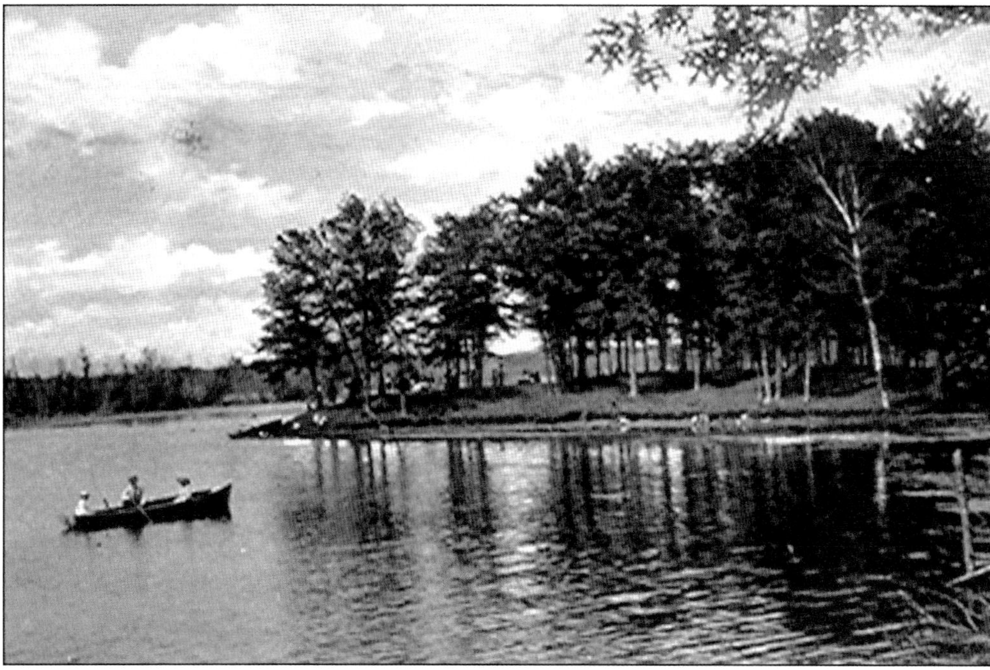

The location of this spot is not determined, but it looks as though it could be near what is now the Wakanda Beach area, on Lake Menomin. (Courtesy of UWSA.)

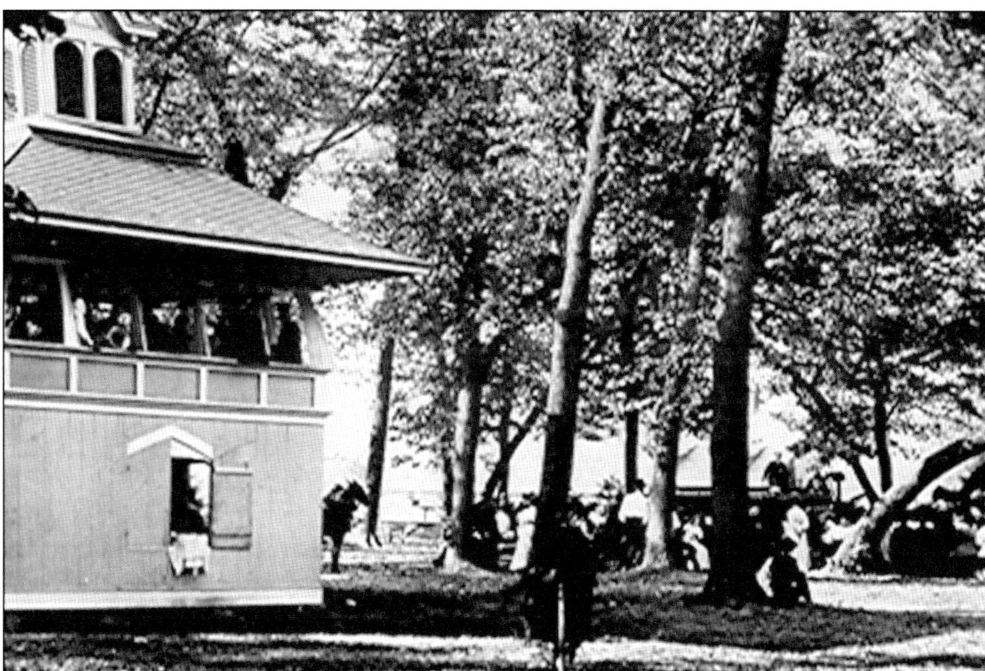

Riverside Park is pictured in the early part of the century. This park is now alongside the Red Cedar Trail, and offers visitors a pleasing place to picnic, bike, and relax. Bicycle groups from the Minneapolis-St. Paul area use the park to stage annual weekend rides such as the Weekend on Wheels. (Courtesy of UWSM.)

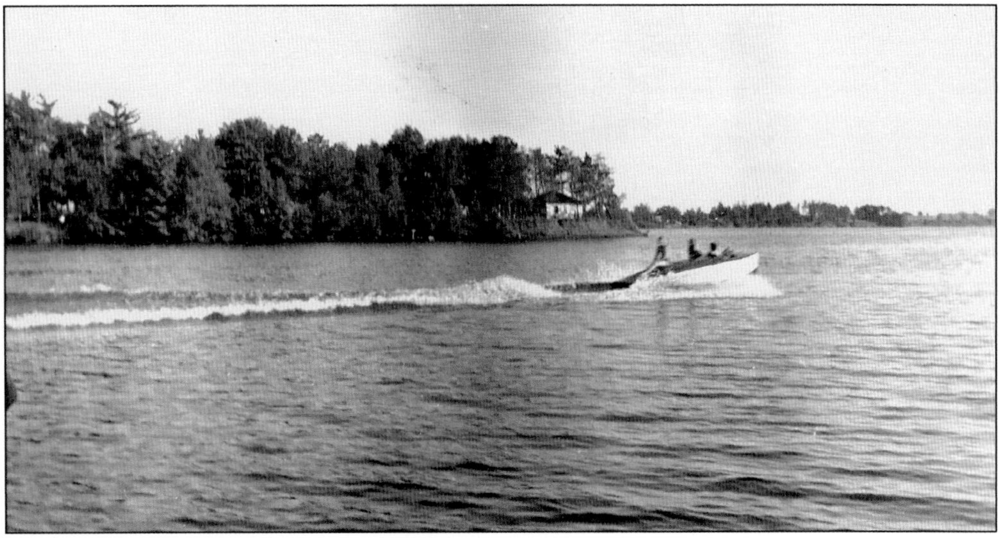

Boating is still popular on Lake Menomin, and sailboats can be seen today on the lake. This image is taken where the Red Cedar River narrows and creates a natural pathway past cottages. (Courtesy of Alta Vasey Morgan.)

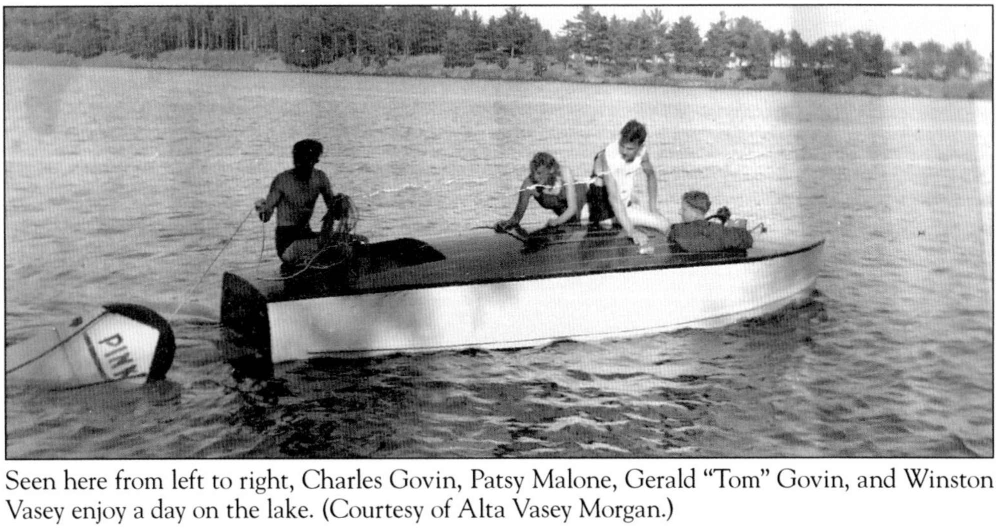

Seen here from left to right, Charles Govin, Patsy Malone, Gerald "Tom" Govin, and Winston Vasey enjoy a day on the lake. (Courtesy of Alta Vasey Morgan.)

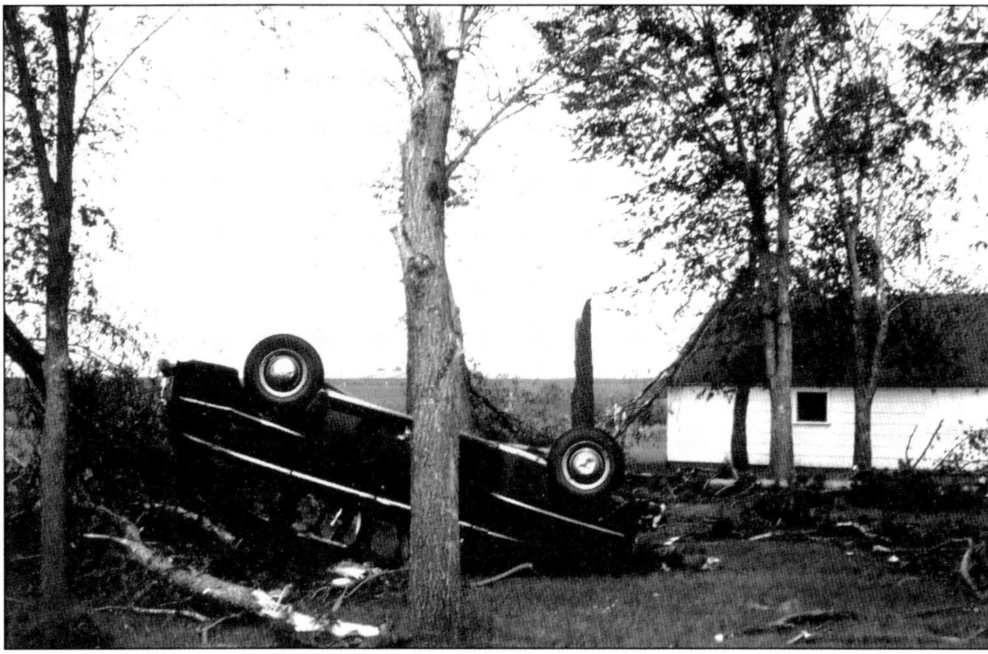

Storms can be quite destructive in this part of the Midwest. The storm of 1980 was such a storm, causing thousands of dollars of damage to homes, cars, trees, and other buildings. It was considered to be a straight-line windstorm, not a tornado, though the destruction caused was just as significant. (Courtesy of Sofi Doane.)

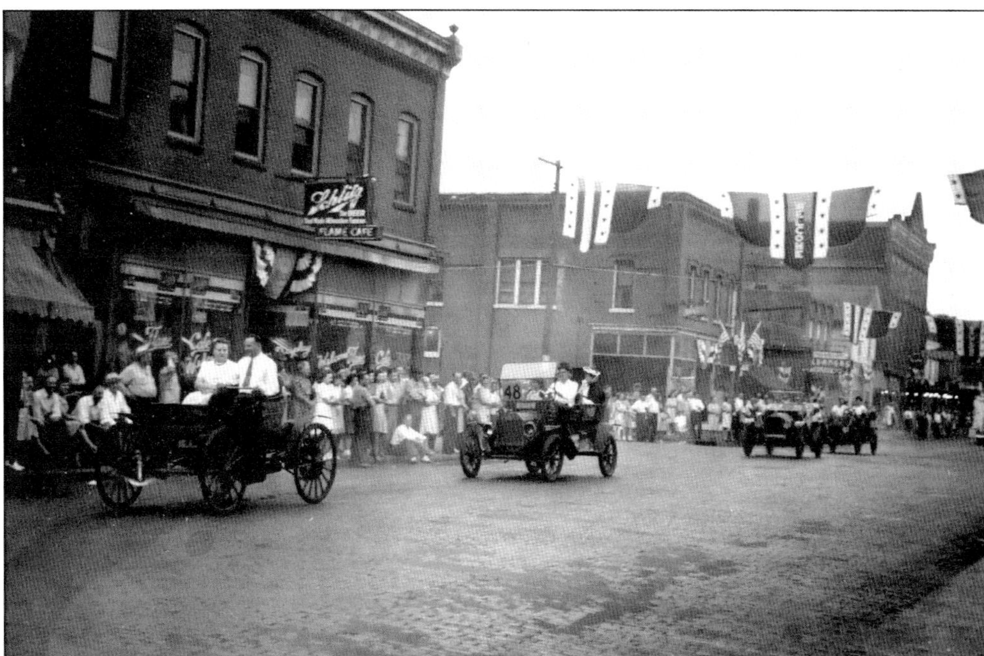

The centennial parade in Menomonie was a community affair. The building in the back, on the left, now houses the Chamber of Commerce. (Courtesy of UWSA.)

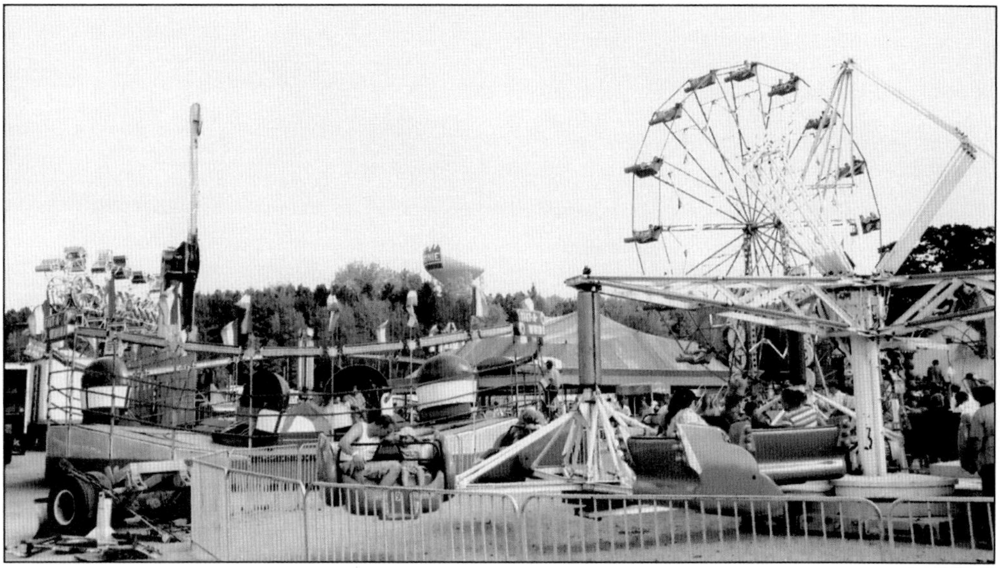

Shown here is the Dunn County Fair, 2006, at the Dunn County Recreation Park. According to fair officials, attendance in this year was one of the largest in many years. Many businesses host booths to give visibility to the community, and 4-H students work hard to get their projects finished for exhibit. The first Dunn County Fair was held in 1886 and organized by 40 local farmers. It continues to this day, offering people a chance to learn and exhibit. (Courtesy of Bruce Dybvik.)

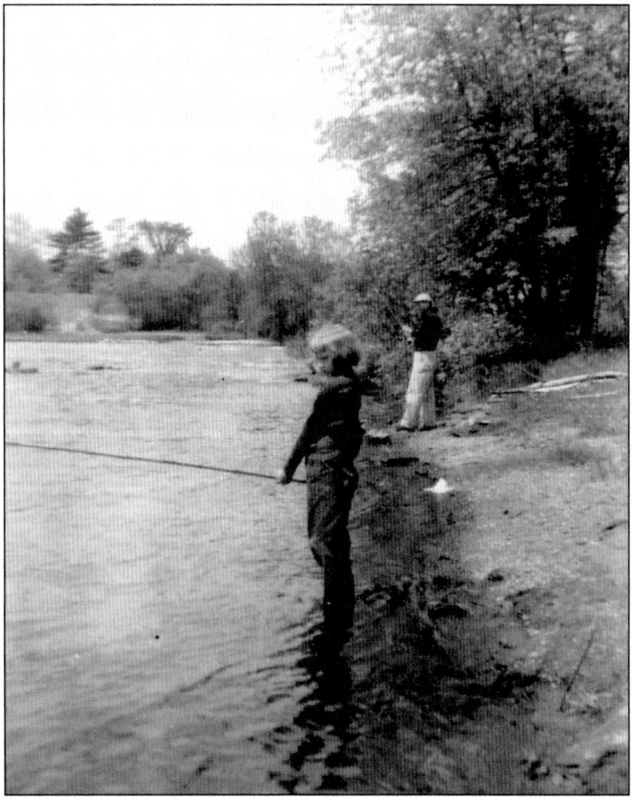

Fishing is always popular on the banks of the Red Cedar River. (Courtesy of UWSA.)

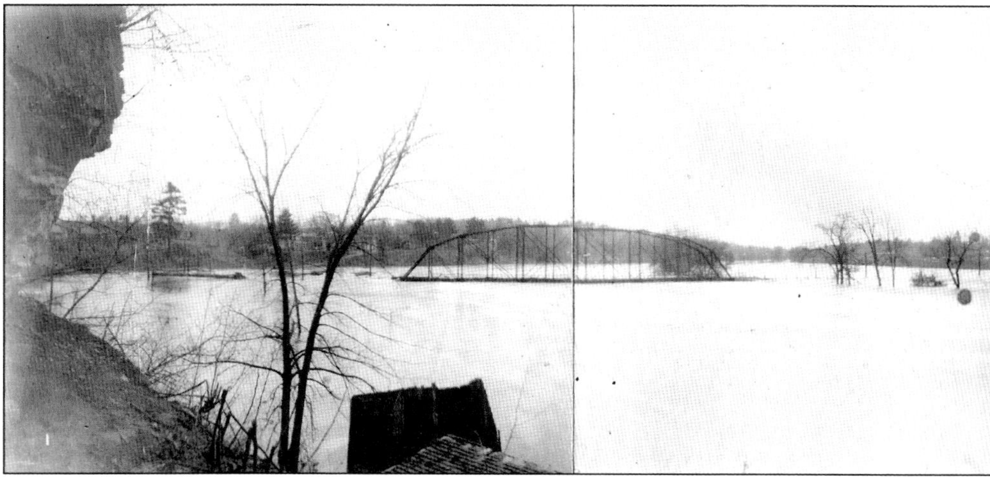

Flooding was common in the early years Menomonie. (Courtesy of Alta Morgan)

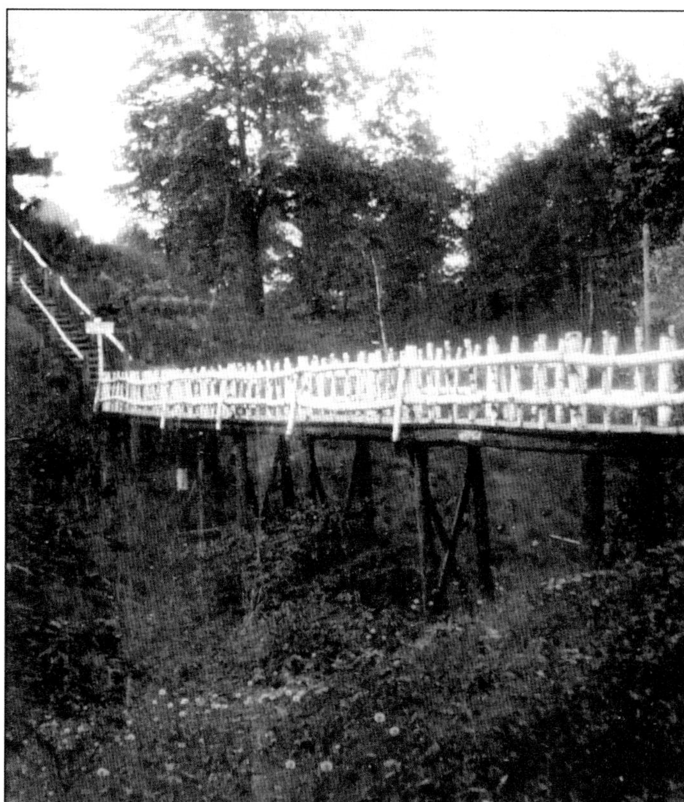

The location of this bridge is unknown, but the back of the photograph indicates a "footbridge in Menomonie." (Courtesy of Mary Shows.)

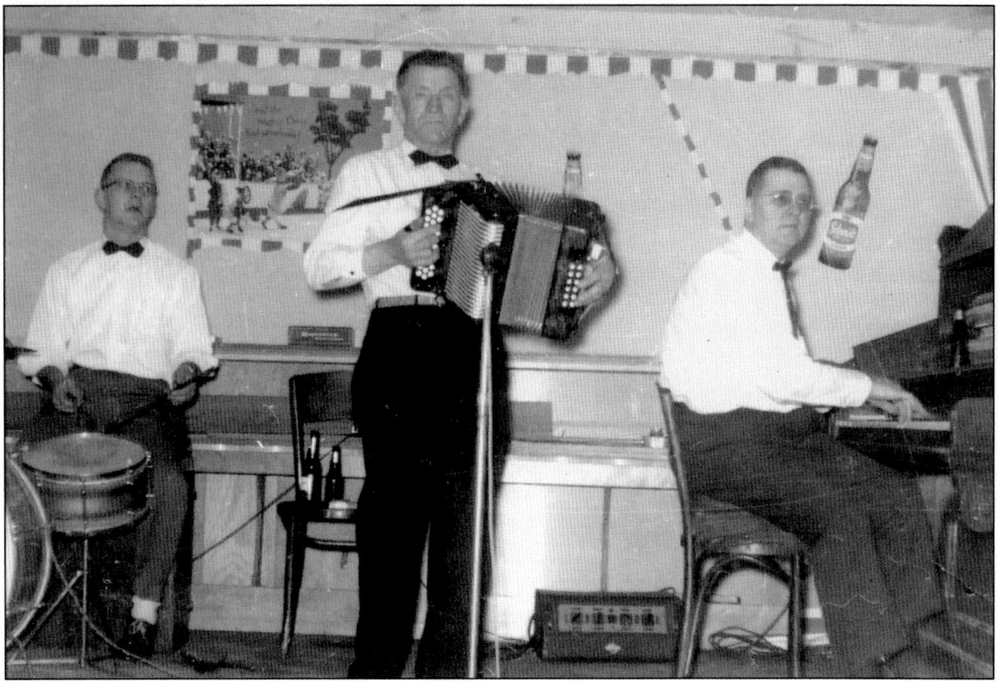

Fred Clements led a popular band that played in the Menomonie, Downsville, and Irvington areas. It was known officially as Fred's Old Tyme Orchestra, and was the first group to play a wedding, at the nearby Crystal Cave in Spring Valley. Pictured here, from left to right, are Don Clements, Helmer Debee, and Fred Clements. (Courtesy of Sofi Doane.)

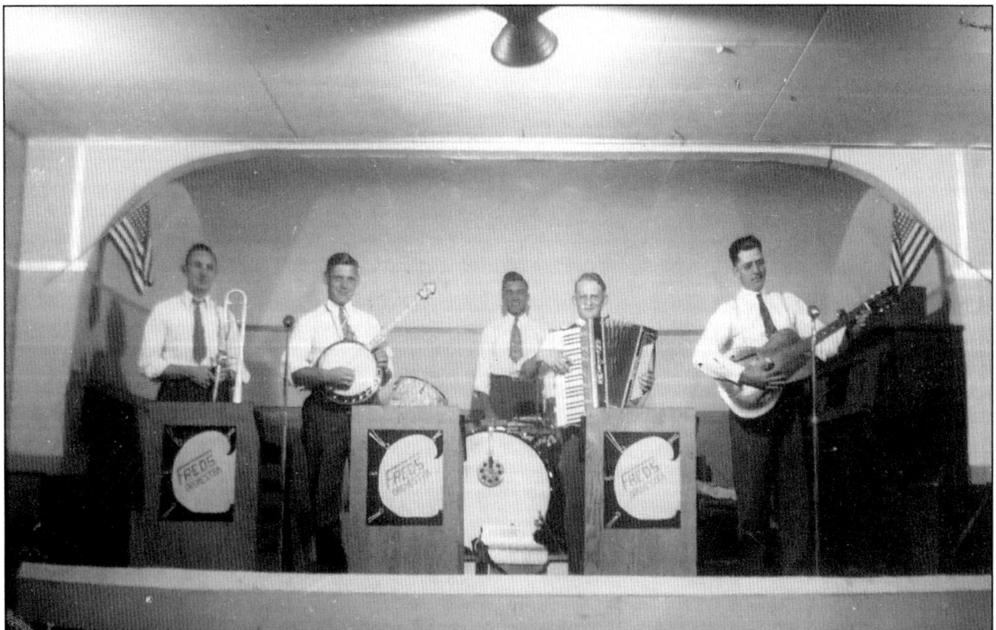

Here is another picture of the orchestra. Members Howard Buss, Paul Krueger, Harland Scheel, Ervin Oebser, and Fred Clements played old time music in Irvington at the Red Rooster and the 400 Club. (Courtesy of Sofi Doane.)

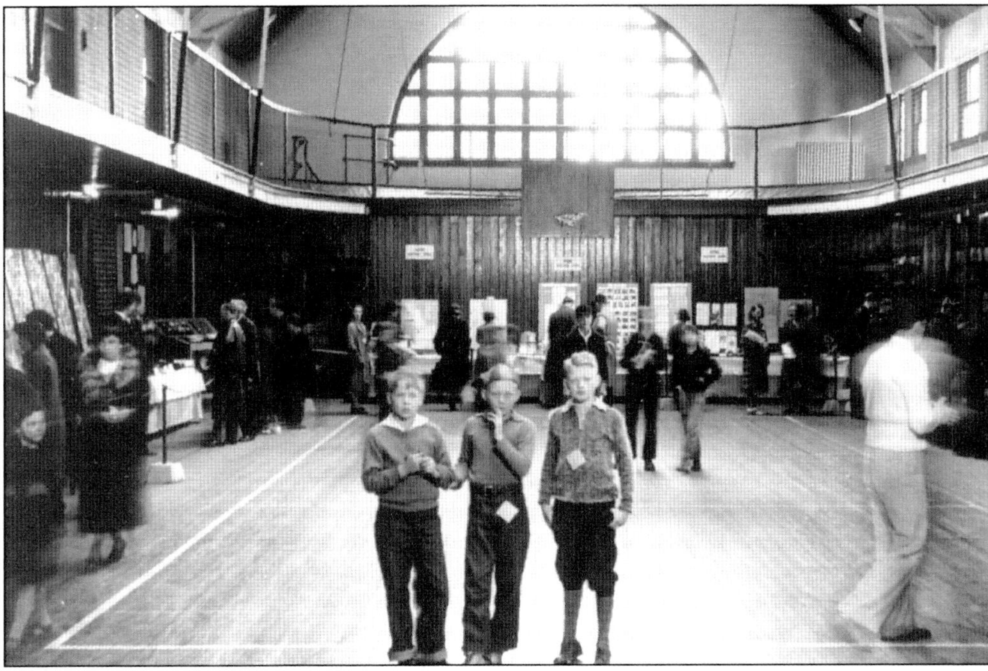

In 1937, a hobby show was held at the Stout Institutes's gymnasium. People of all ages attended and shared their particular interests. This gym and the accompanying natatorium were considered state of the art in 1901. (Courtesy of UWSA.)

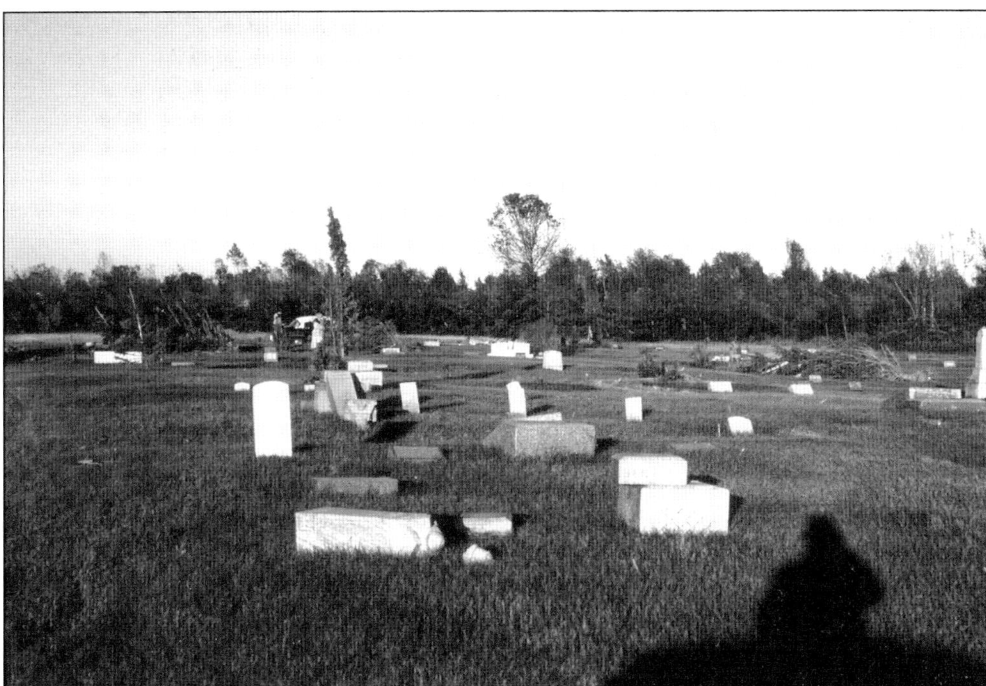

The storm of 1980 did damage to cemeteries, as well as buildings and cars. Here headstones scatter the ground. (Courtesy of Sofi Doane.)

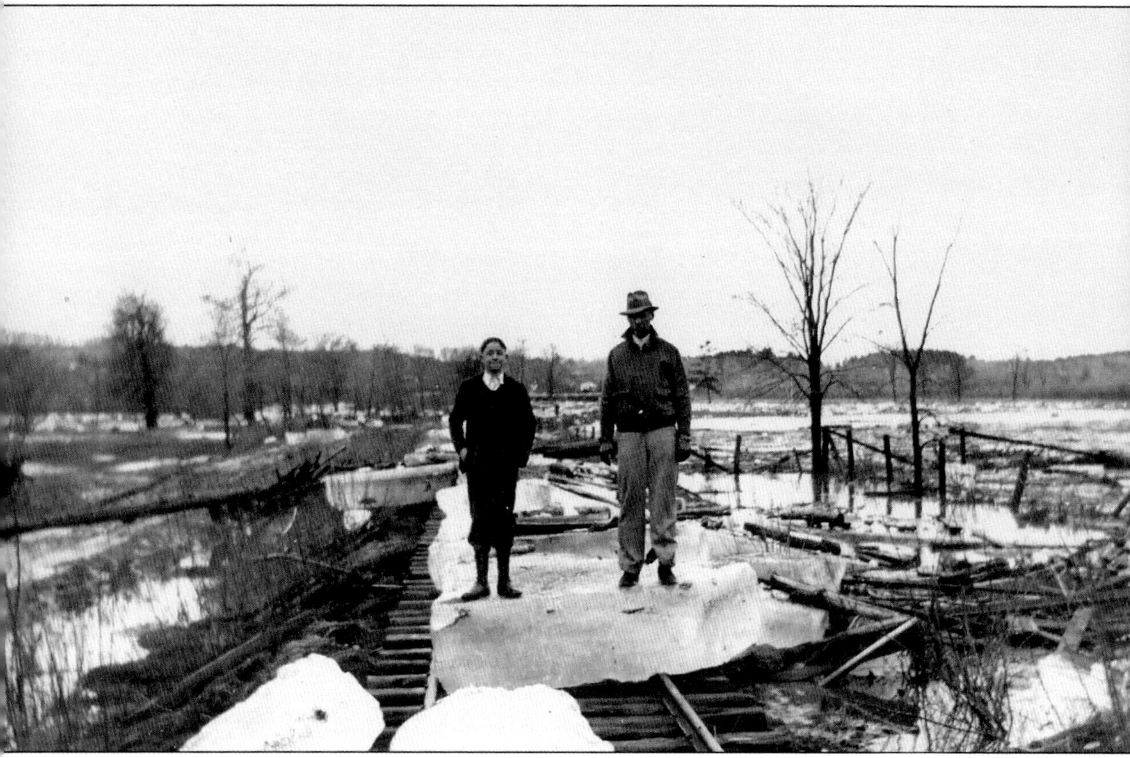

Two unidentified people brave the ice flows and stand on the railroad tracks after the flood subsided. The worst floods of the region were considered to be in 1880 and 1905. Dams at Colfax and the Wilson Mill on Elk Creek were destroyed, and the shingle mill at Cedar Falls was carried away. Many farms on the river bottoms were covered with water, causing much damage. (Courtesy of Alta Morgan.)

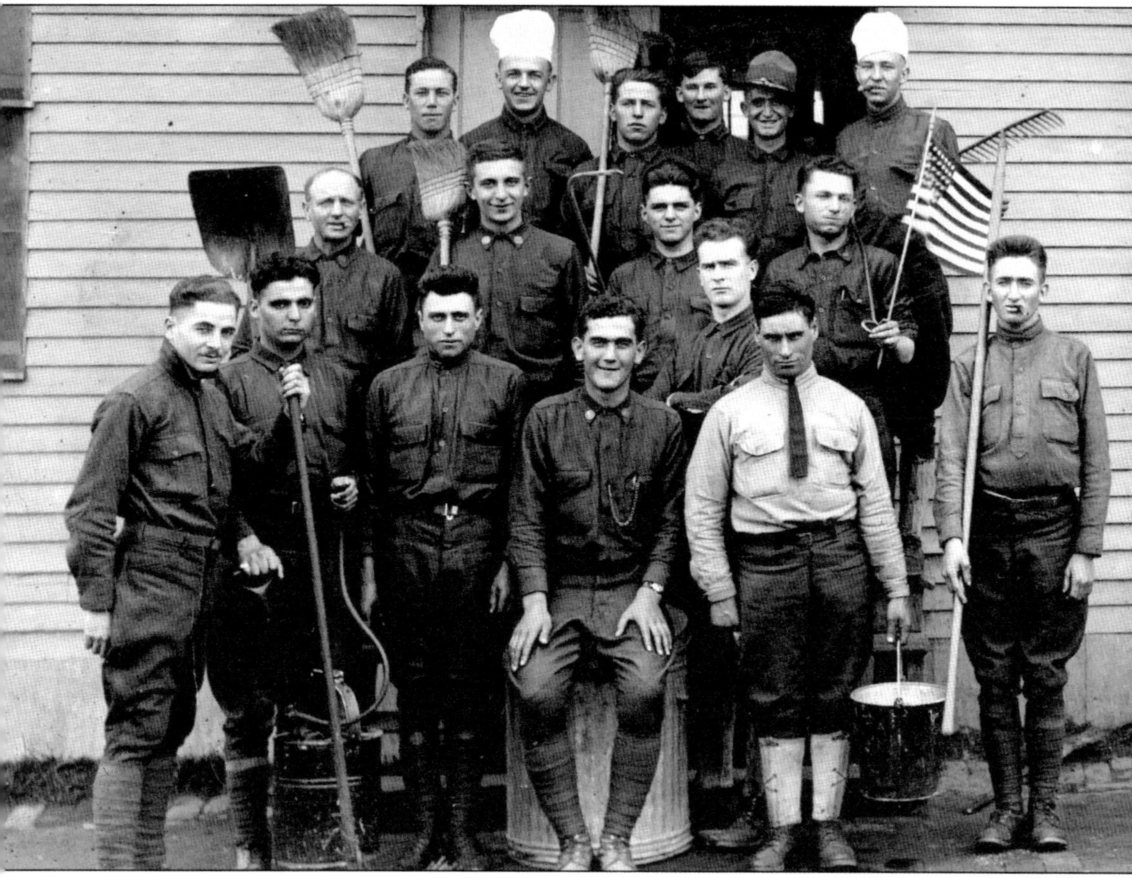

Menomonie has a history of military commitment. This photograph of the "kitchen guys" was taken in 1918 at Camp Meigs, in Washington, D.C. An organization of Spanish American War veterans was formed after the close of the war, and in 1877, Company A, 128th Infantry, was formed, also known as the Ludington Guard. The unit was named after the governor of the state at that time, Harold Ludington. (Courtesy of UWSA.)

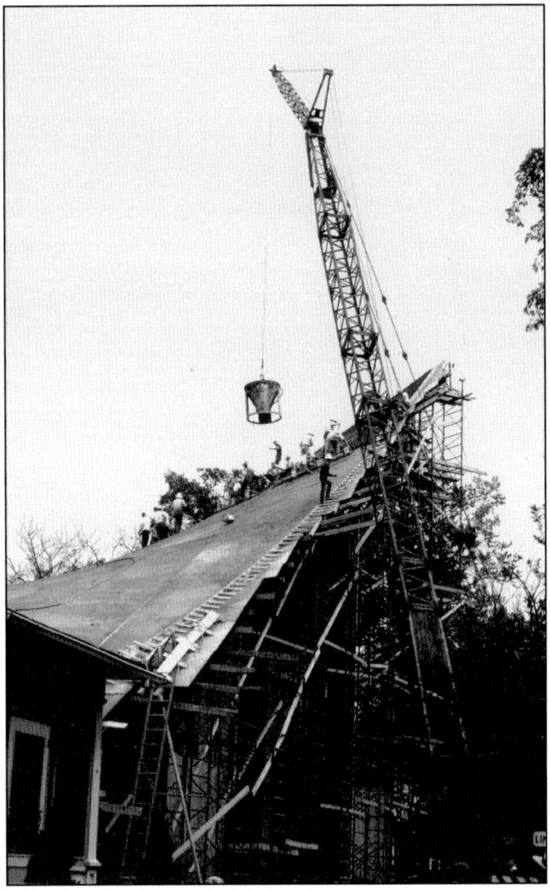

The roof of St. Joseph's Catholic Church in Menomonie is impressive with its pitch and form, but after the storm of 1980 took much of it away, parishioners had to muster courage to climb to the top and help repair the damage. (Courtesy of Sofi Doane.)

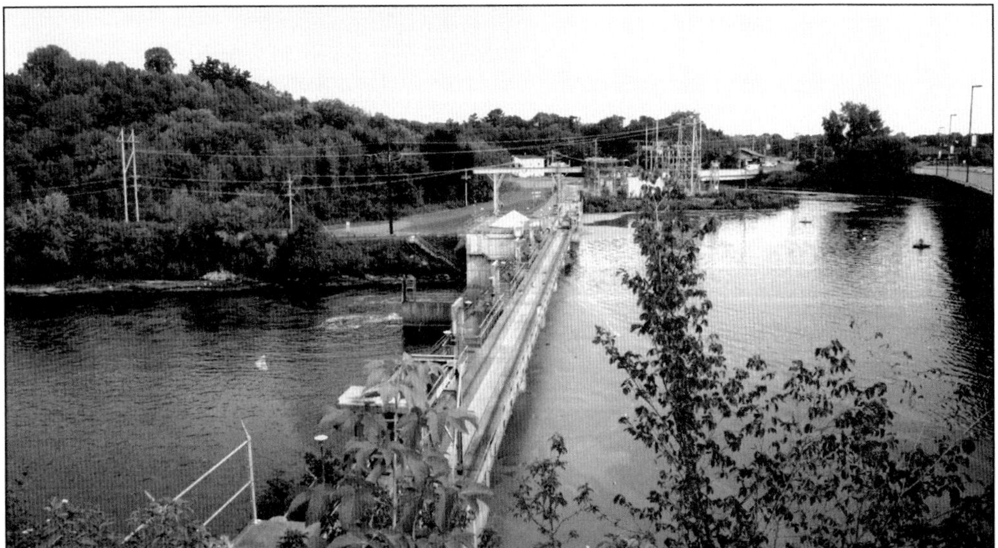

This 2006 view is of the dam over the Red Cedar River, which forms Lake Menomin. A walking trail, called Stokke Trail, now meanders along the river to the south and connects with the popular Red Cedar Trail. (Courtesy of Bruce Dybvik.)

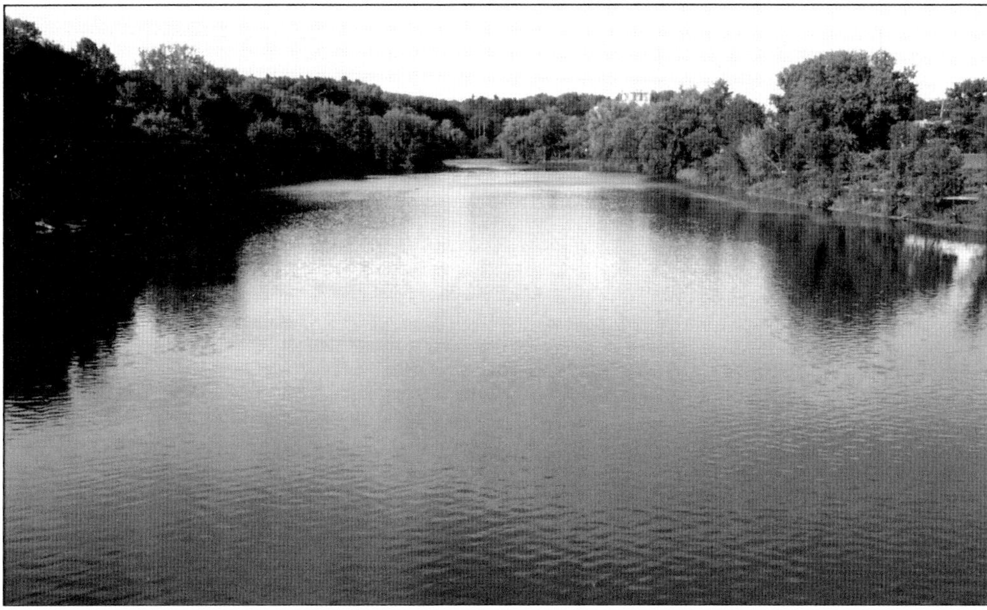
The Red Cedar River is seen on a quiet Saturday in September of 2006. This view looks south, where the river continues to wind to Downsville and beyond. (Courtesy of Bruce Dybvik.)

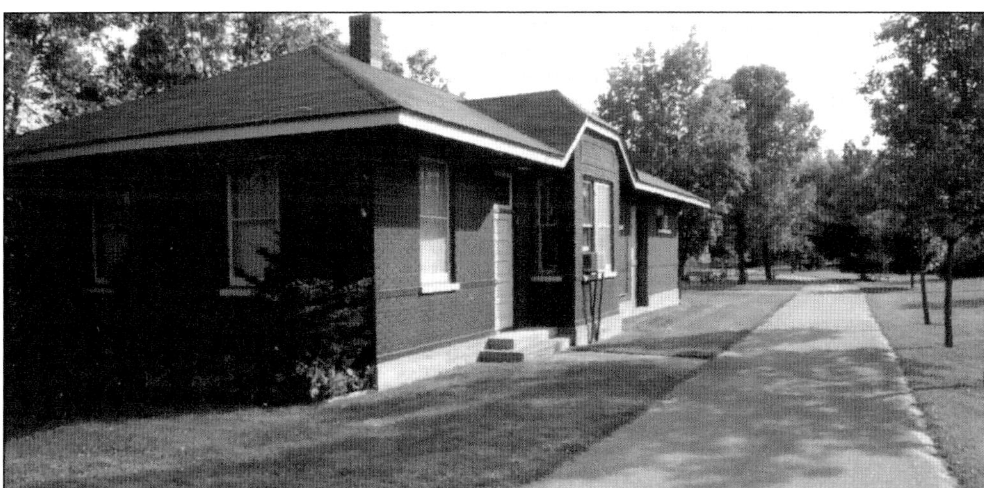
This beautiful brick building is headquarters for the Red Cedar Trail. It is considered to be one of the most vibrant trails in the state, as it follows the river on one side and a mixture of cliffs, wetlands, and prairie on the other. (Courtesy of Bruce Dybvik.)

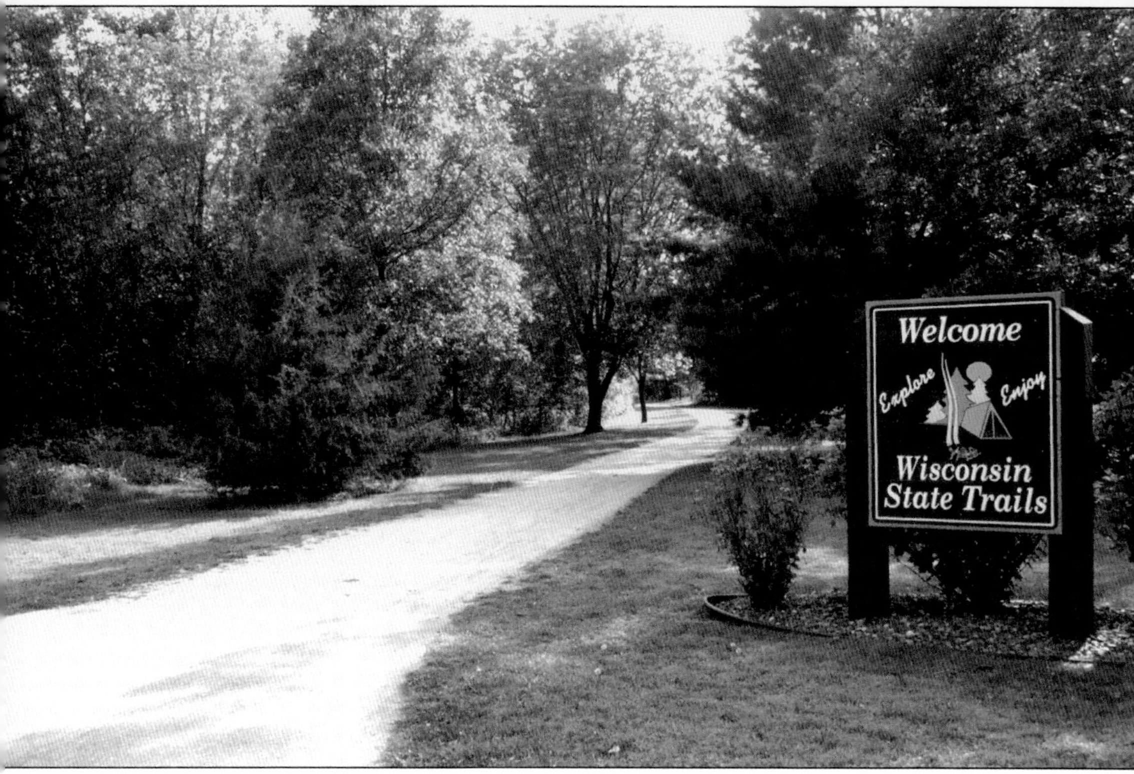

The beginning of the Red Cedar Trail, just off Highway 29, is on the west side of Menomonie. The trail is beautifully maintained throughout the year. In warm weather it offers a comfortable, flat ride on crushed gravel, and in the winter it is always kept groomed for cross-country skiing. (Courtesy of Bruce Dybvik.)

Four

COMMERCE AND CRAFT

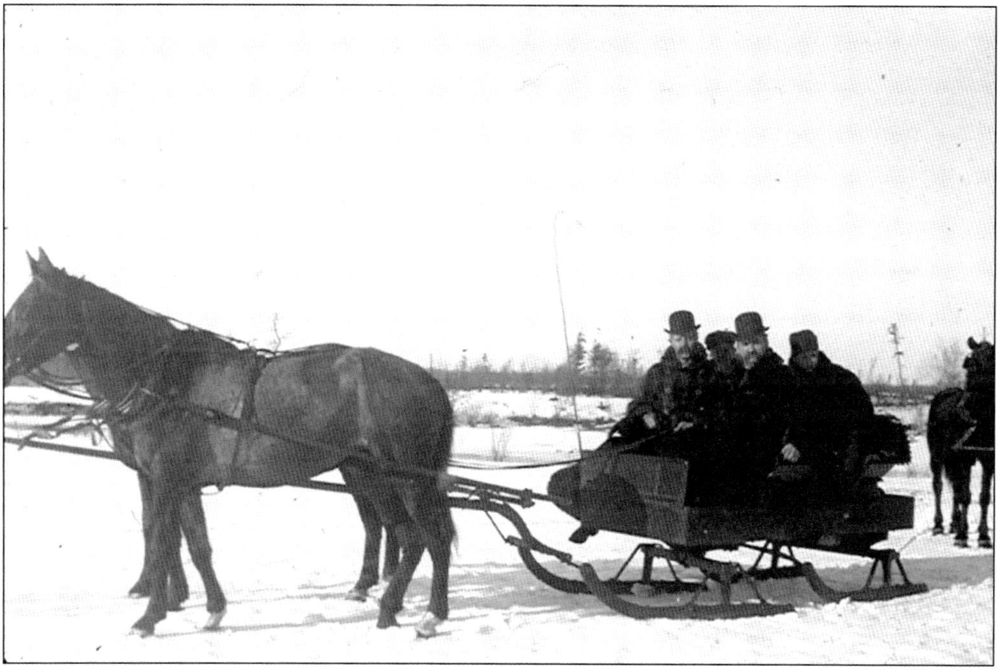

Executives of the largest lumber company in the world at the time, Knapp, Stout, and Co. Company, traveled by sleigh to survey the work crews and make sure the lumber projects were progressing in a timely manner. Each man had his own area of expertise, but all worked together to make the company successful. (Courtesy of UWSA.)

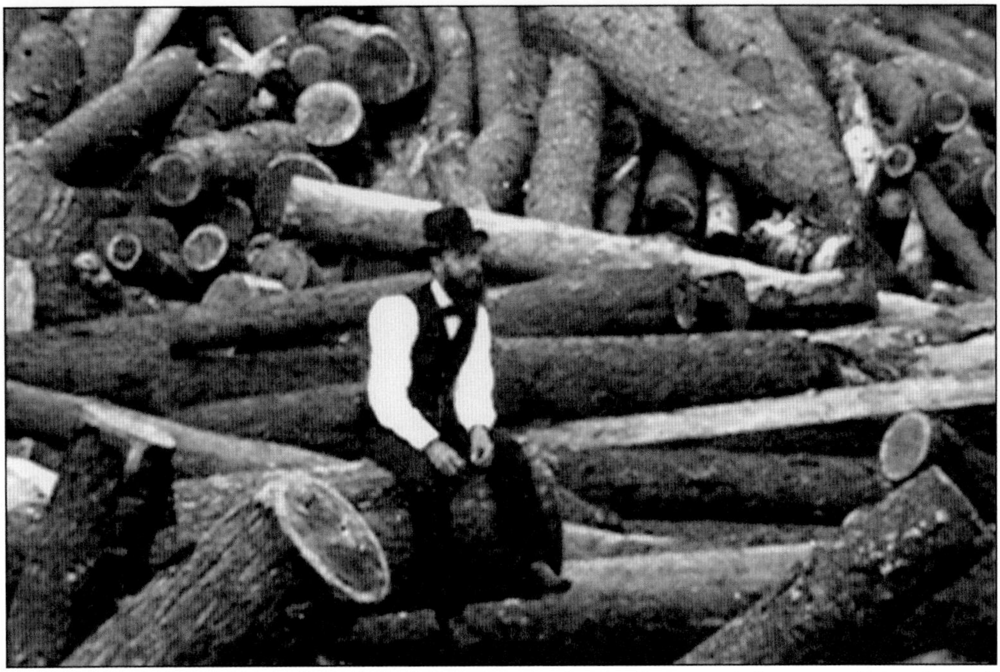

This photograph gives an idea of just how massive the timbers were that were being logged. (Courtesy of UWSA.)

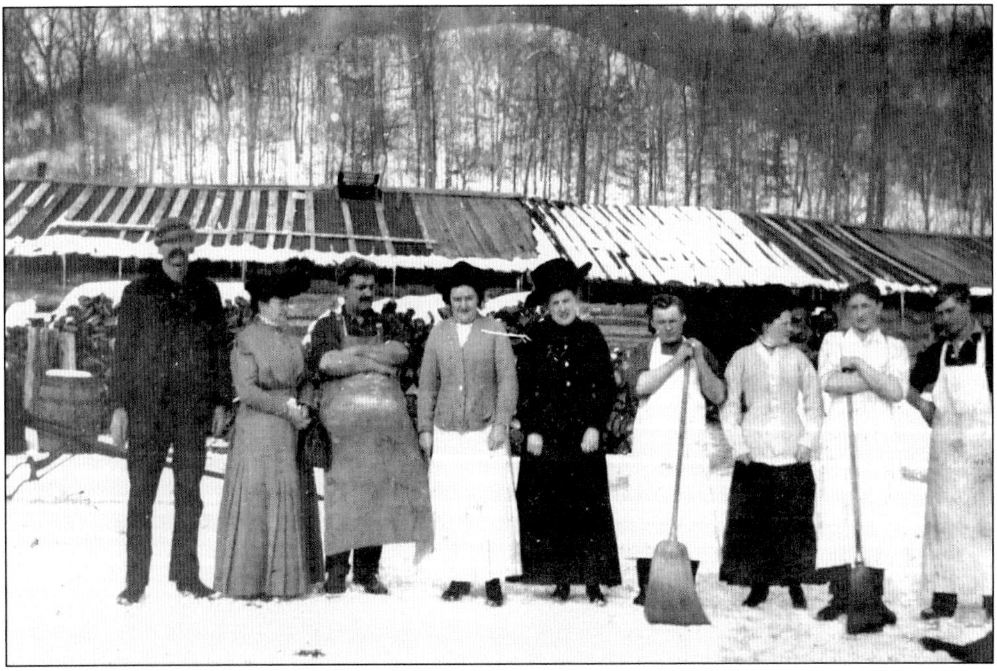

A logging camp at Weston was located west of Menomonie. In 1889, William Starr of Eau Claire bought around 14,000 acres, or half the area of Weston Township, and persuaded the Omaha railroad to put in a spur line. He then built a planing mill and began lumbering. This was the beginning of the town of Weston, where lumber operations continued until 1910. Once they subsided, so did the growth of the town. (Courtesy of UWSA.)

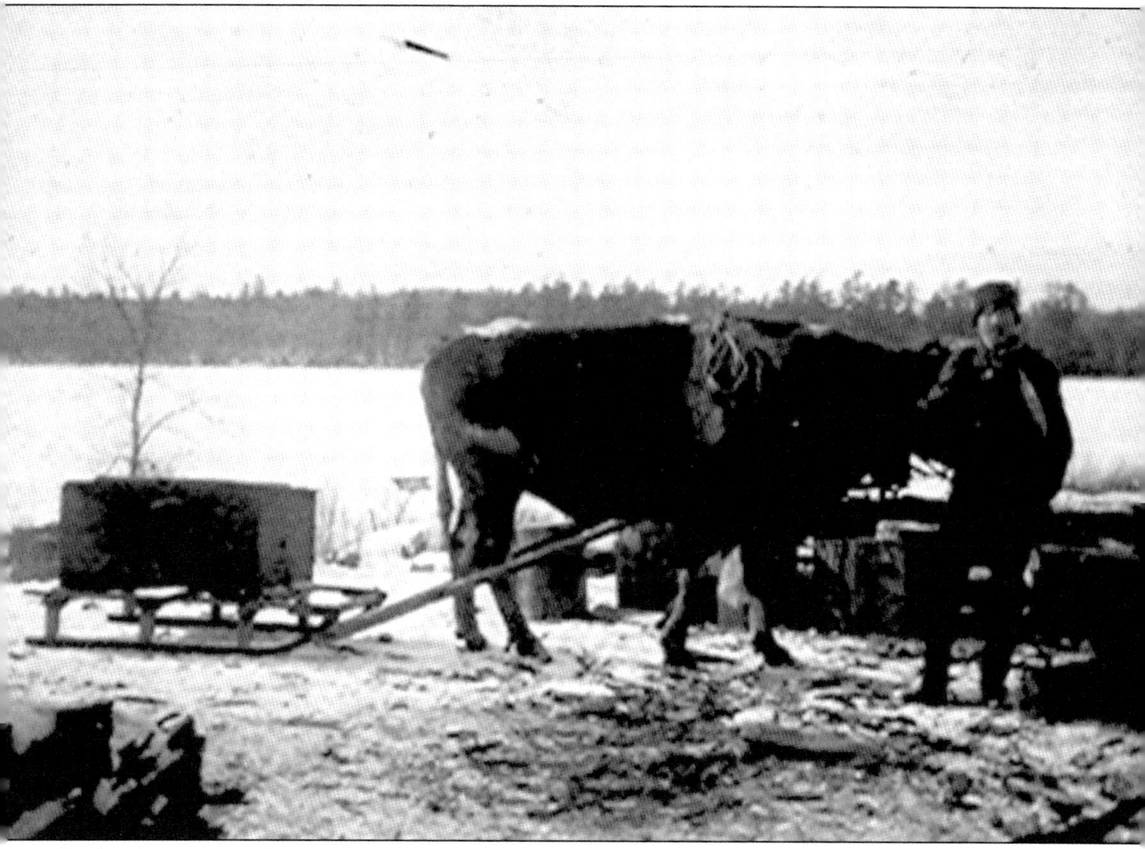

The lumberman's café was a lunch sled pulled by livestock. It was important to bring lunch to the men, so that work could continue without the interruption of having to travel back to camp. (Courtesy of UWSA.)

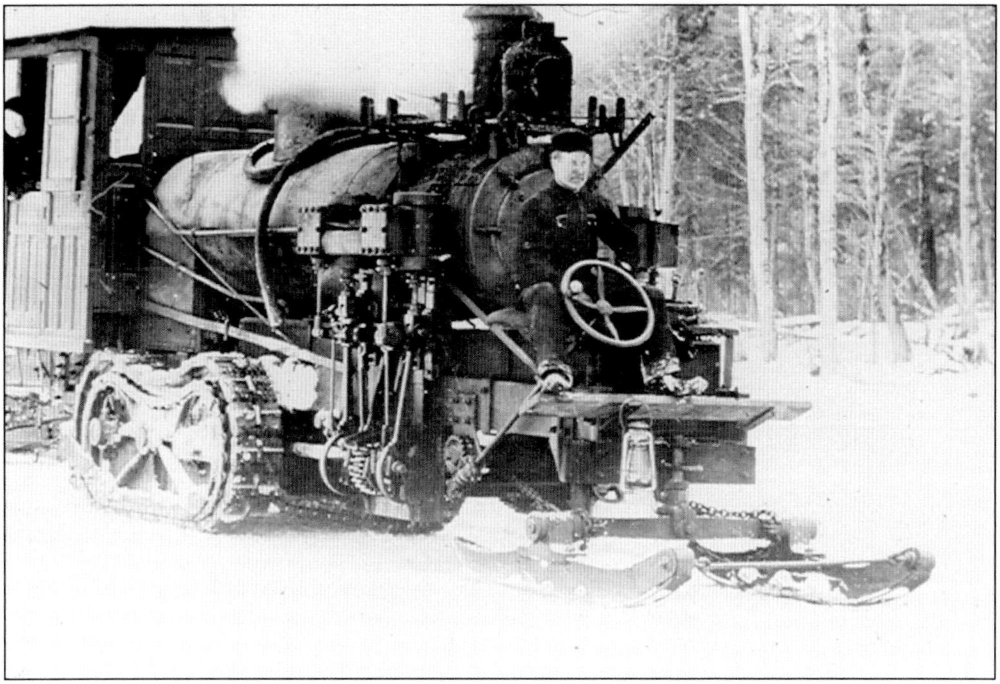

Sometimes the engine-powered machines needed skids in order to continue to operate in the heavy snow of Wisconsin winters. (Courtesy of UWSA.)

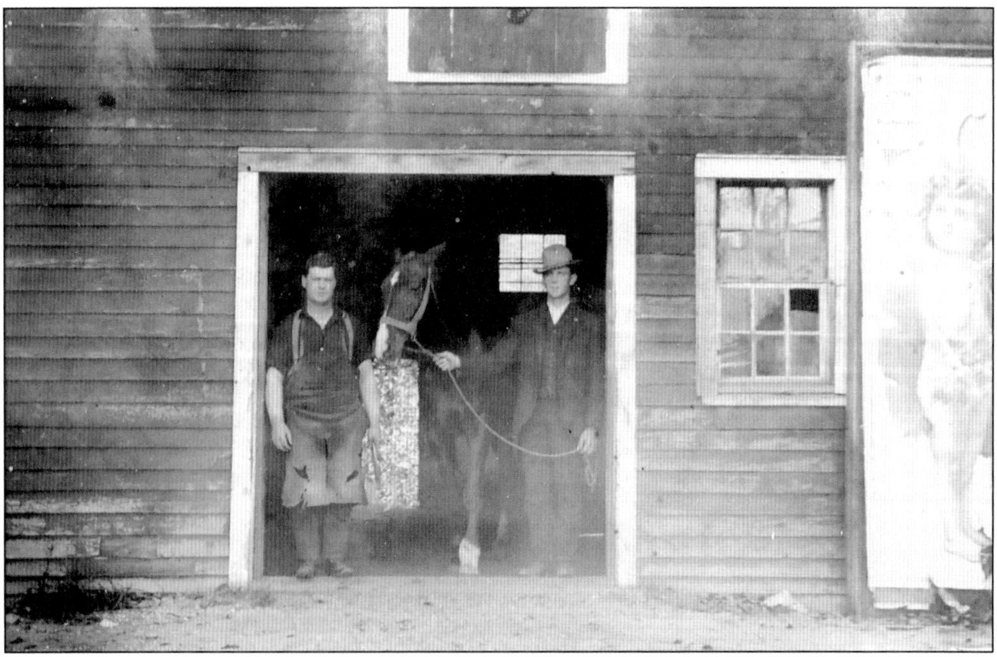

This image shows Patrick James Galvin (left) and friend in the door of Patrick's blacksmith shop. Galvin owned a shop in Menomonie until April 1907. (Courtesy of Mary Galvin Shows.)

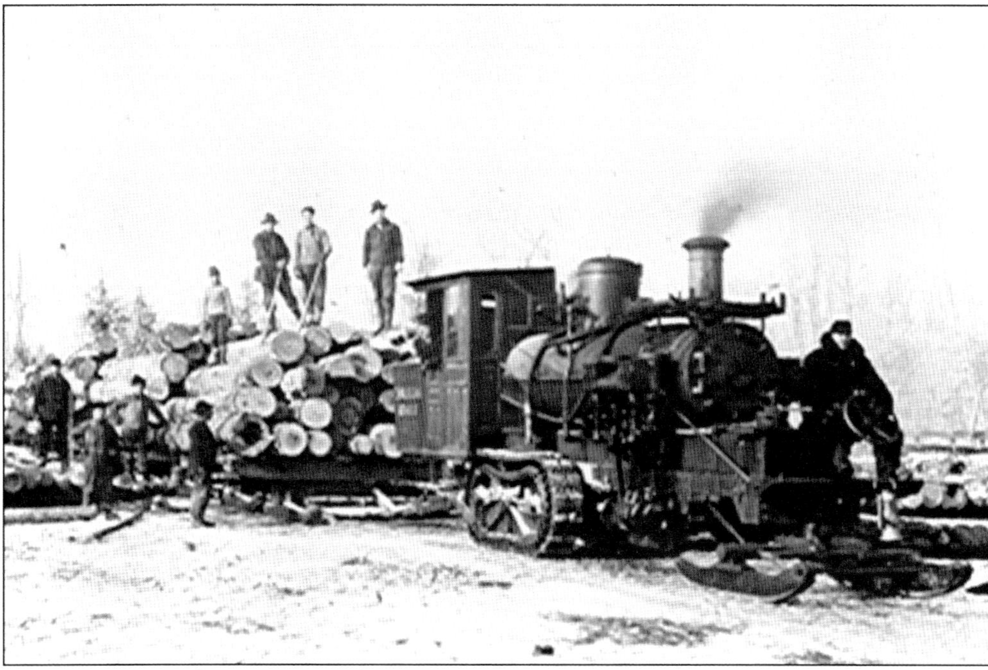

With the advent of engine power, horses were no longer worked as they had been. Lumber could be transported much faster out of the woods and to the rivers or directly to mills for processing. (Courtesy of UWSA.)

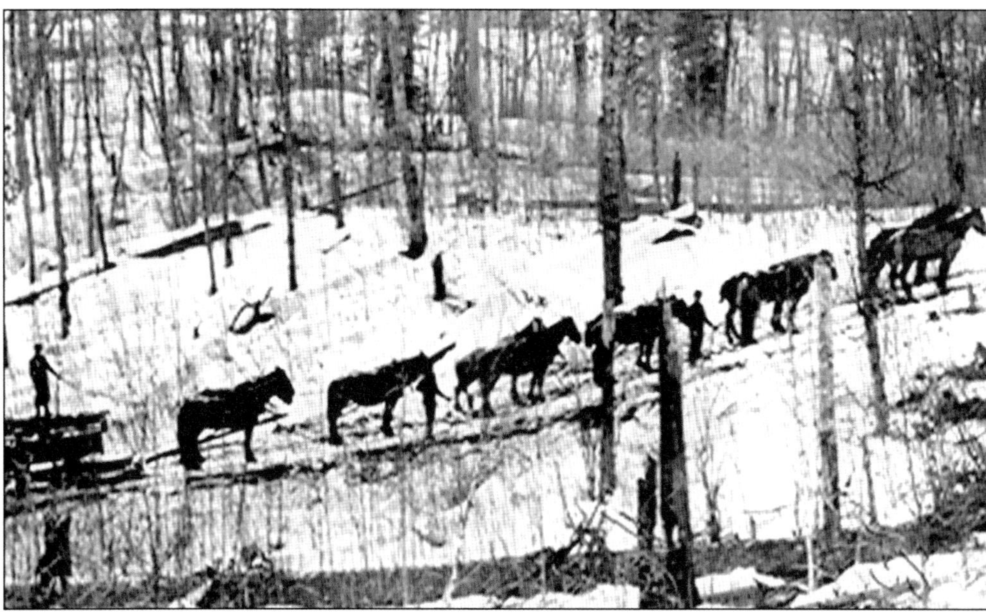

Here is an example of the kind of natural "horse power" that was needed to haul giant, felled logs from the woods. A team of 12 horses pulls its load uphill. (Courtesy of UWSA.)

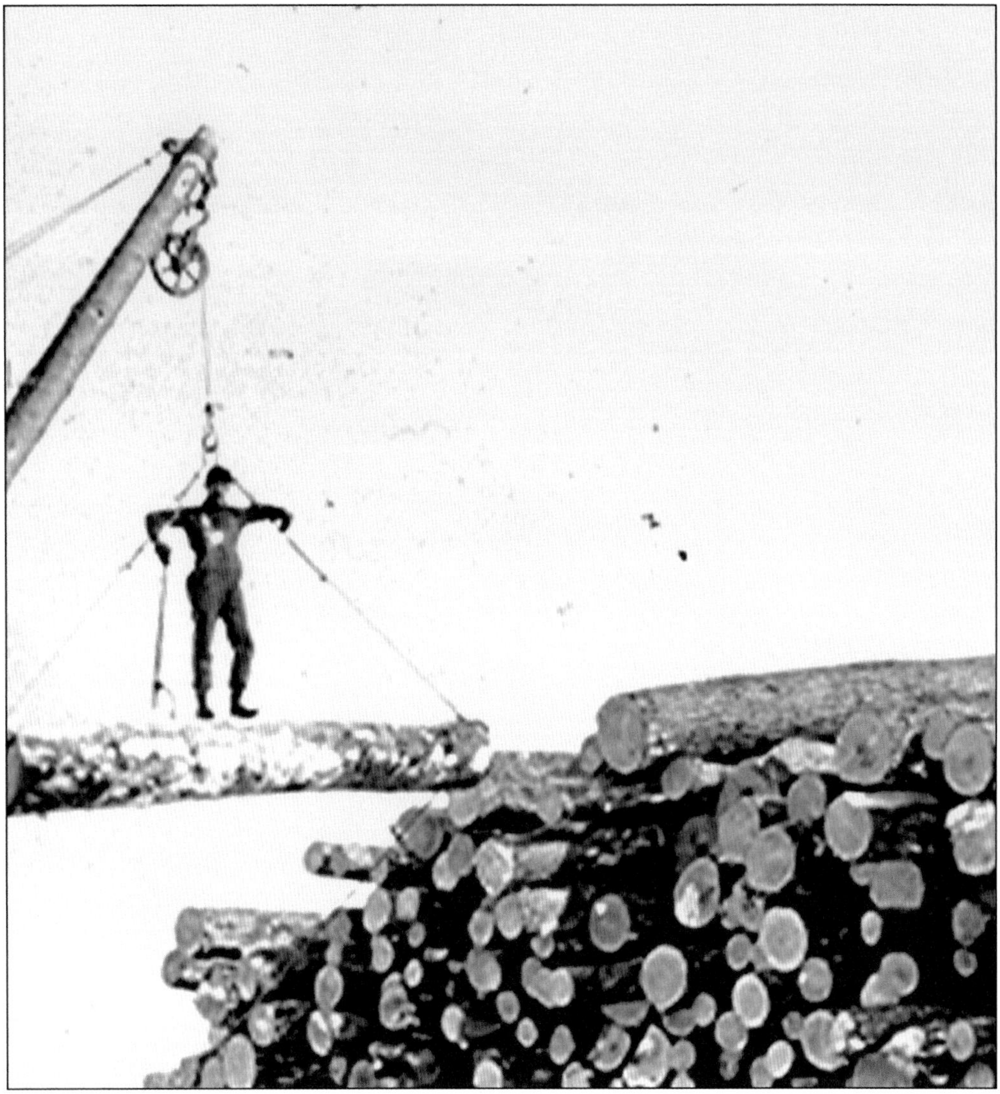

Lumbermen were asked to do work that could be very dangerous; a man guides a log into place by standing on it and giving directions to the operator. (Courtesy of UWSA.)

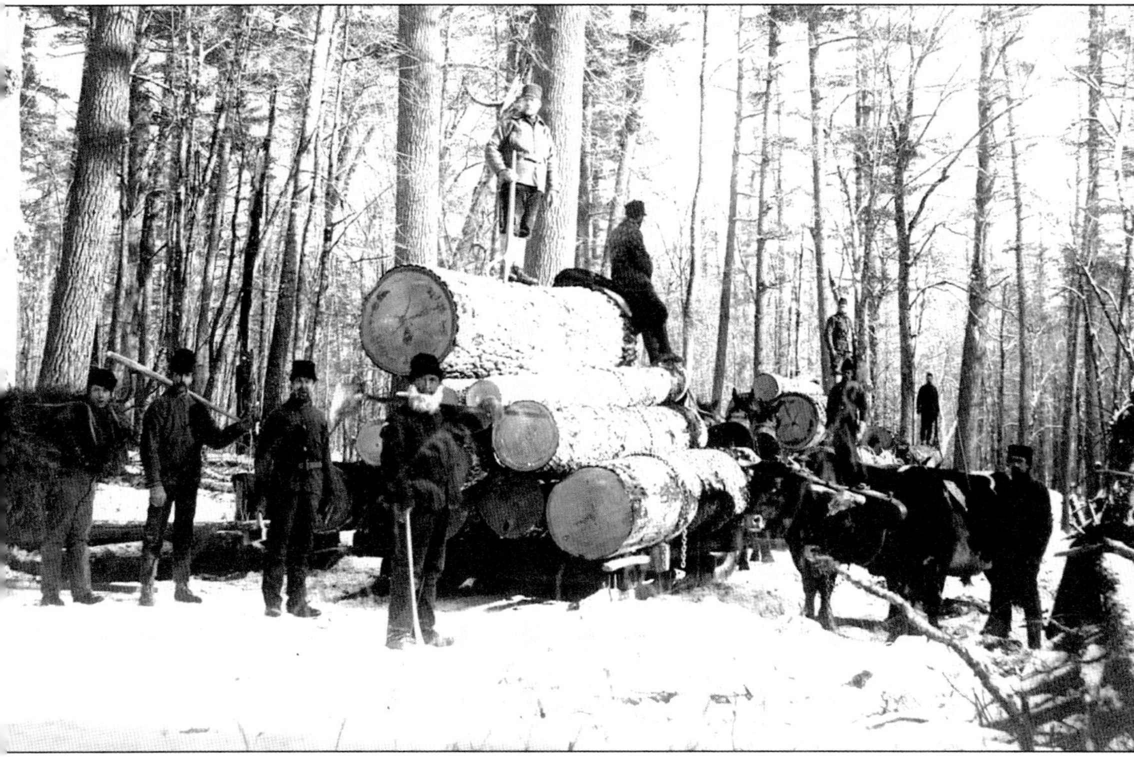

Here is another example of the size of trees felled (the animals needed to do the work) and the size of a lumberjack crew. (Courtesy of UWSA.)

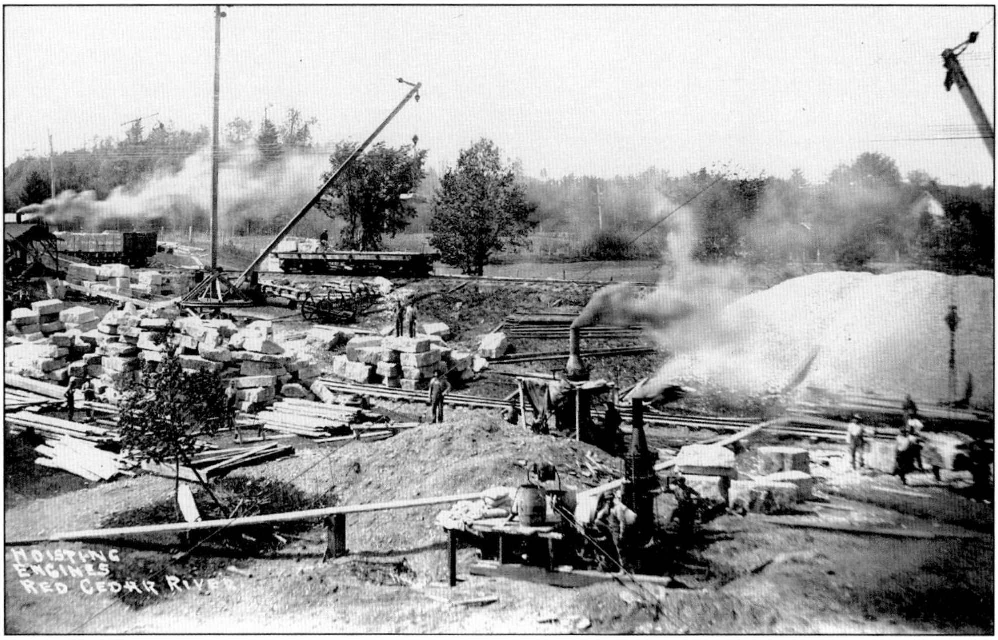

Pictured here is an active mill, where trees are made into a marketable product before being shipped further down river, to their retail or construction destination. (Courtesy of UWSA.)

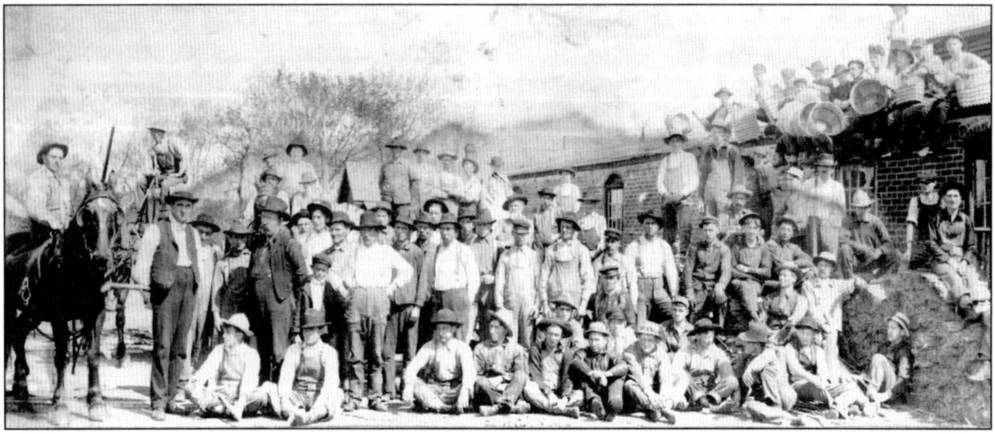

Irvington, just south and west of Menomonie, was once a thriving little town. It even boasted a basket factory. Pictured are the employees, some of them with baskets. (Courtesy of Sofi Doane.)

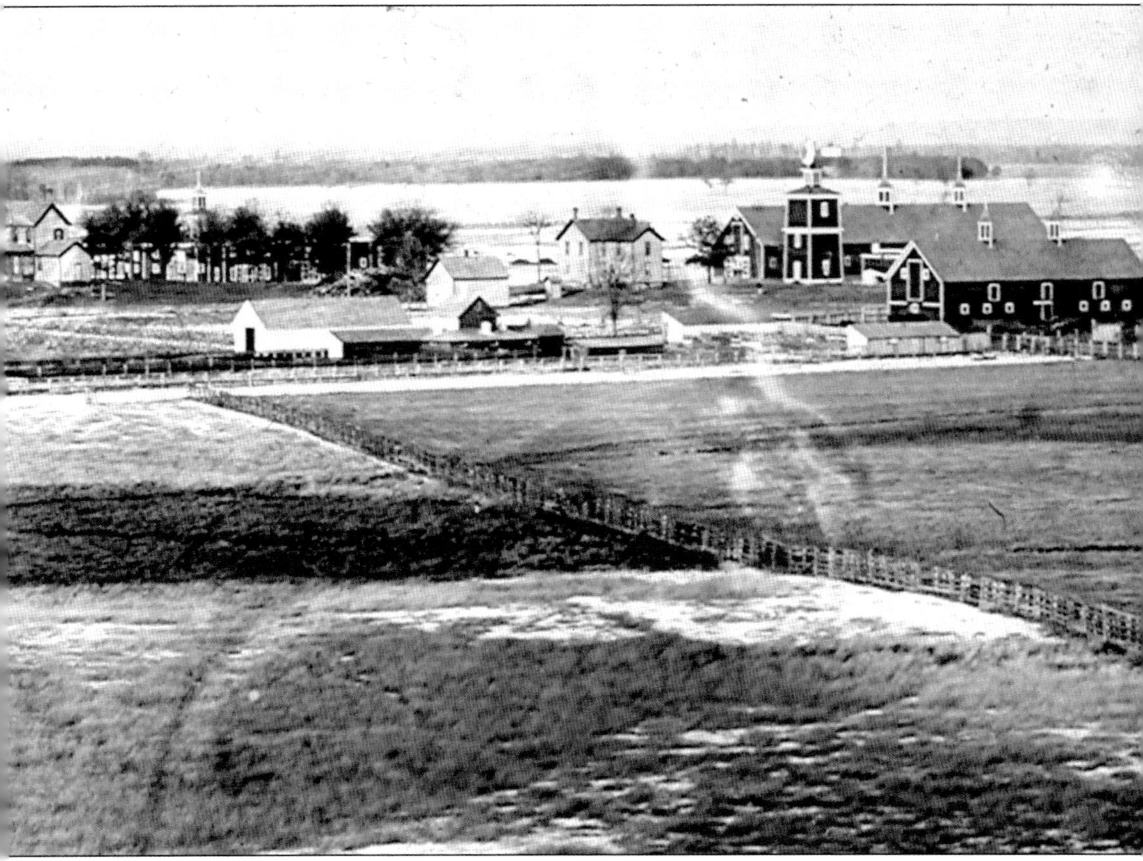

The Oaklawn Stock Farm was an innovative and highly respected breeding farm for horses. Owned by Capt. Andrew Tainter, it featured several new processes, including an octagonal barn, a covered racetrack, running water from a water tower, and a giant windmill. Every building on the farm had fire hydrants and water faucets. (Courtesy of UWSA.)

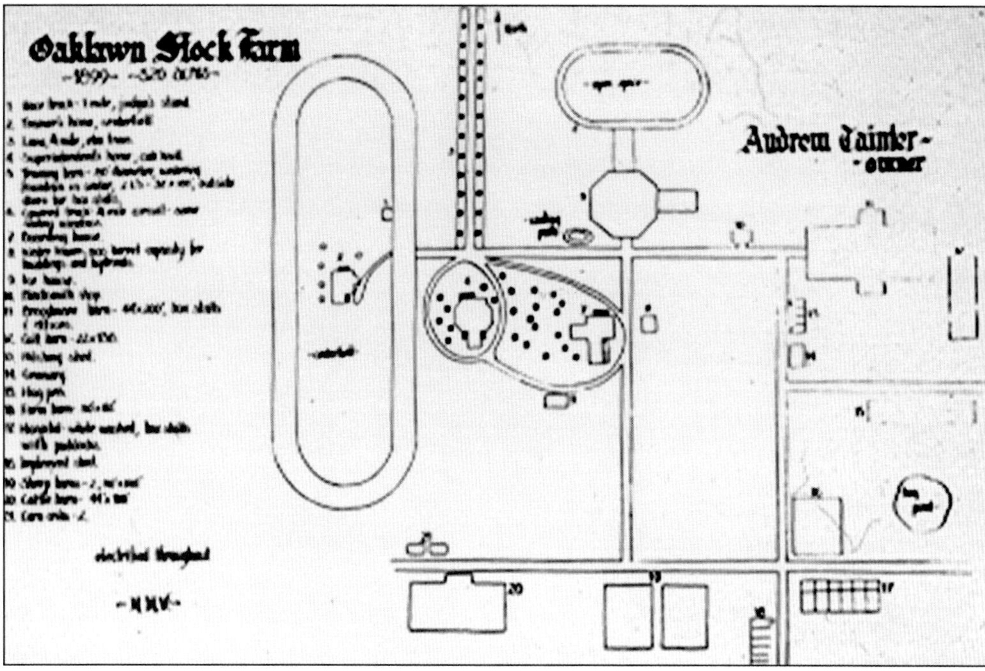

This is a diagram of Capt. Andrew Tainter's estate. He built the farm for over a decade, until his death in 1899. His daughter, Fannie, and son, Louis, inherited the estate, and the farm stayed in the family until 1948, when it was sold to the John Dale family; they sold it to the Stout Foundation in 1968. The Stout Technology Park now occupies over 100 acres of the land. (Courtesy of UWSA.)

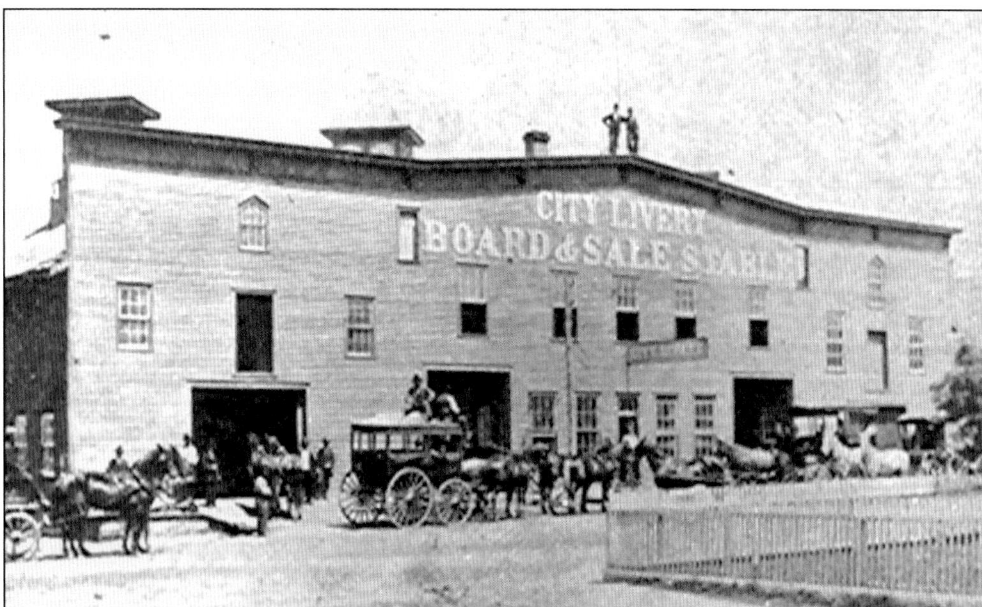

Livery stables were an important part of the Menomonie community in the 1800s and 1900s. With the advent of the engine, they declined in numbers, but in their heyday they were critical to the success of many businesses. (Courtesy of UWSA.)

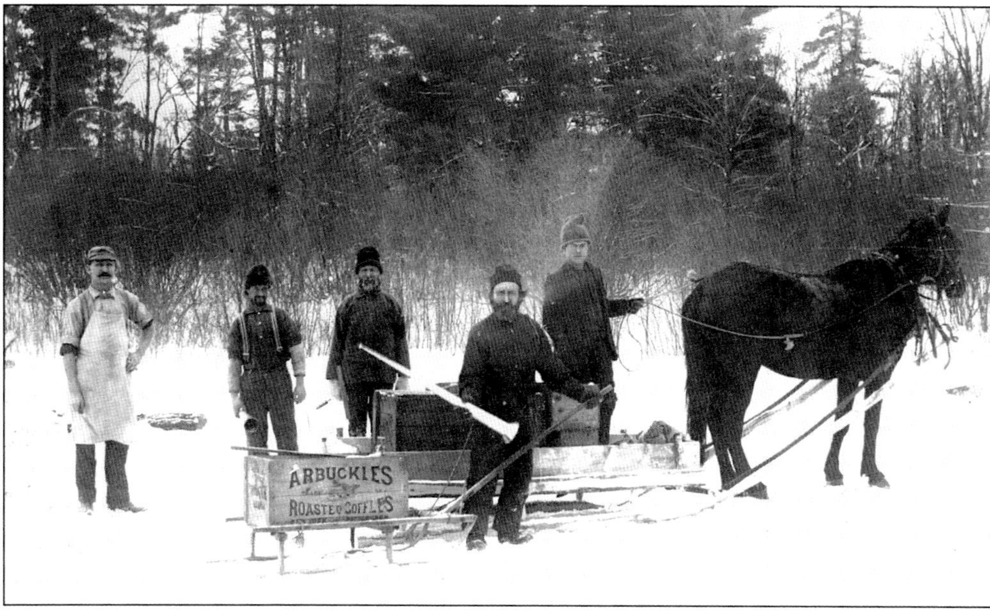

Pictured is another example of "cookies" lunch cart for the lumbermen in the field. (Courtesy of UWSA.)

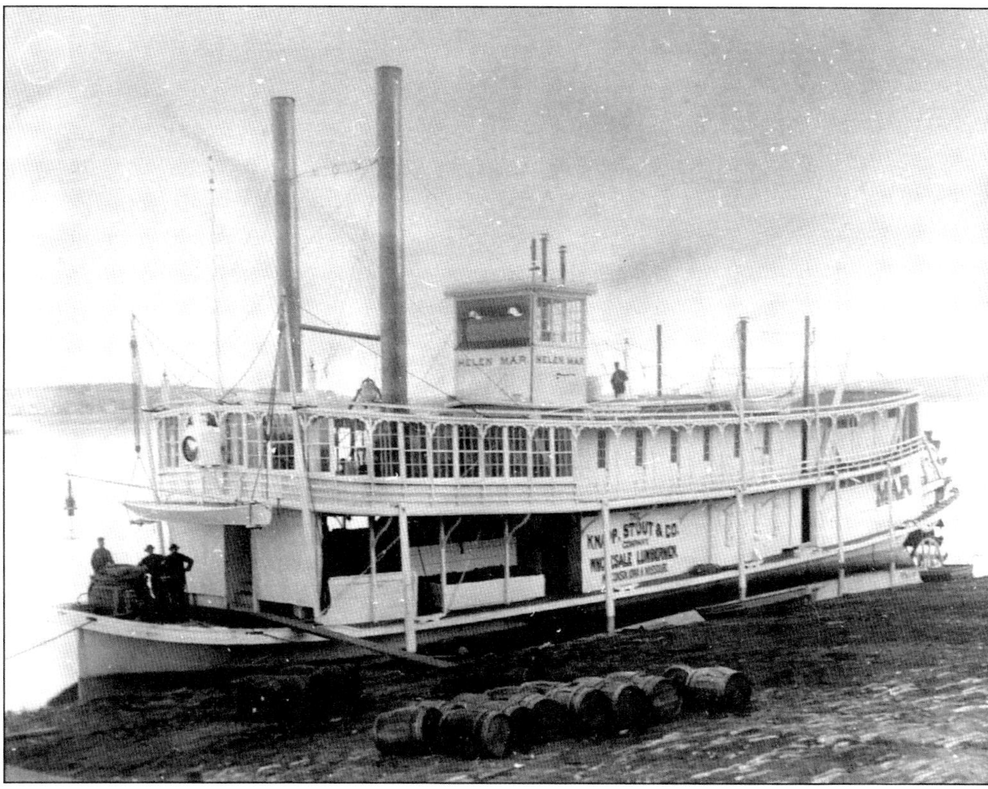

The *Helen Mar* was one of the steamships owned by Knapp, Stout, and Co. Company. This boat carried passengers and freight, as well as shuttling lumber up and down the river. (Courtesy of UWSA.)

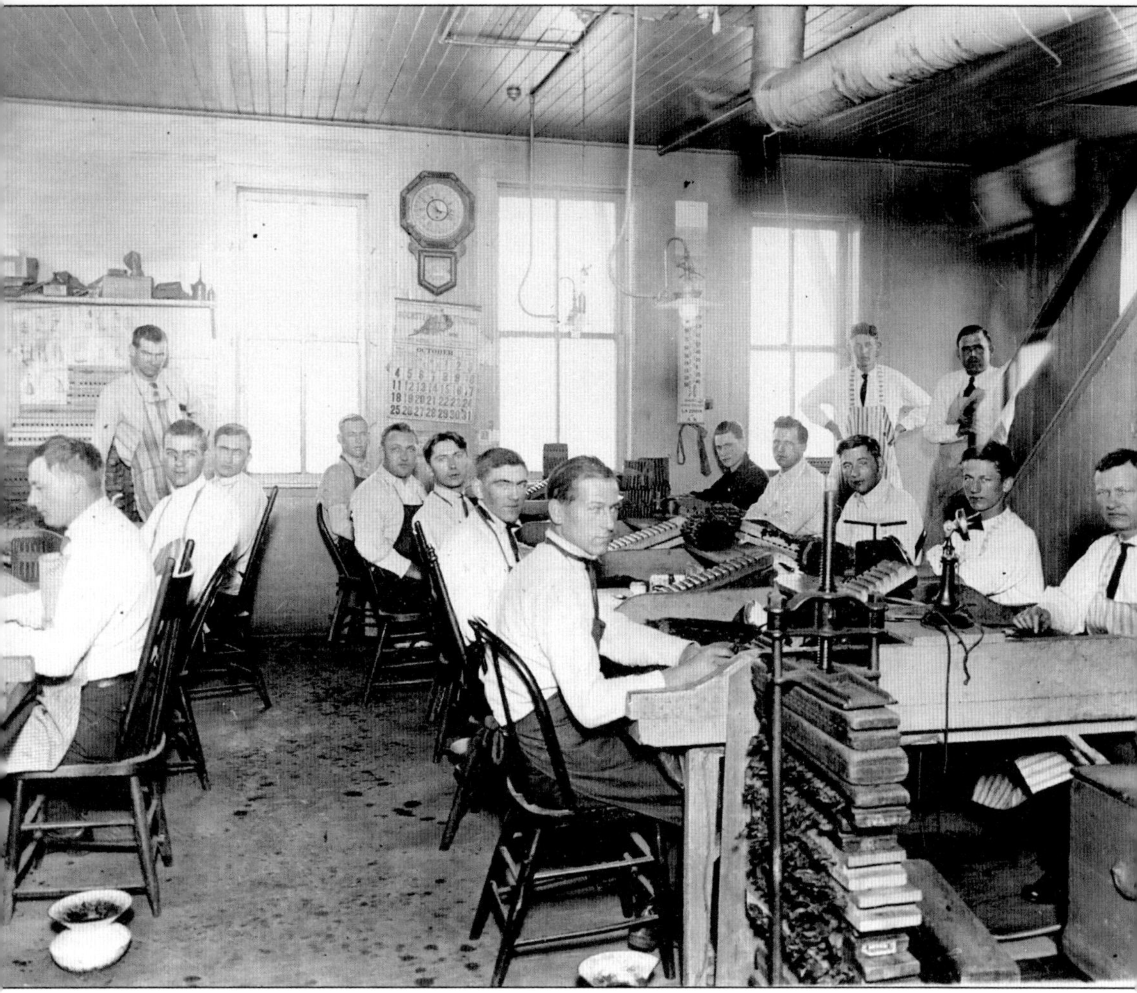

This image shows the Anderson Brothers Cigar Factory in 1914. Otto Anderson and his brother Al bought the factory in 1893 from the Diamond Company. They relocated to the corner location of Broadway Street, Crescent Avenue, and Fourth Street and, until 1925, made enough cigars to call itself the leading cigar factory in northern Wisconsin. Employees hand-rolled the cigars and could turn out over 300 per day. (Courtesy of UWSA.)

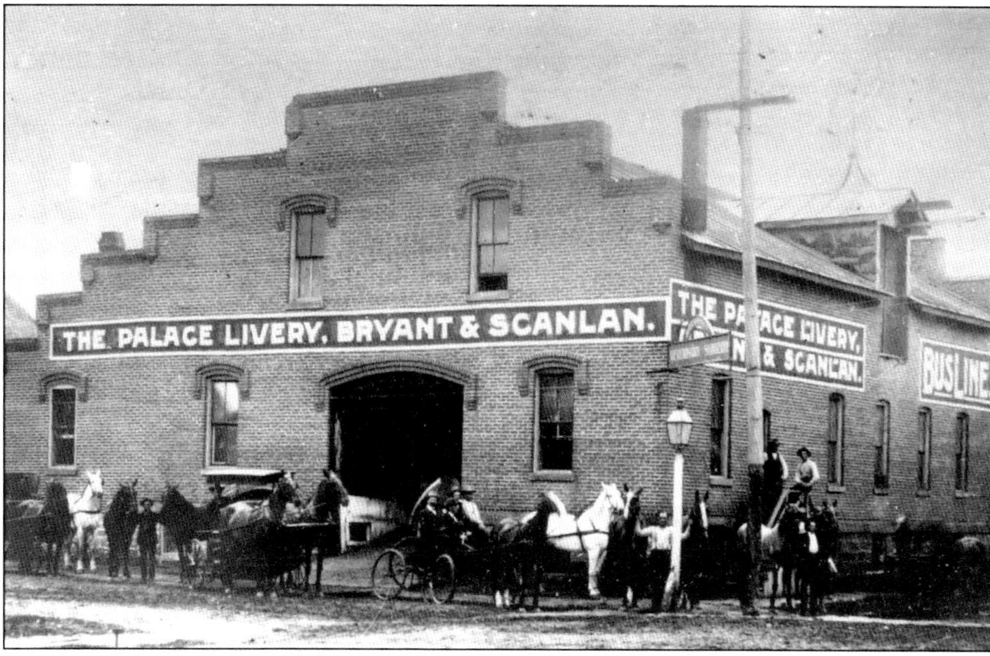

Here is another livery establishment. There was such a need for livery services that more than one operation could survive at a time. (Courtesy of UWSA.)

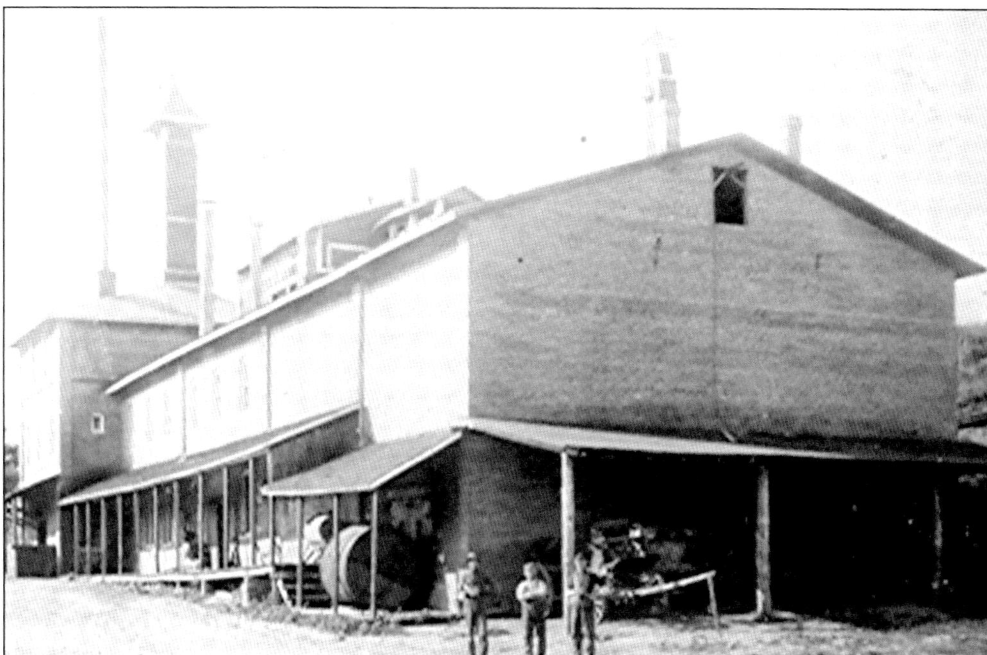

The Burkhardt Brewery was built on what was then known as Hudson Road, now Meadow Hill Drive, on the west side of Menomonie. It was started by Gottfried Burkhardt, from Switzerland, in the 1870s and was a leading brewery for many years before Burkhardt took ill. His son took over the business in 1895 and ran it for a few more years before the brewery closed. (Courtesy of UWSA.)

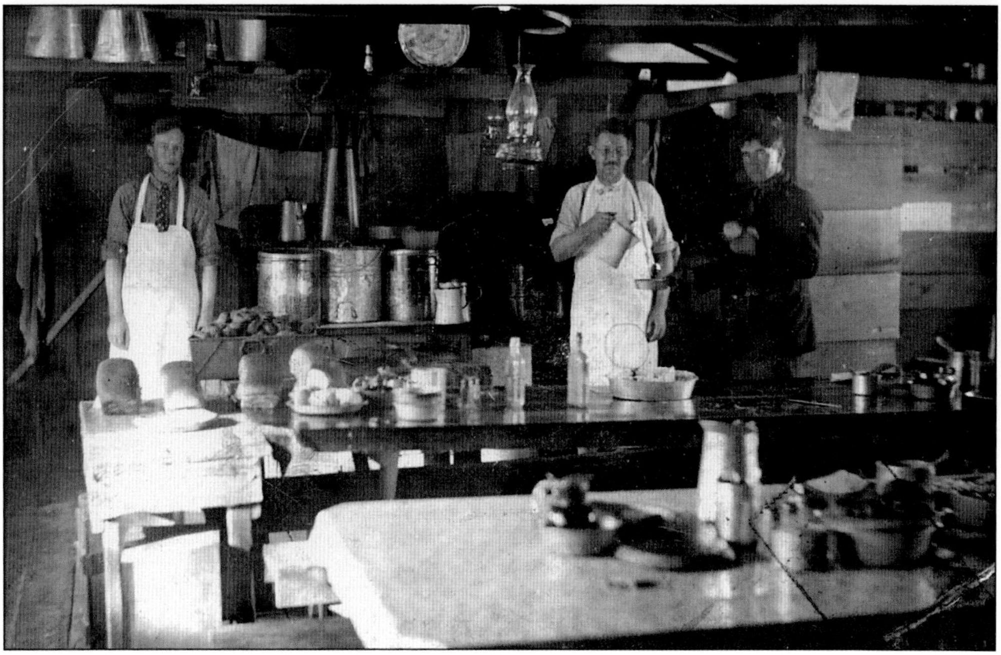

This photograph was taken in 1907, at the Weston Lumber Camp. The kitchen and dining areas were probably the most important places in camp. It took a crew of "cookies," or men who fed the crews, to keep the kitchens running. (Courtesy of UWSA.)

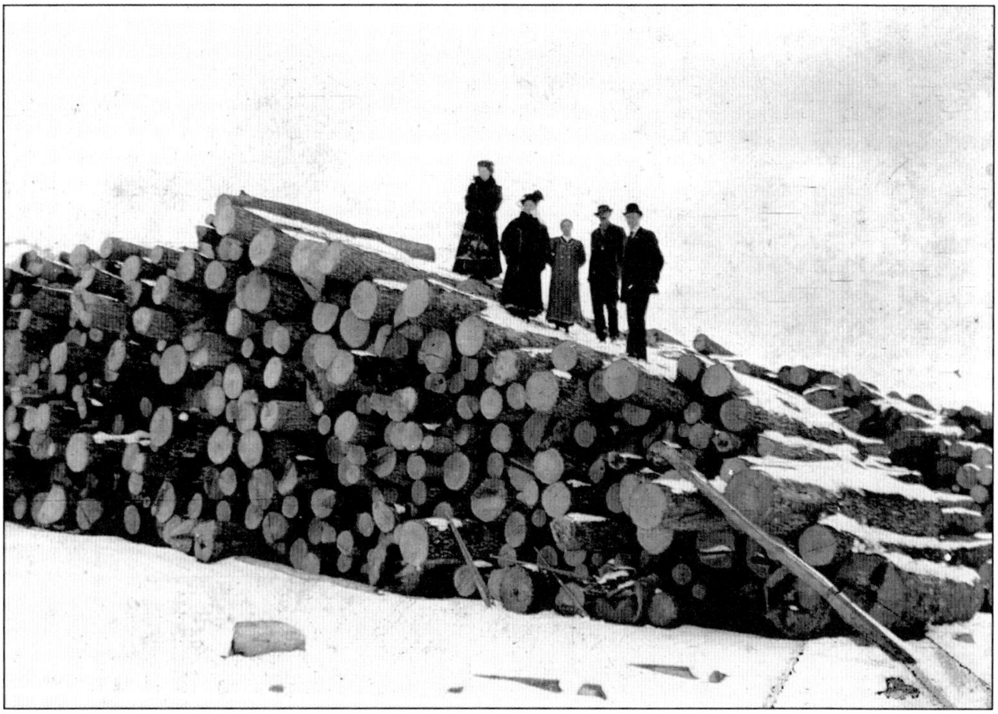

Logs harvested from the Weston Lumbering Camp, 1907, near Downsville, logs are stacked in rows waiting to be sent to the mill in Menomonie. Three teachers and two other citizens braved the stack to stand on top. (Courtesy of Louis Frank, Fred Miller, Lawrence Crank; UWSA.)

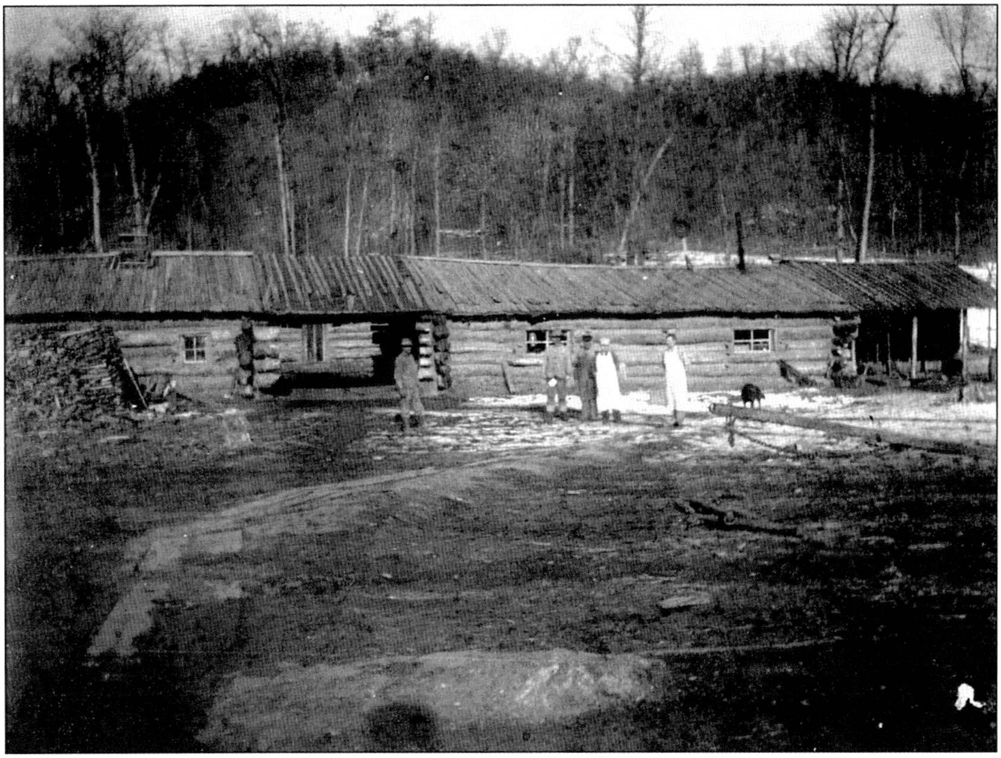

The Weston Lumber Camp No. 2 in 1900 was one of the larger lumber operations. It was located on the south fork of Knight's Creek in the town of Weston. (Courtesy of UWSA.)

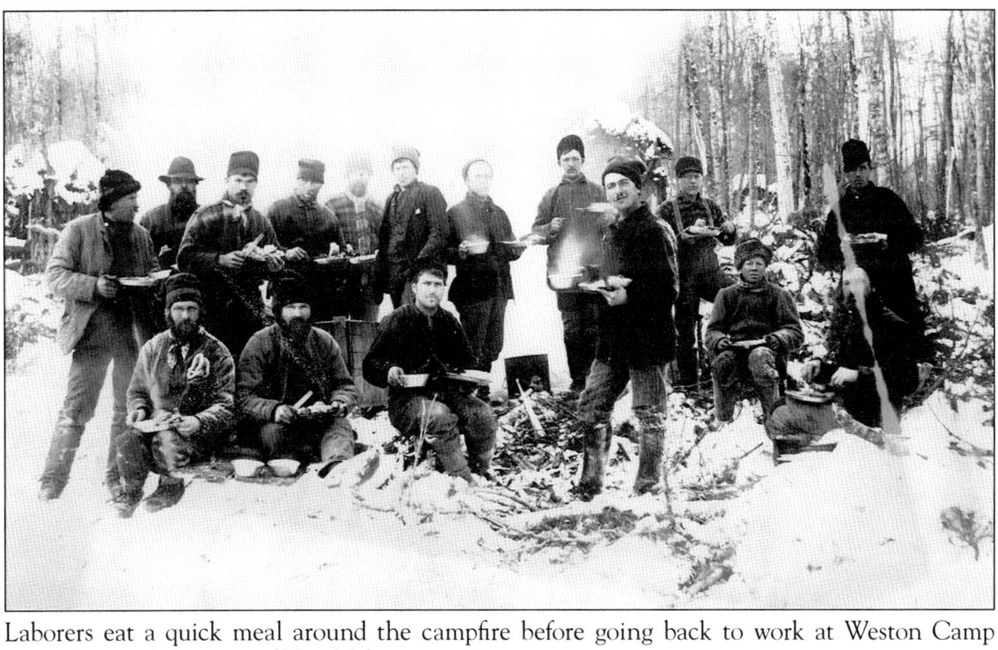

Laborers eat a quick meal around the campfire before going back to work at Weston Camp around 1900. (Courtesy of UWSA.)

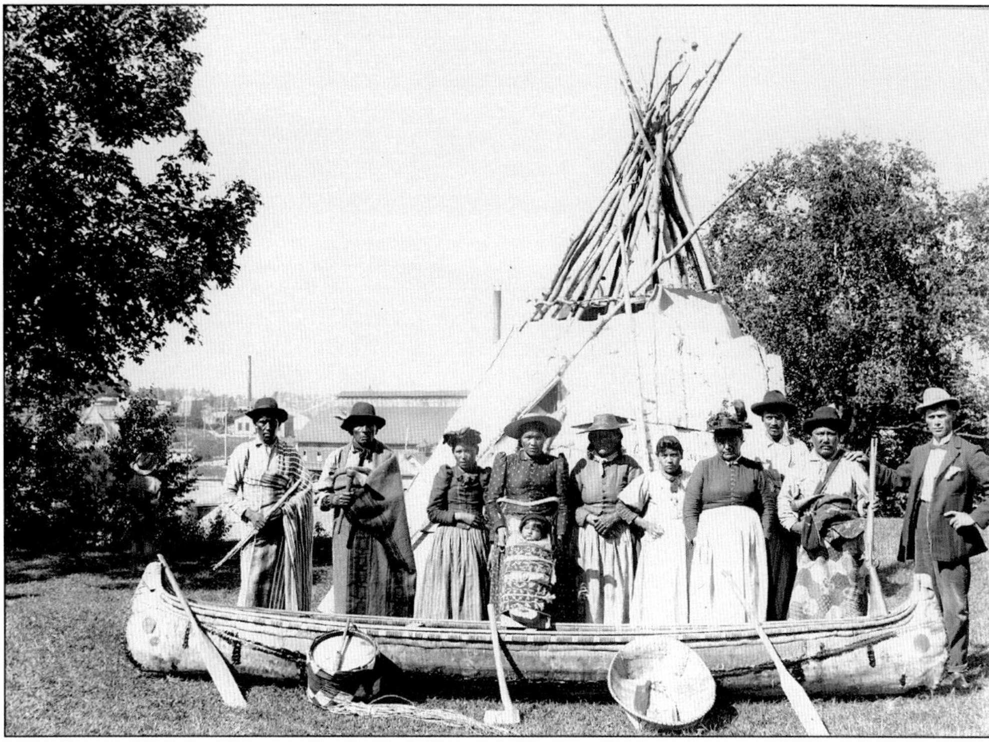

Shown here is the Knapp, Stout, and Co. Company 50th anniversary picnic, held on the lawn of the Stout home on August 12, 1896. Pictured are some of the Native American workers from the company. (Courtesy of UWSA.)

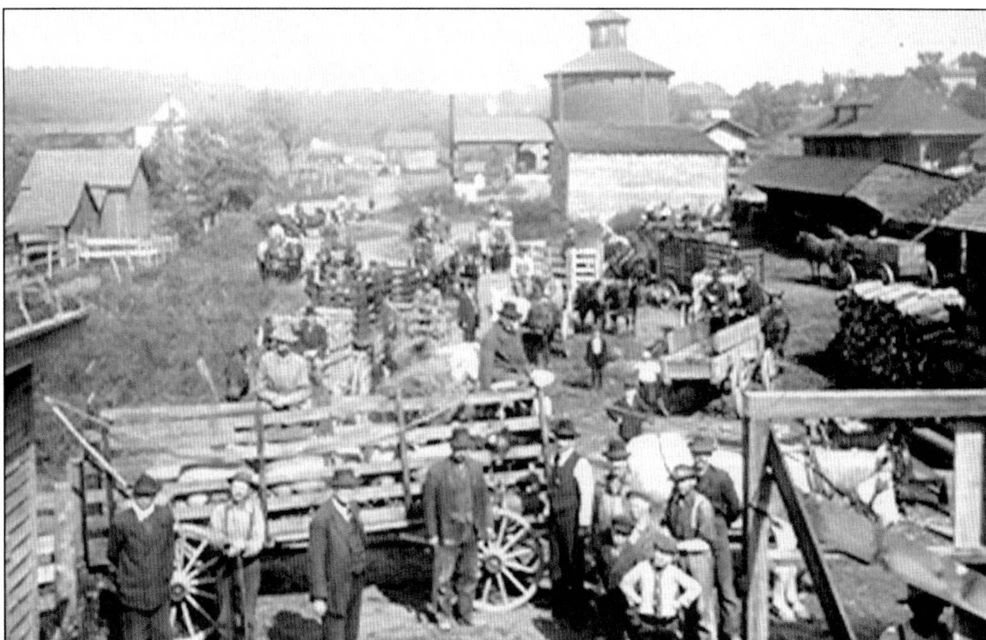

It is just another busy day at the stockyards, near Highway 29 in Menomonie. (Courtesy of UWSA.)

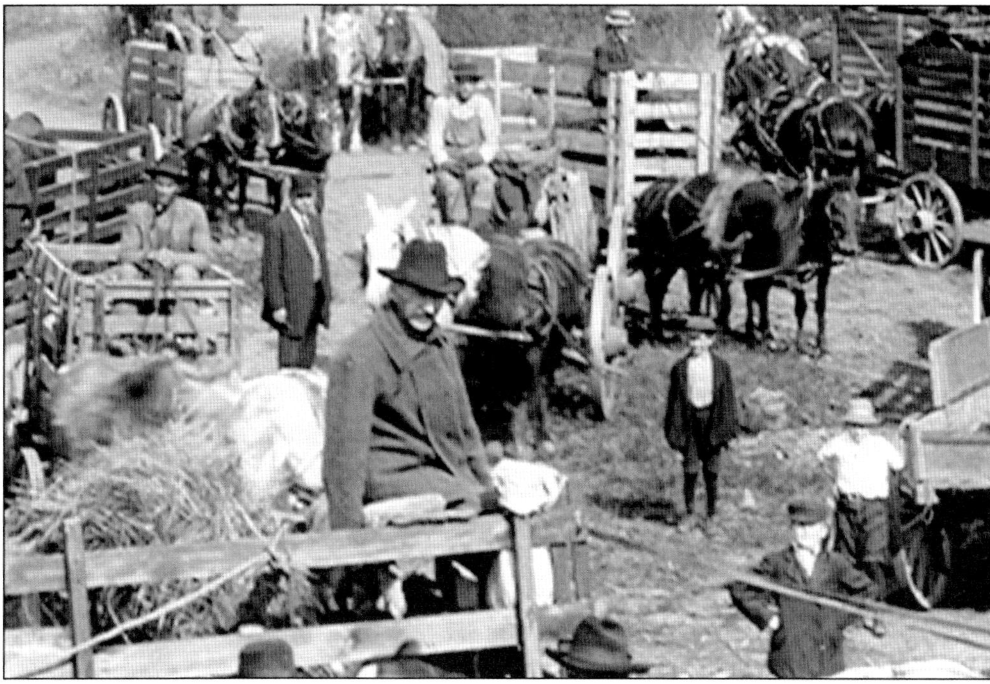

There was much more to the Menomonie economy than lumbering, as evidenced by the number of livestock and farmers attending the sale. (Courtesy of UWSA.)

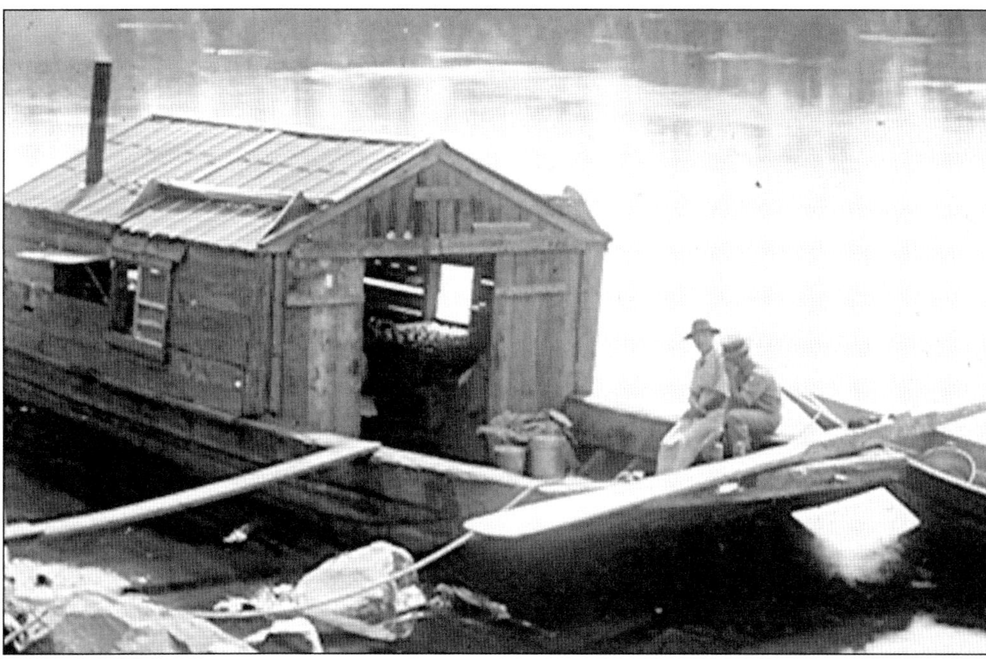

Two unidentified people enjoy their houseboat on the Red Cedar River. The Red Cedar River is a critical part of the history of Menomonie. (Courtesy of UWSA.)

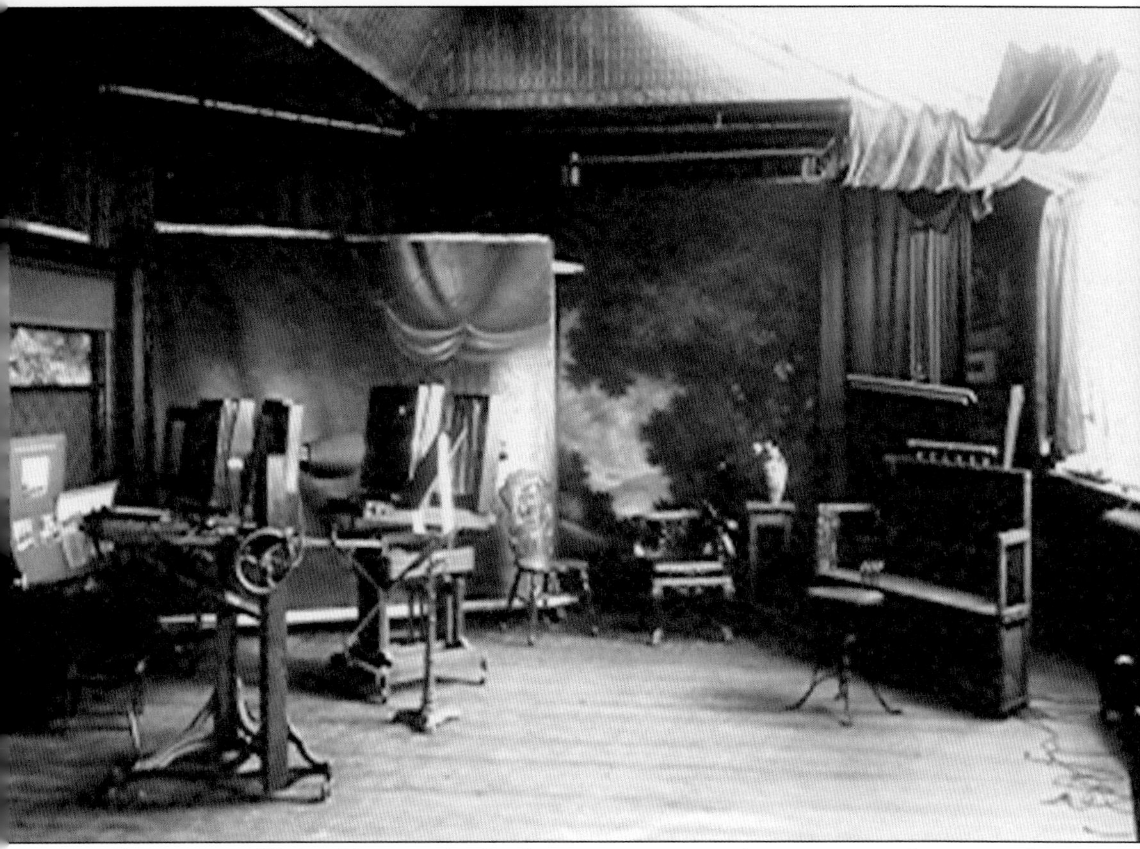

The interior of Belair Photography Studios was a mixture of equipment and intrigue. George Belair was born in 1881 and attended school in Menomonie. He worked for a short time for the local paper, *Dunn County News*, but then moved toward the more artistic venue of studio photography. He studied art under Prof. Jacob Miller of Menomonie, and in 1899 opened his studio, which grew to be considered the best-equipped photographic art studio in northern Wisconsin. (Courtesy of UWSA.)

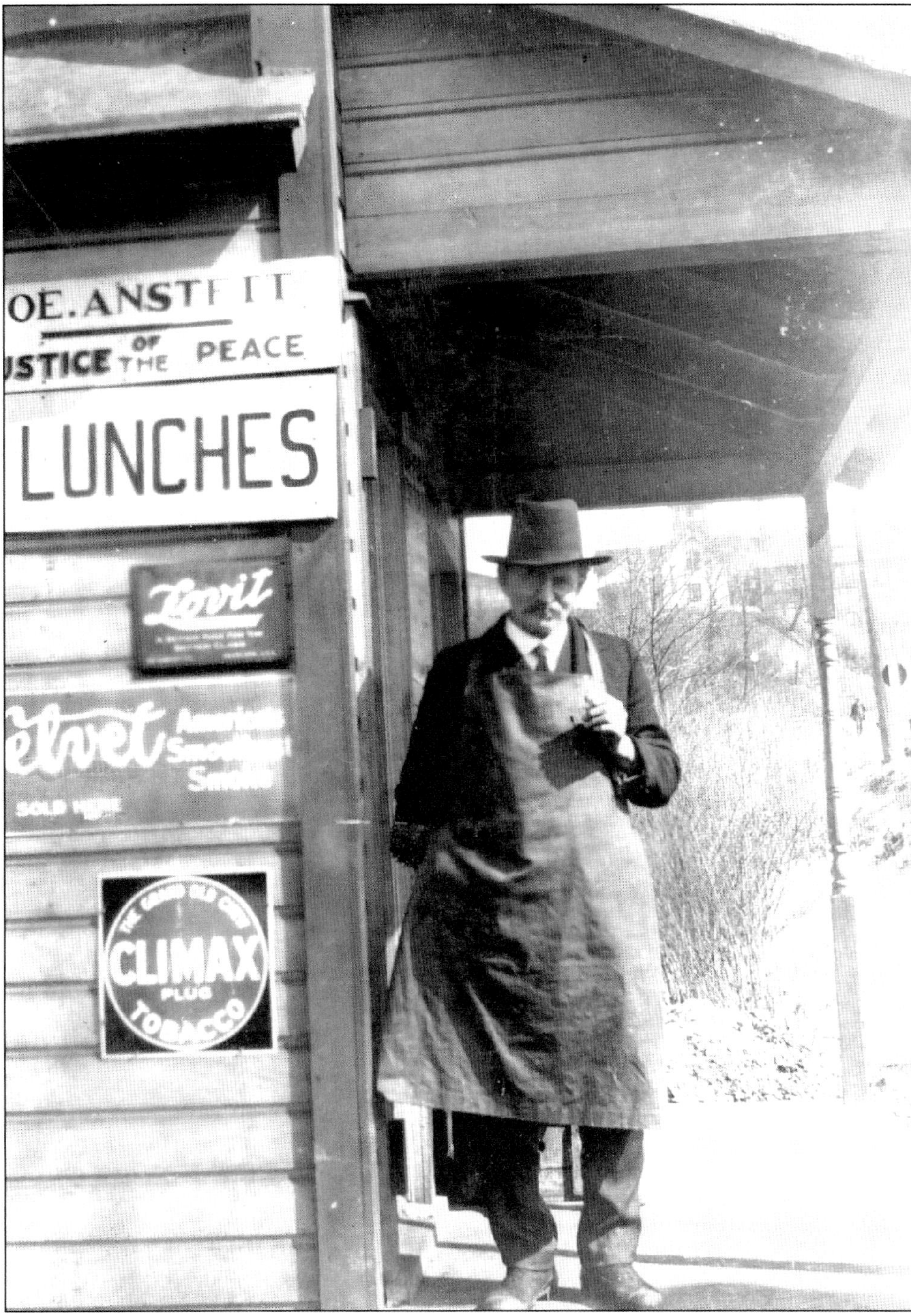

A proprietor stands outside his store adjacent to the train depot in Menomonie. Trains were a major part of the landscape for years. In 1871, the West Wisconsin Railway arrived in Menomonie, from the east. The Chicago, Milwaukee, and St. Paul Railway moved in 10 years later, opening the way to easier travel to places such as Madison and Milwaukee, as well as smaller towns along the way. The old depot still stands today, abandoned, near the Red Cedar River.

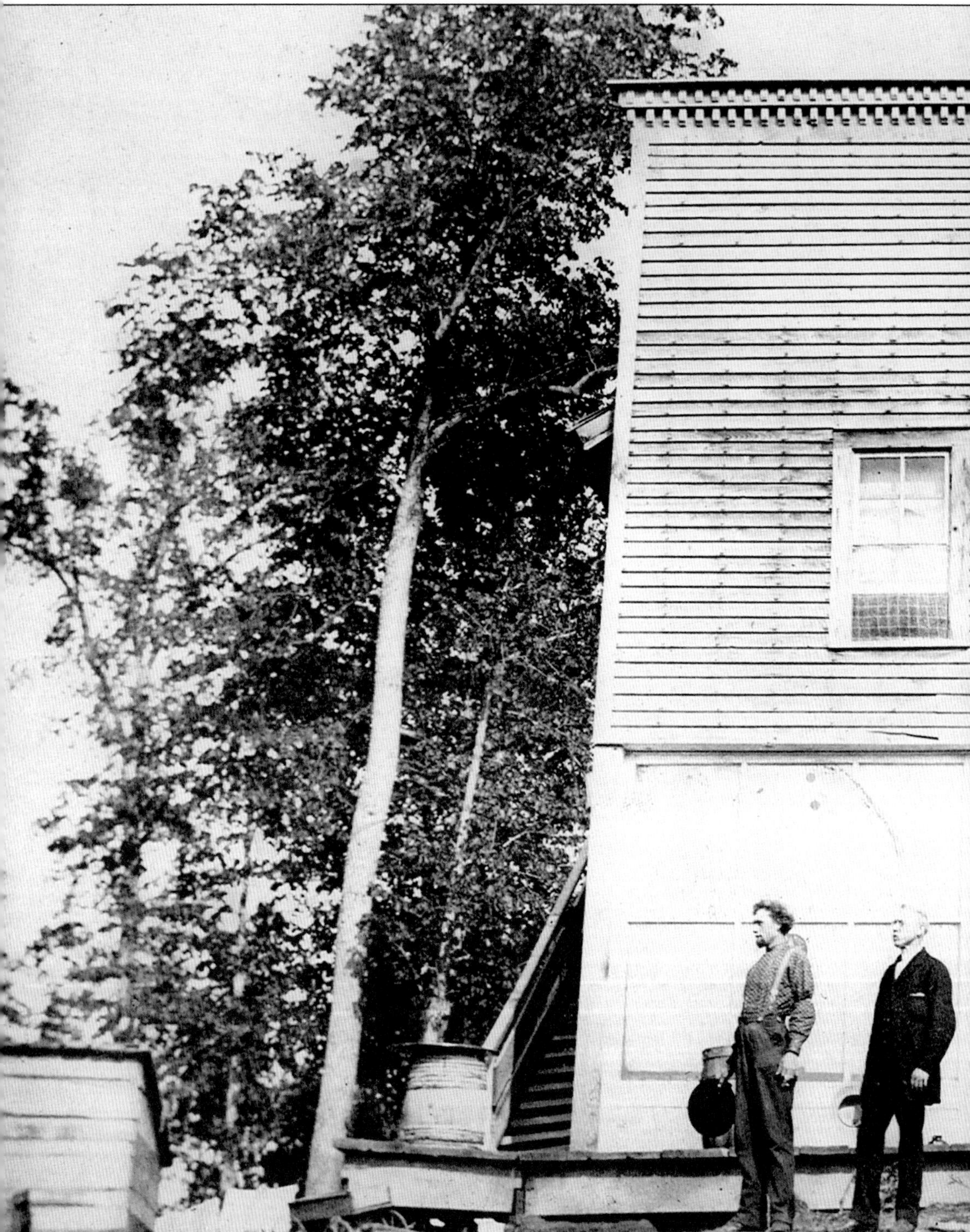

The Downing store was one of two mercantile businesses in town. Downing was an incorporated village in the southwest corner of the town of Tiffany. It was on the " Soo" railroad line, so it naturally grew to host several businesses, as well as a post office, civic center, saw and gristmill,

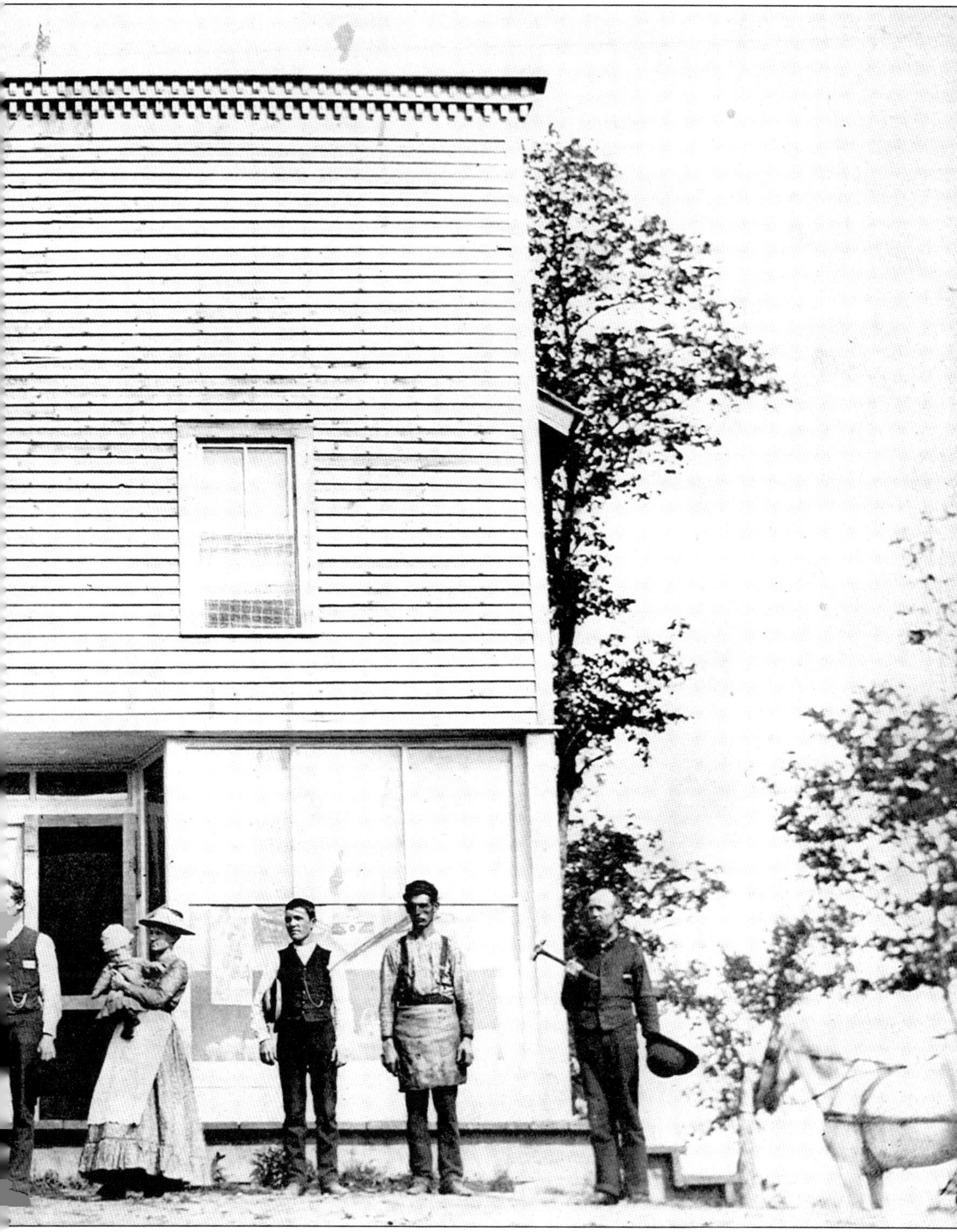

and bank (the Bank of Downing). The surrounding area was, and still is, rich in small farms. (Courtesy of UWSM.)

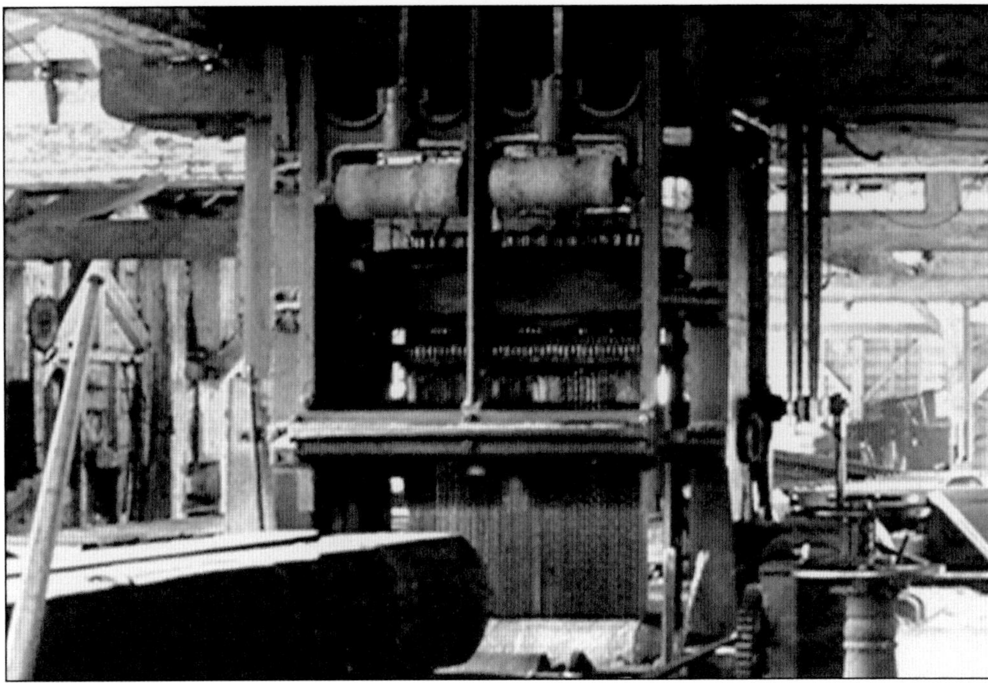

The Menomonie mill held massive equipment designed to speed the process needed to get products to retail markets.. (Courtesy of UWSA.)

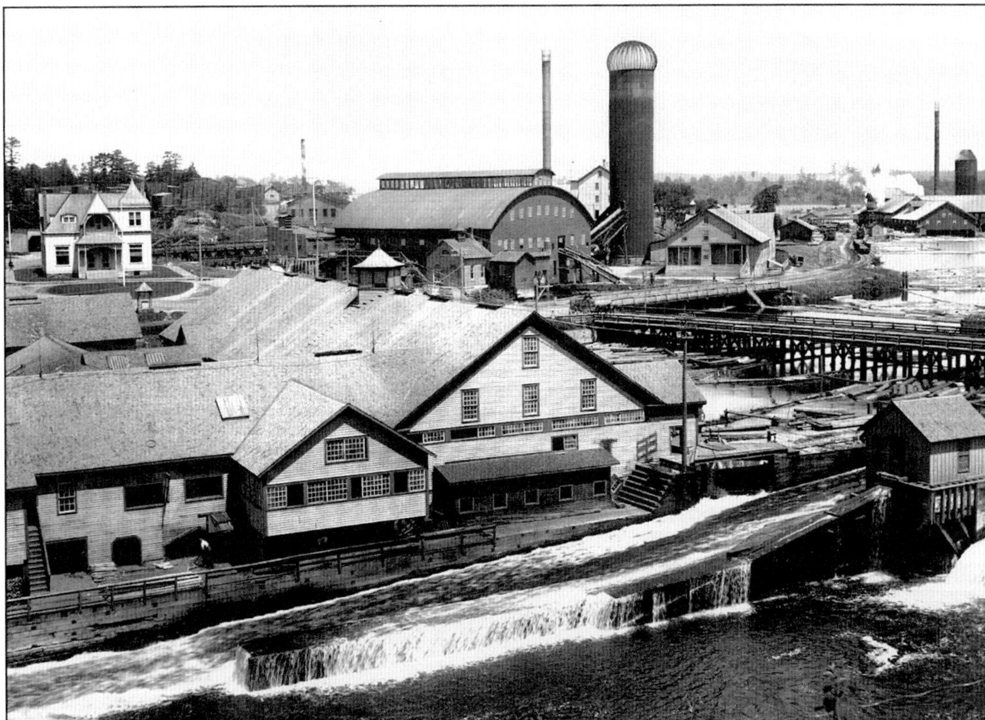

Seen here are the mill, with the office building, shingle mill, and sawdust burner. Every step of the lumbering process had its own process and equipment. (Courtesy of UWSA.)

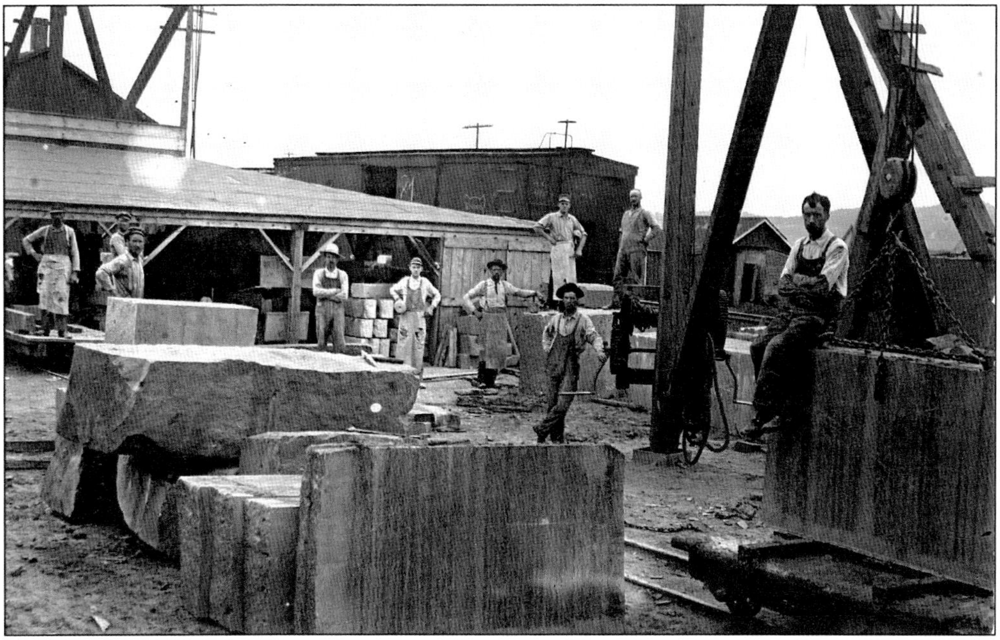

Brick making and granite quarrying were the other industries that grew up in Menomonie. There were, at one time, five brickyards in town, all located on the west side near what was then Hudson Road. Notice the huge granite stones waiting to be cut. (Courtesy of UWSA.)

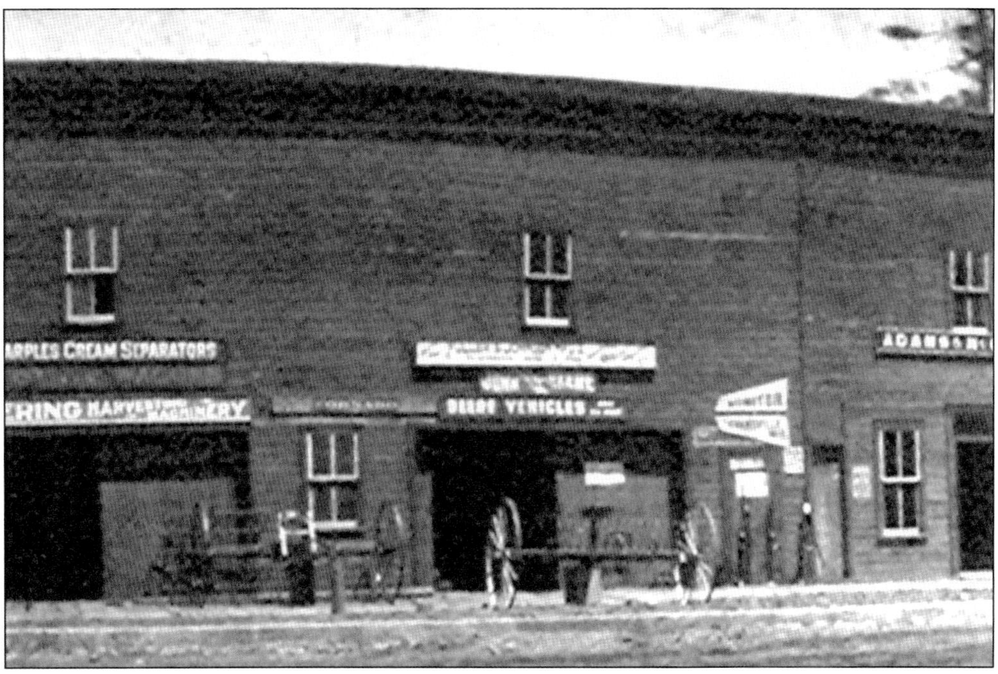

This building, in the early part of the 19th century, housed several different operations. The exact location of the building is not determined, but it is likely that it was near the downtown area, where most business concerns congregated. (Courtesy of UWSA.)

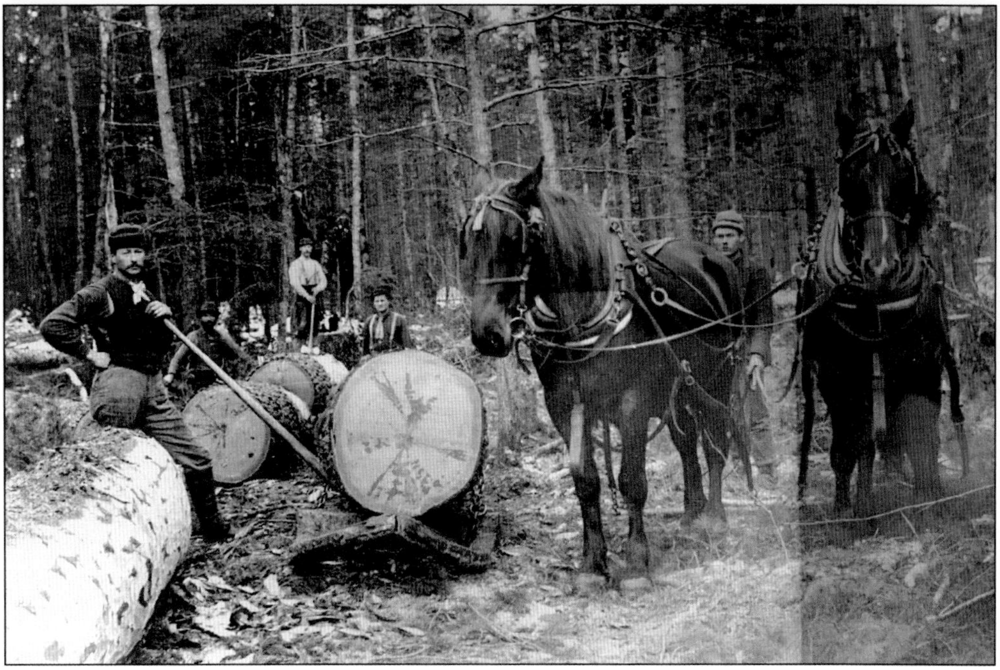

Horses were a major factor in lumbering, until the advent of the train systems arrived in town. Liveries, stables, and other businesses were critical to the care of the workhorse during this period in time. (Courtesy of UWSA.)

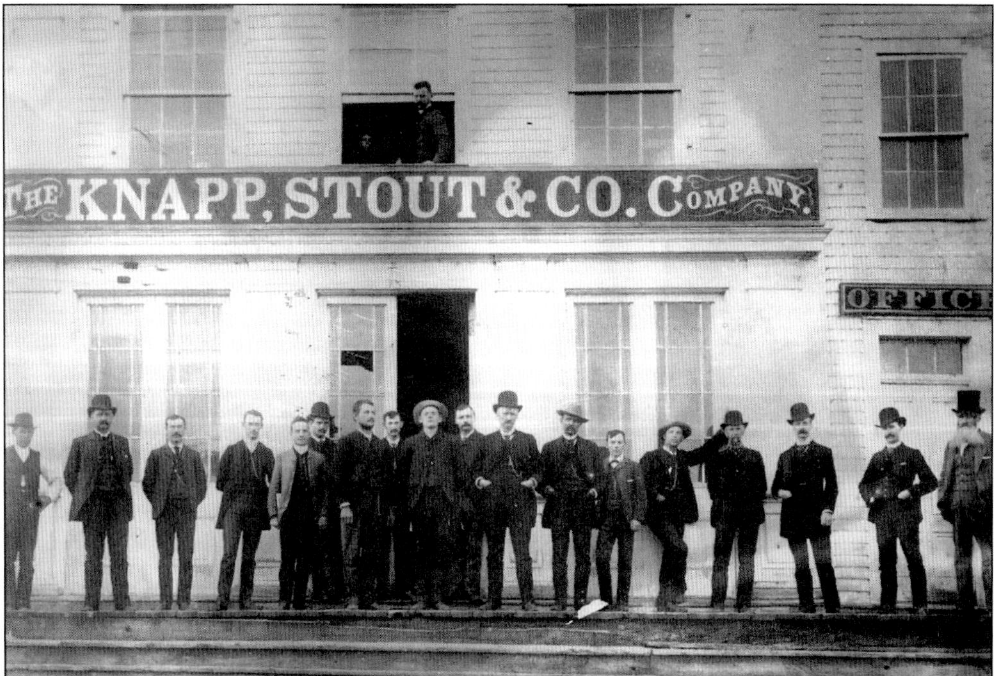

Shown here is the Knapp, Stout, and Co. Company in front of the company store and offices. This photograph was taken in 1882 and includes the clerks and managers of the different company departments. (Courtesy of UWSA.)

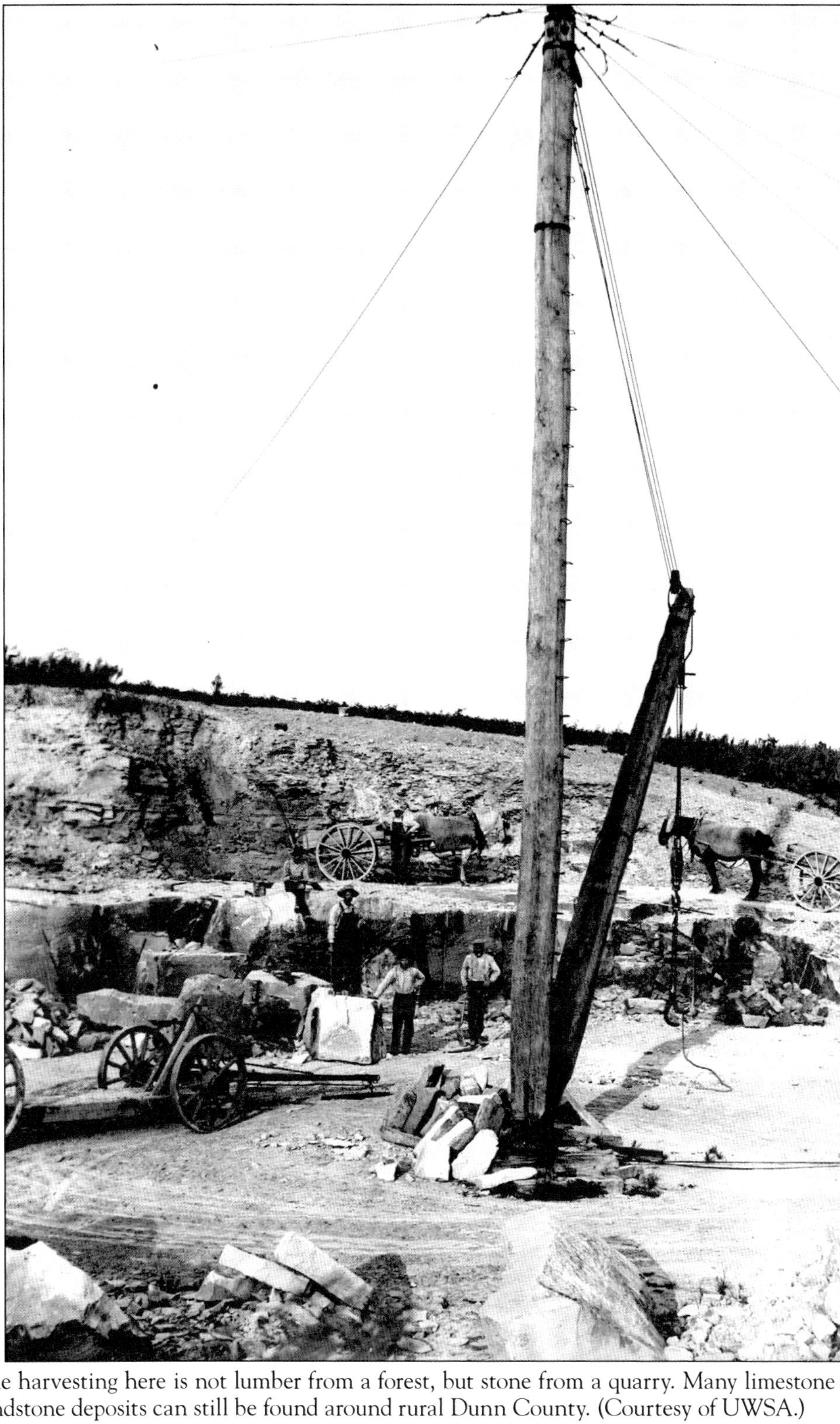

The harvesting here is not lumber from a forest, but stone from a quarry. Many limestone and sandstone deposits can still be found around rural Dunn County. (Courtesy of UWSA.)

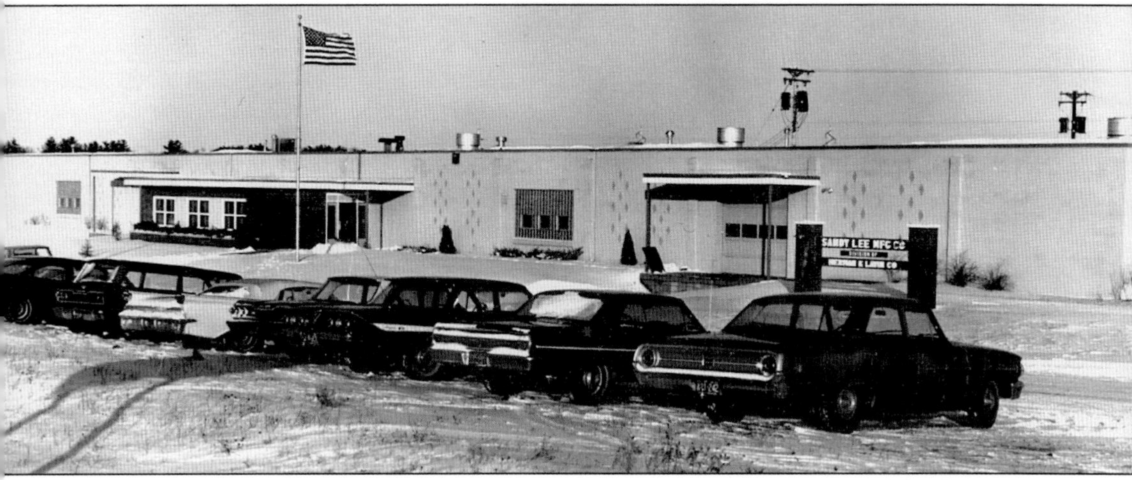

The Lee manufacturing building, around the 1950s, was an early resident of the industrial park concept. Menomonie is home to several well-known industries, including Andersen Windows, Cardinal Glass, Phillips Plastic, and 3M, as well as many small, independent businesses and services. (Courtesy of UWSA.)

Five

EDUCATION AND LEARNING

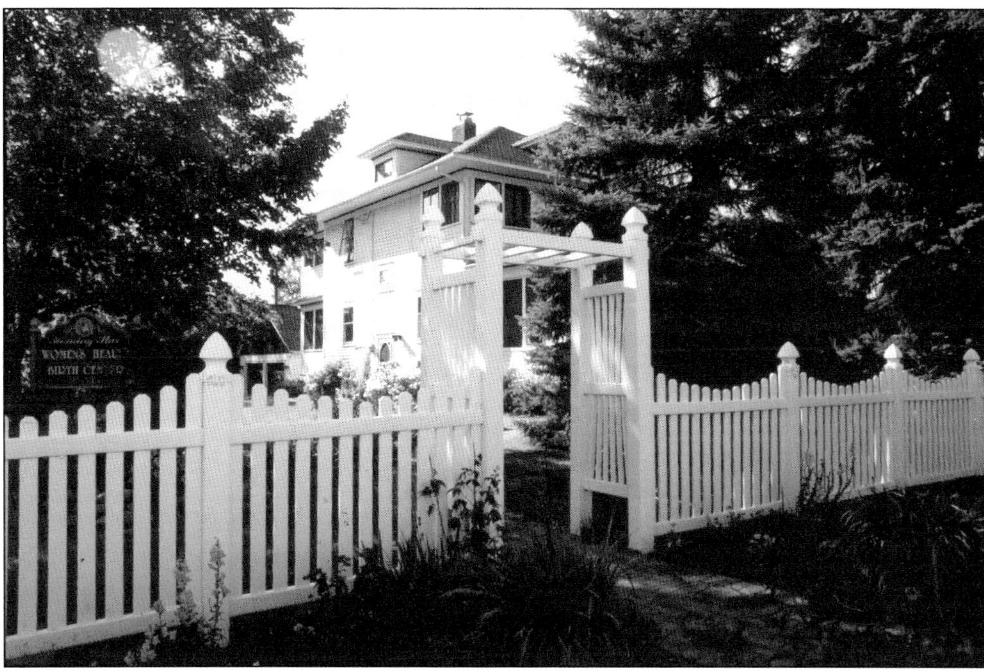

The Morning Star Women's Health and Birthing Center, on Stout Road and Thirteenth Avenue in Menomonie has been revived as a birth center, having once been the Molitor Maternity Hospital in the late 1800s and early 1900s. Today it again serves families in a home-based, yet professional setting. In September 2003, Paula Bernini Feigal, a certified midwife, purchased the home from the Grundrigs and opened the center. The house had been a private home for 42 years. (Courtesy of Bruce Dybvik)

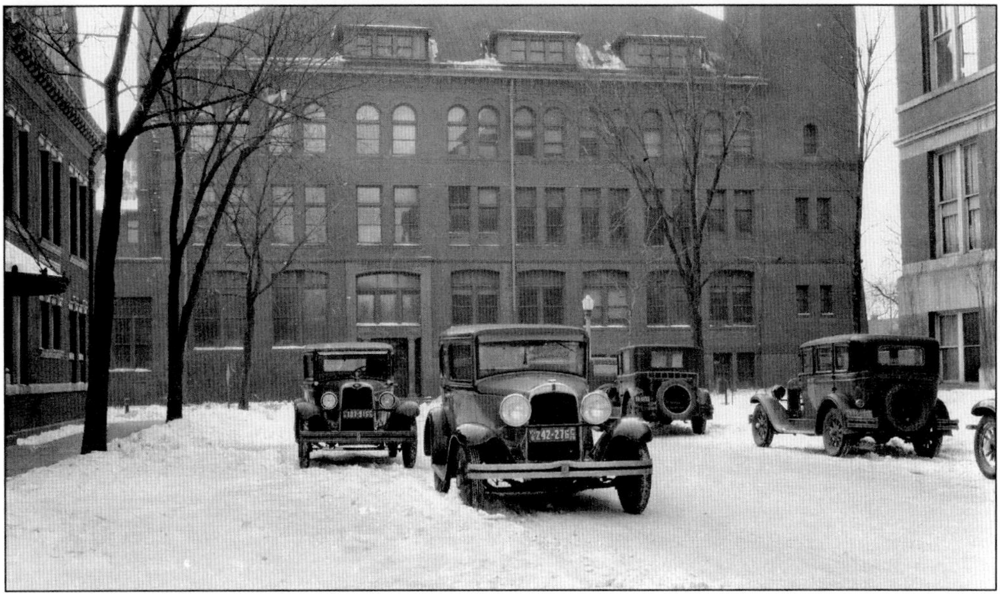

This is the campus of Stout Institute around 1915, with Bowman Hall taking center stage. The buildings are all brick, adding to the practical, but sturdy feel of the school. The Stout Institute and Menomonie High School buildings stood side by side for years, until fire destroyed the first Stout tower building. (Courtesy of UWSA.)

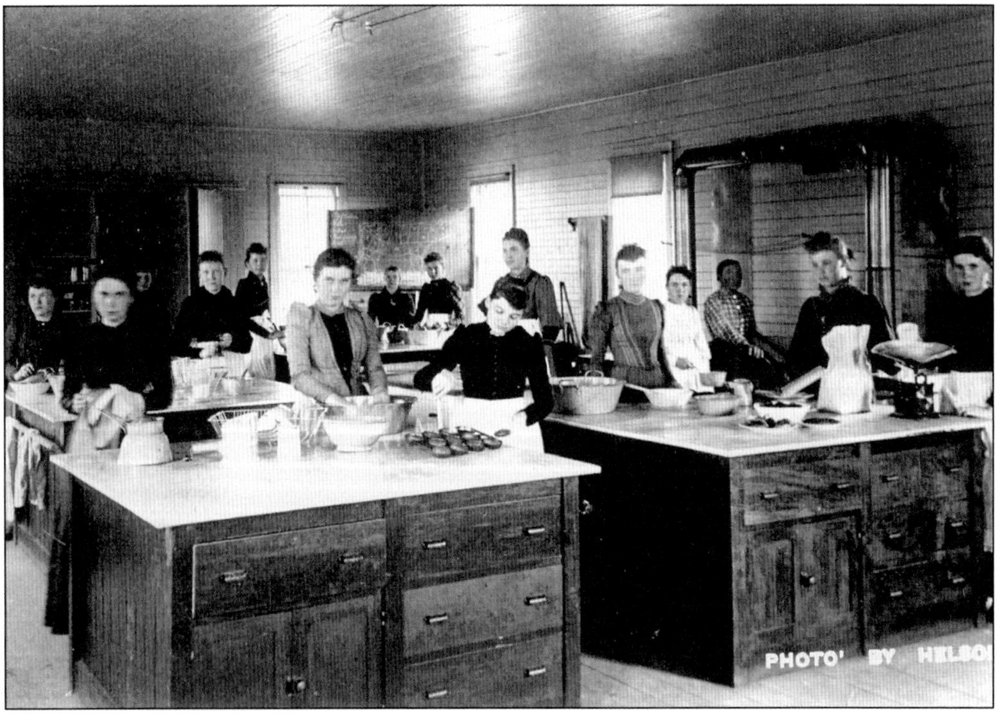

Women are trained in food science in an 1890s foods class at the Stout Manual Training and Domestic Science School. One of the primary focuses of the school, started by James H. Stout, was to train students to learn functional skills through hands-on activities. His philosophy was often equated to that of John Dewey. (Courtesy of UWSM.)

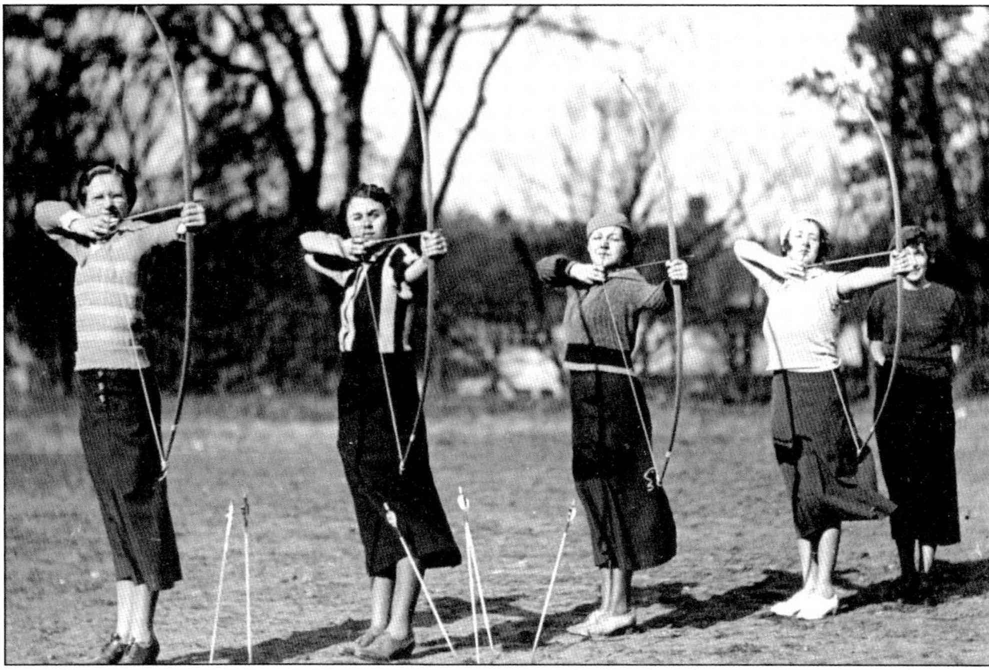

Archery began gaining support at Stout in 1933 as an intramural program and became one of the more skilled sports for women. In 1935, Katherine Watson won the spring championship with a score of 359. Ruth Graham placed second, and Marine Schultz placed third. (Courtesy of UWSM.)

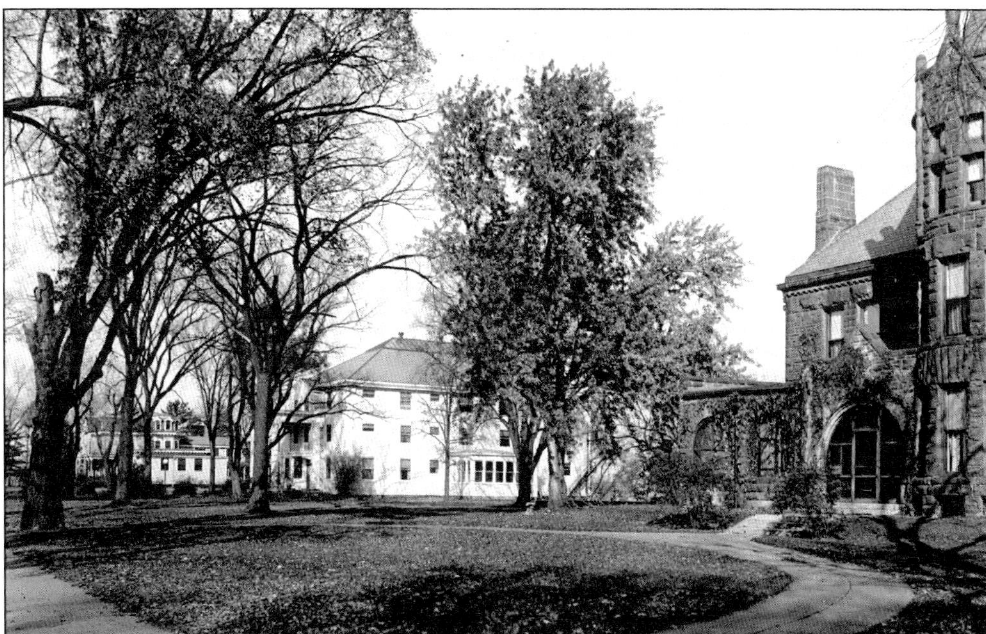

The girl's dormitories on the north side of town are pictured here in 1939. The building in the foreground, the Louis Smith Tainter house, still stands but the other two have been demolished and replaced by the Jeter-Tainter-Callahan complex. (Courtesy of UWSM.)

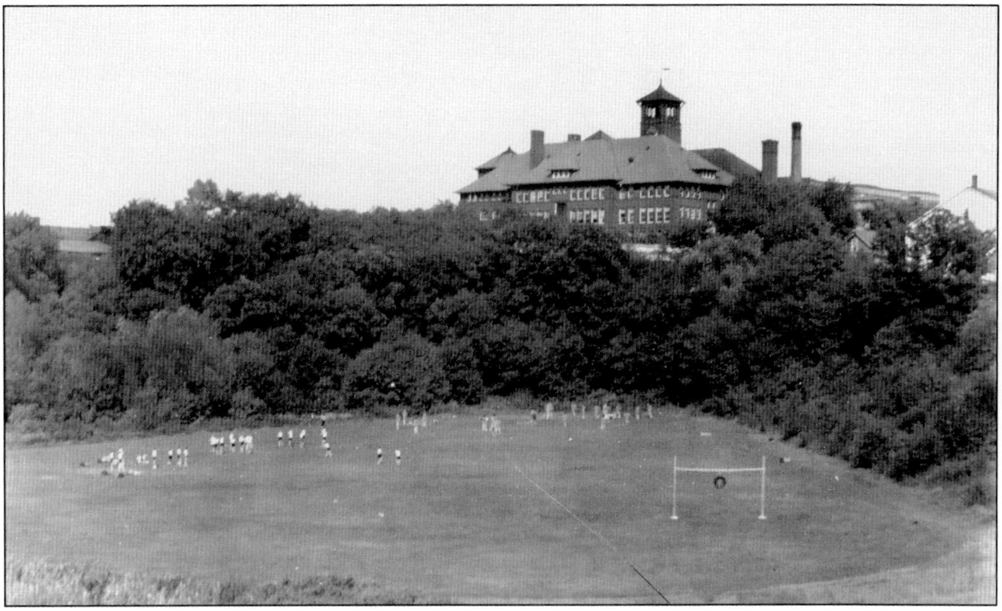

Menomonie High School is pictured in 1945. It was part of the Stout Institute for many years, since the vision of James H. Stout was to include different levels of students in his manual and training programs. (Courtesy of UWSA.)

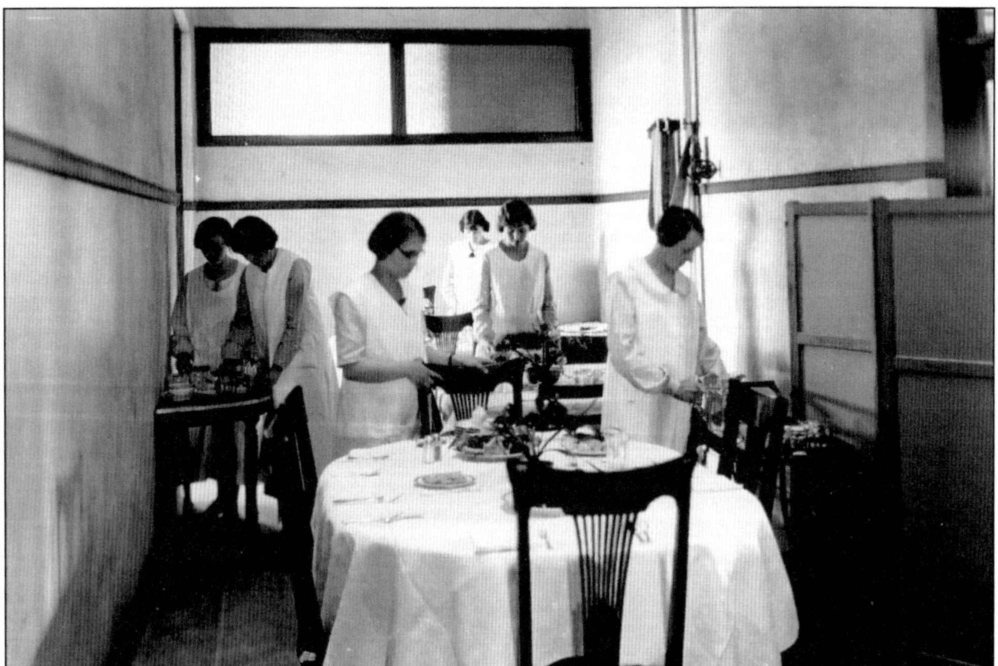

A women's meal planning class is pictured around the late 1890s. Women were taught the "domestic sciences," while men were offered classes in manual training such as woodworking, metal work, and other crafts. (Courtesy of UWSA.)

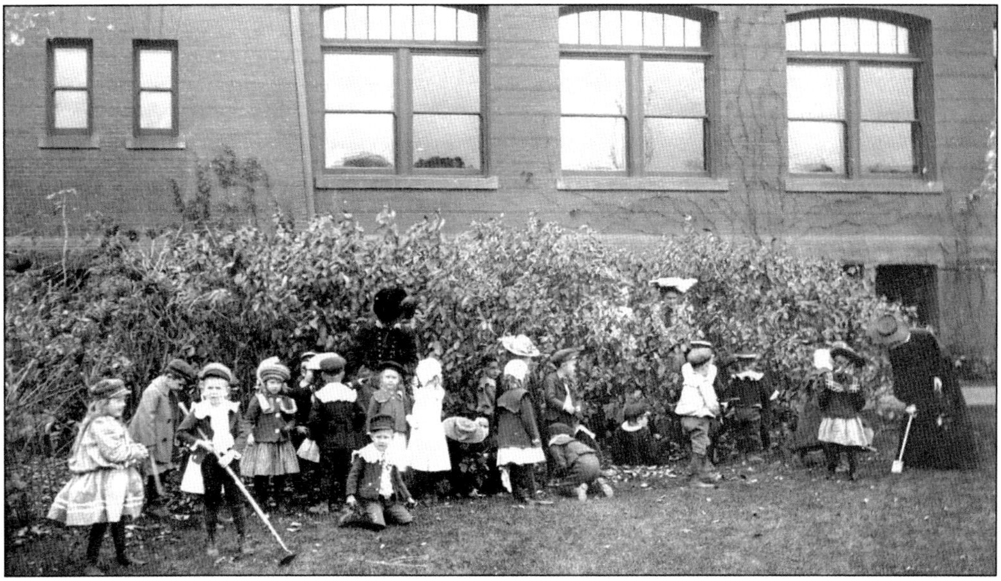

In 1901, Stout added a kindergarten to their rooms at Coddington and North School, in addition to equipping rooms at Central School to train teachers to teach kindergarten. The tradition continues to this day with University of Wisconsin–Stout's highly respected early childhood programs and child care training facilities. (Courtesy of UWSA.)

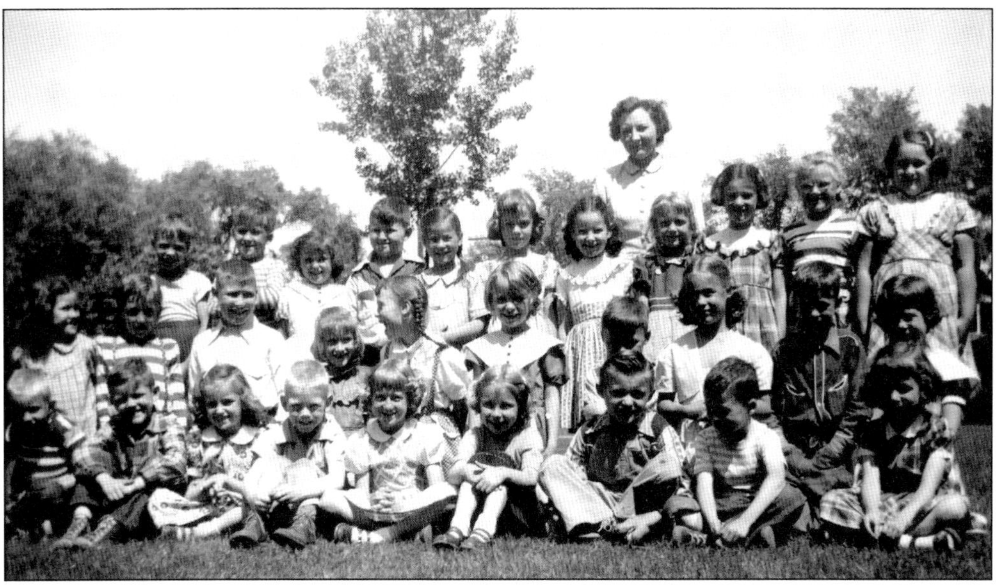

A class poses with their teacher, Mrs. Marvel Meisner, in front of East School in 1950. (Courtesy of Gary Hinrichs.)

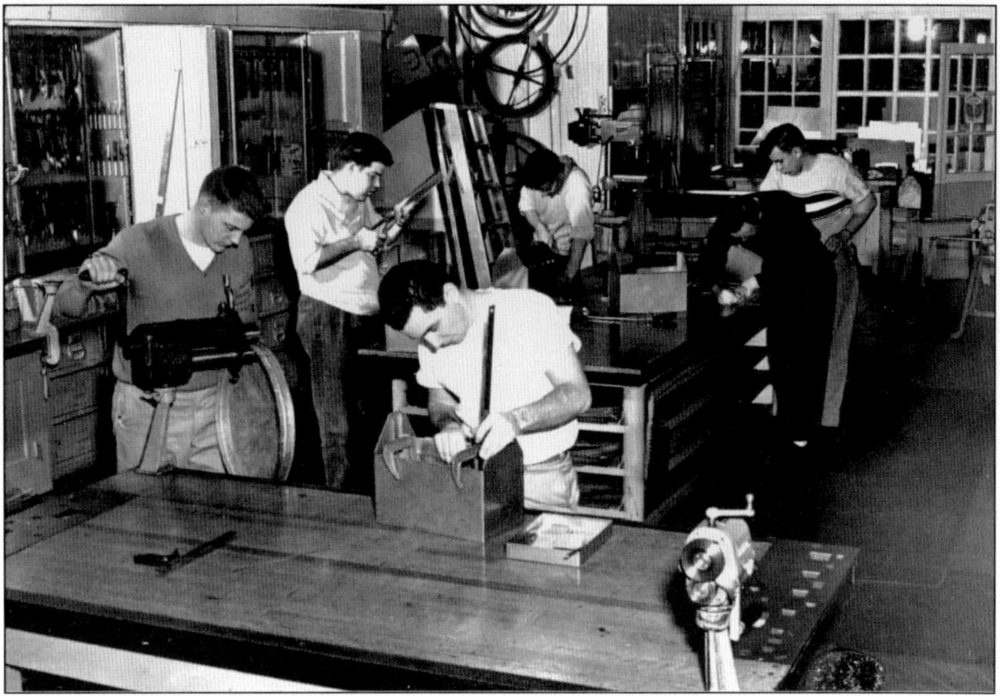

In the woodworking classes, men learned hands-on skills in crafts needed to earn a living. Univerity of Wisconsin–Stout continues its strong reputation in training and skill development through many undergraduate and graduate programs. (Courtesy of UWSA.)

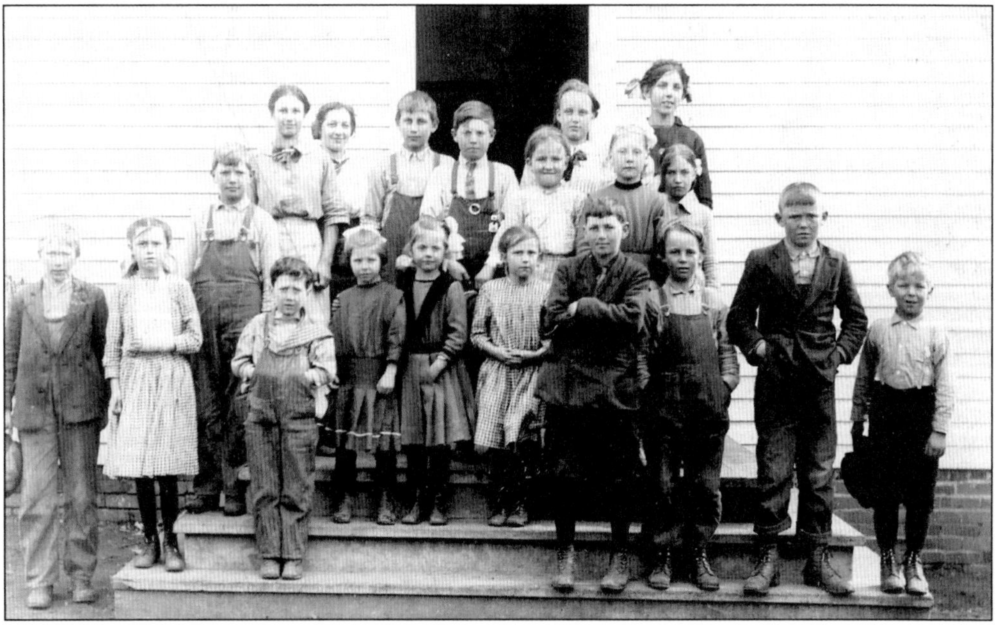

On April 21, 1914, the entire class of West Springbrook School gathered outside to have their photograph taken by Melvin S. Bradford. (Courtesy of Gary Hinrichs.)

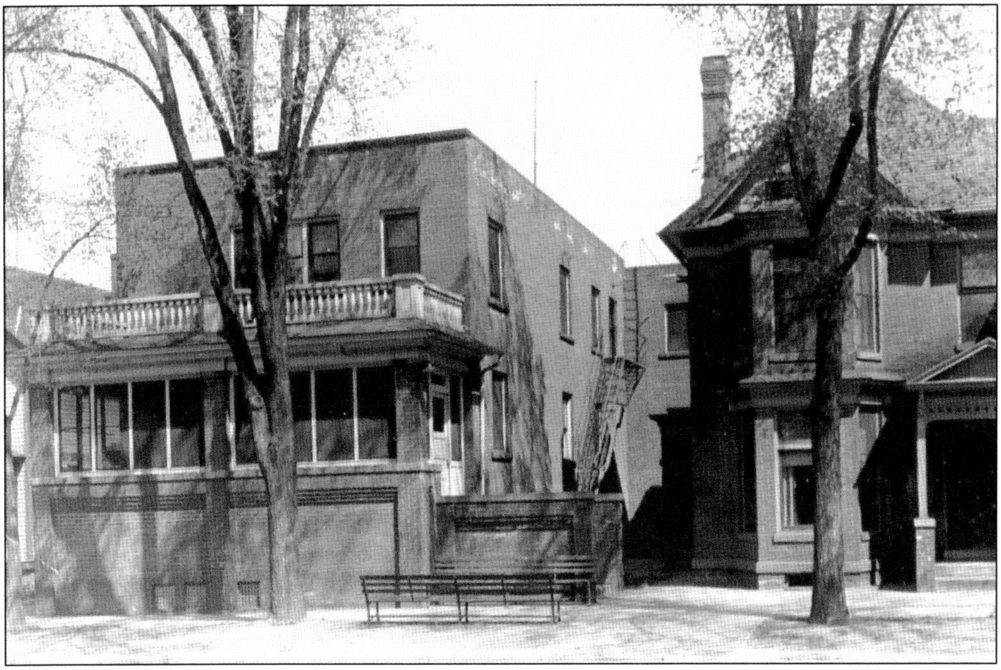

Lynwood Hall, on the left, was a men's dorm. In 1935, in the *Stout Tower*, the official Stout yearbook, the list of members includes President Harry J. Kubalek, Vice President Steve F. Giovanni, and hostess Mabel Davison. (Courtesy of UWSA.)

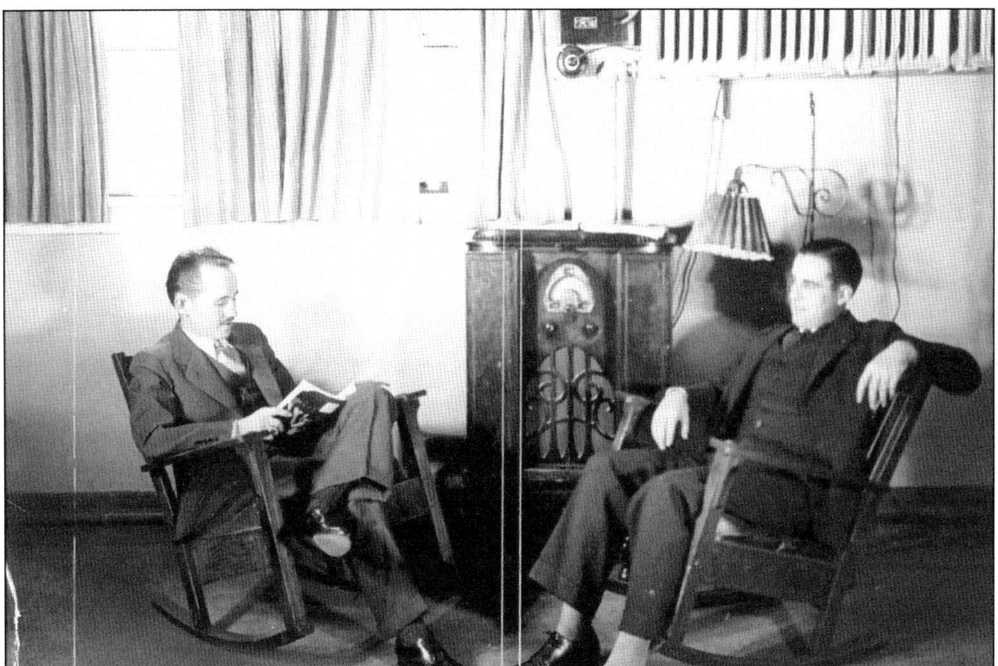

This is the view inside Lynwood Hall, in the recreation room, around 1931. (Courtesy of UWSA.)

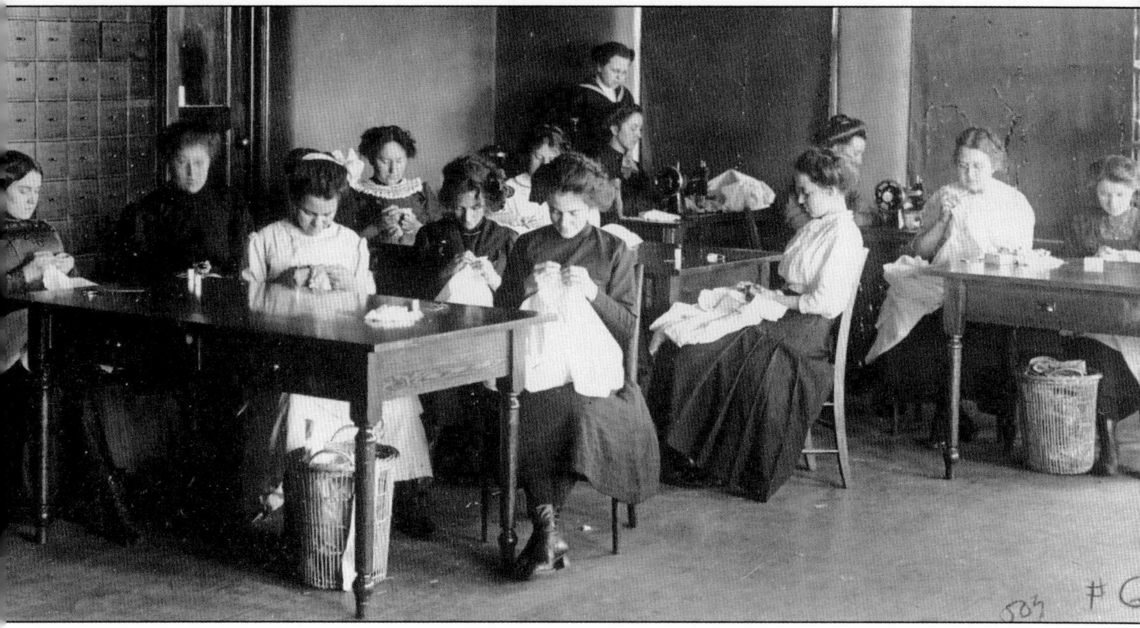

James H. Stout was a leading citizen of Menomonie. Out of his vision grew the concept of training students to learn manual and domestic arts. Here the women's sewing class of 1917 is an example of his vision in action. (Courtesy of UWSA.)

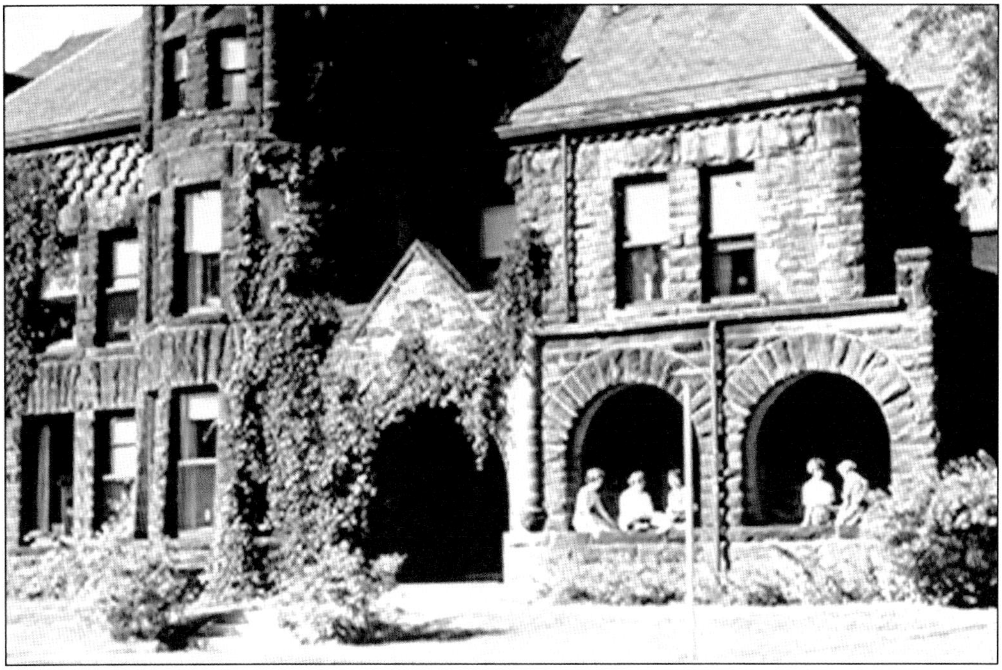

Students take a break on the steps of the original Louis Smith Tainter home, now a part of the Stout campus. (Courtesy of UWSA.)

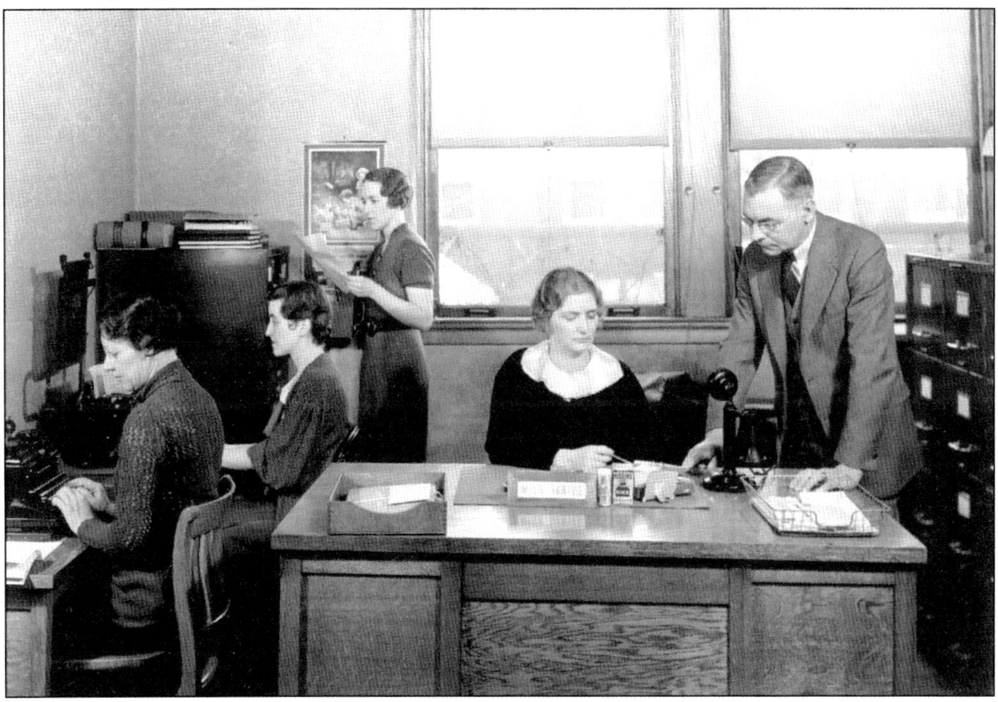

Pictured is the office of the president in 1935. Burton Nelson was acting president from 1923 to 1945, during which time accreditation was achieved so that bachelor degrees could be awarded. In 1935, master's degree programs were also instituted in home economics, vocational, and industrial education. (Courtesy of UWSA.)

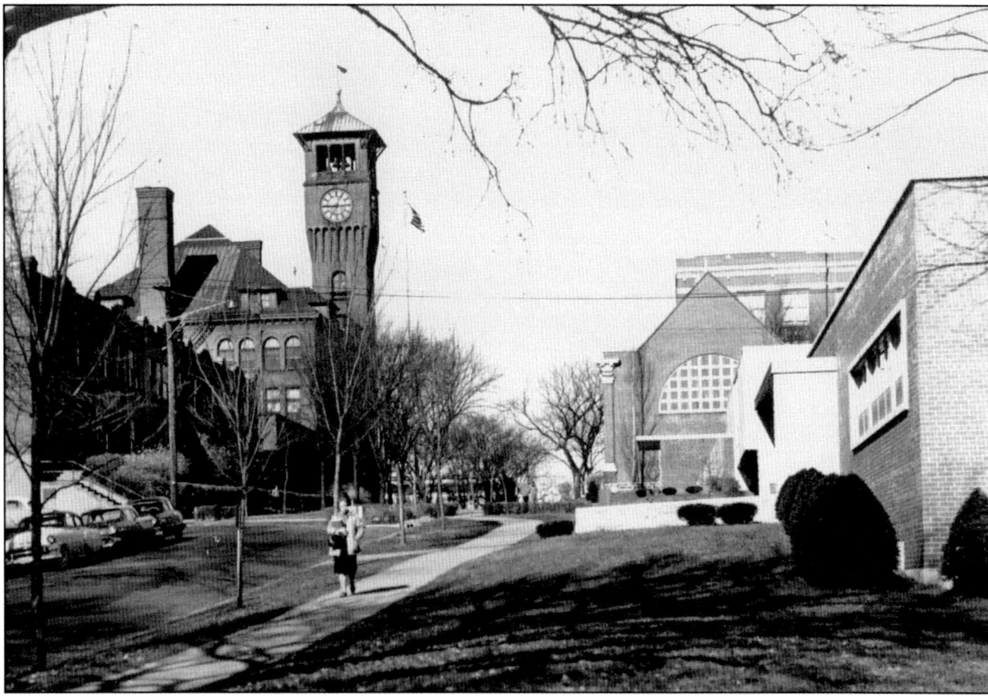

The Stout campus is seen here in the 1950s. Note the clock tower on Bowman Hall, a landmark for all who attend the school. (Courtesy of UWSA.)

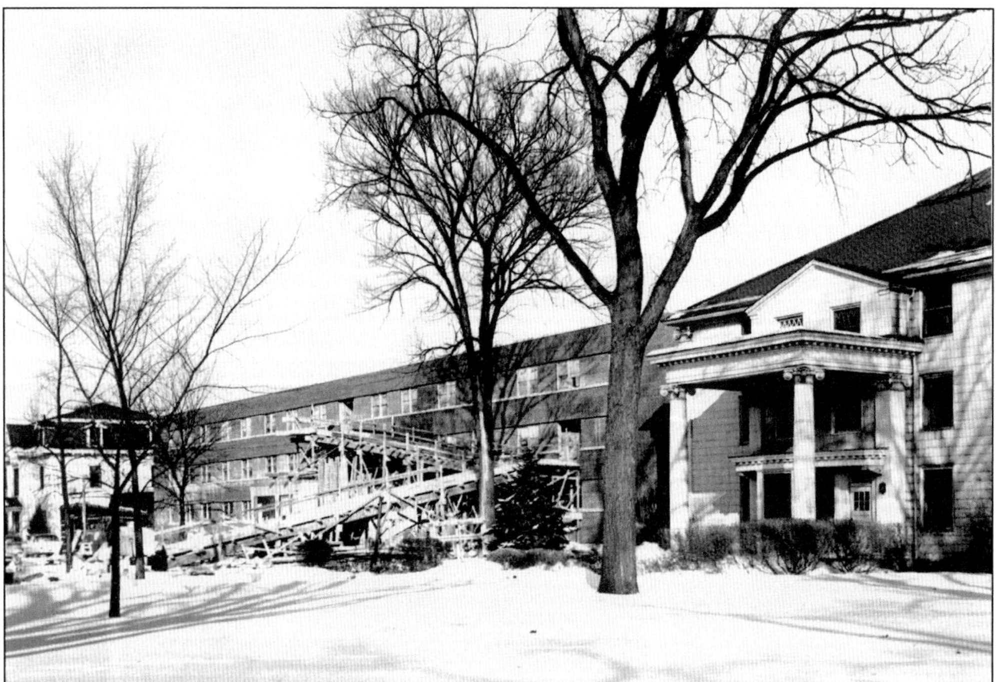

Making way for progress, the girl's dormitories on the north side of campus were torn down in 1956 to build the new complex of Jeter-Tainter-Callahan. It is interesting to note that the new buildings were erected before demolishing the old. (Courtesy of UWSA.)

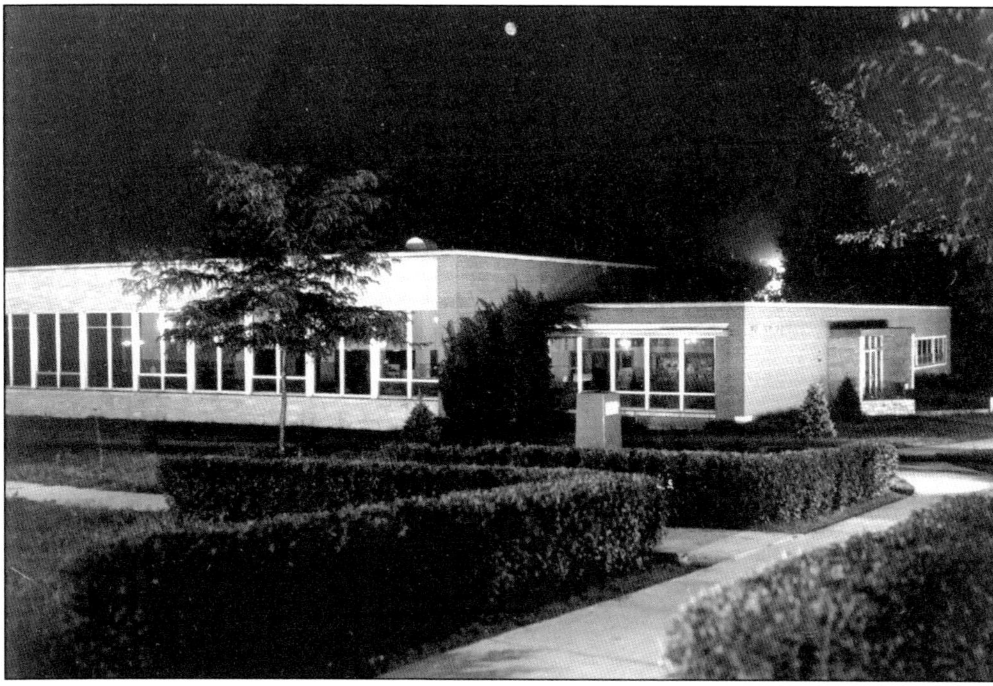

A student union was added to the Stout campus during the tenure of President Verne Fryklund. After World War II ended, it was a time of building and change, which brought increased enrollment and expanded campus facilities to the school. (Courtesy of UWSA.)

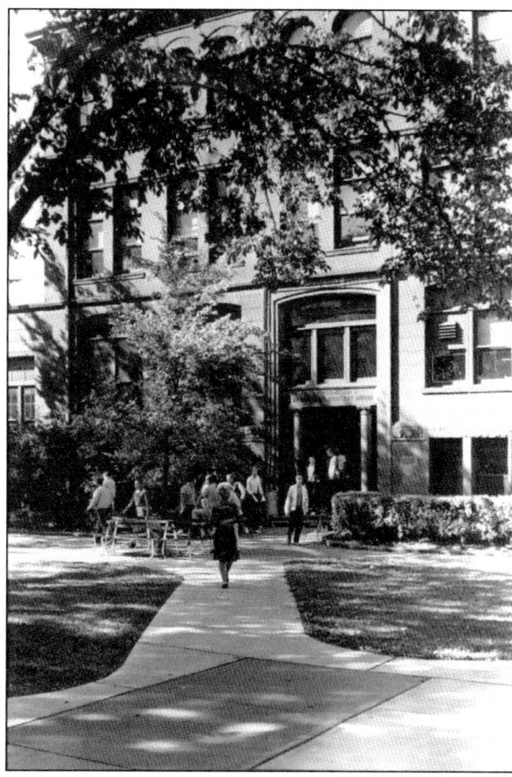

Bowman Hall, a magnificent brick building, continues to stand as a primary landmark for the University of Wisconsin–Stout. Walkways, such as the one pictured, now connect most of the buildings on campus, creating an inclusive and picturesque setting. (Courtesy of UWSA.)

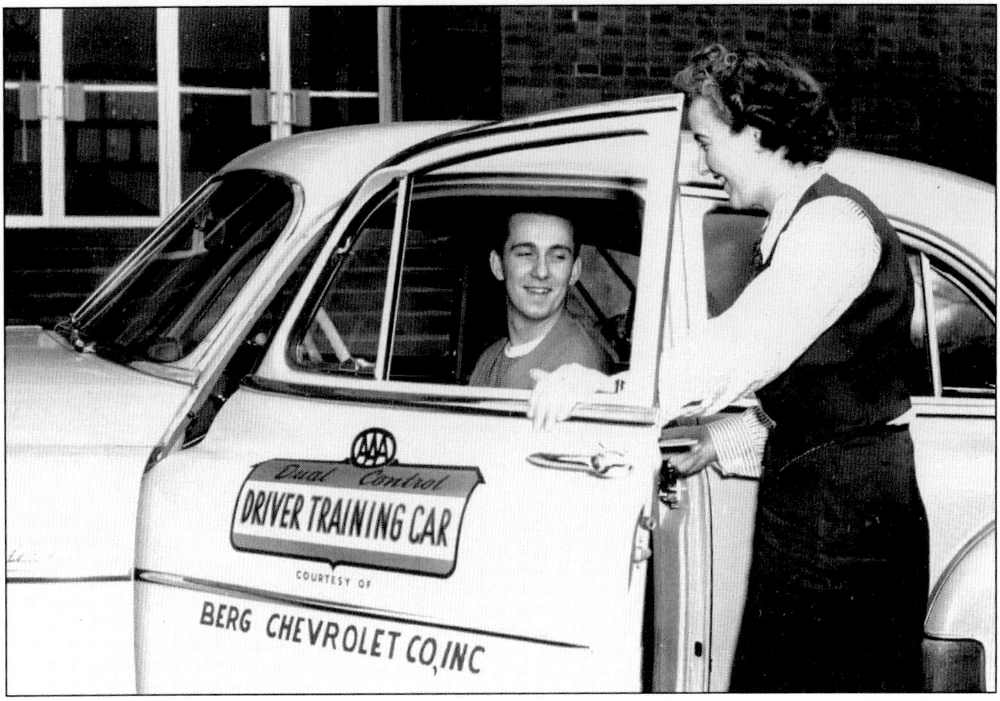

A 1951 driver's education car at Stout offered rural students the chance to earn their license. (Courtesy of UWSA.)

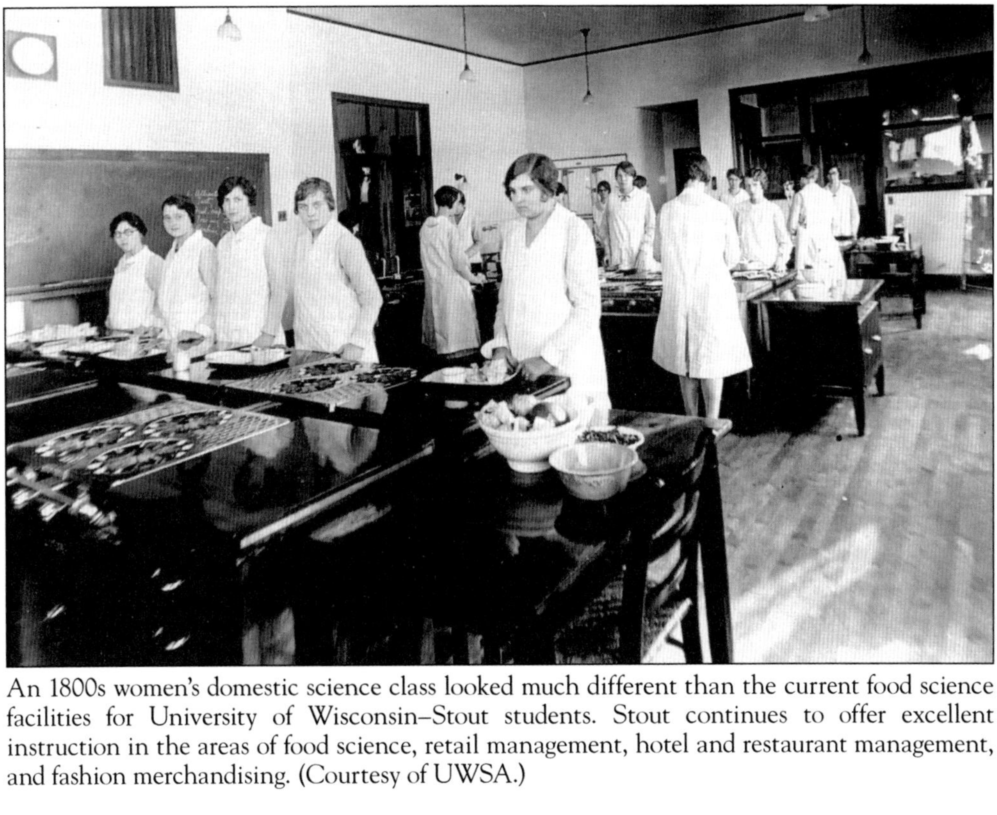

An 1800s women's domestic science class looked much different than the current food science facilities for University of Wisconsin–Stout students. Stout continues to offer excellent instruction in the areas of food science, retail management, hotel and restaurant management, and fashion merchandising. (Courtesy of UWSA.)

The well-known Stout clock tower as it stands in 2006, on Bowman Hall, continues to provide a landmark for the university complex. It is visible throughout Menomonie. (Courtesy of Bruce Dybvik.)

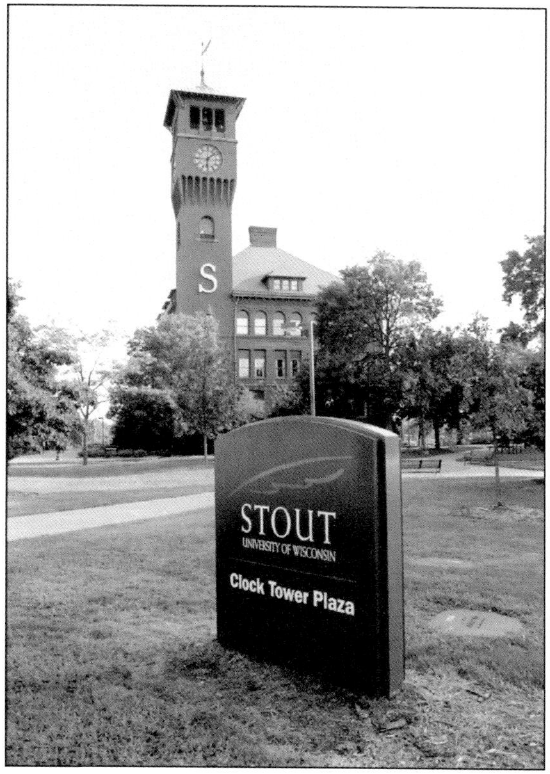

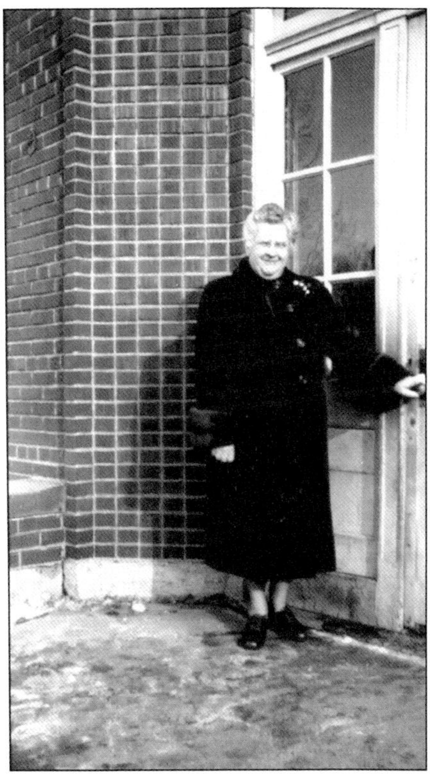

Miss Catts, second grade teacher, stands in front of the East School on Valentine's Day, 1952. (Courtesy of Sofi Doane.)

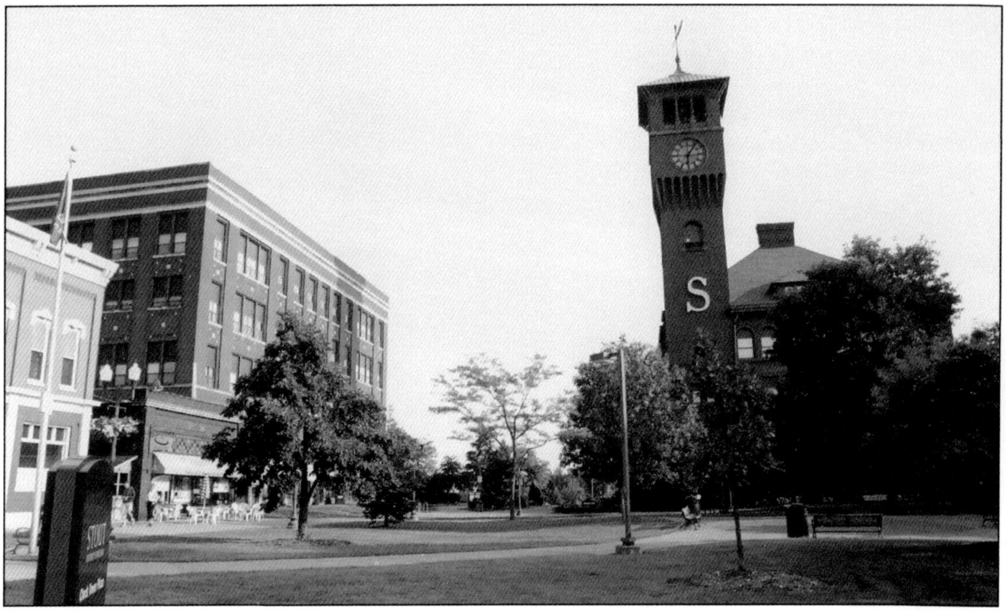

University of Wisconsin–Stout recently added the *S* to its well-known tower. In the foreground is the Stout Tower Commons. Harvey Hall stands, a tribute to craftsmanship in building, to the back left of the photograph.

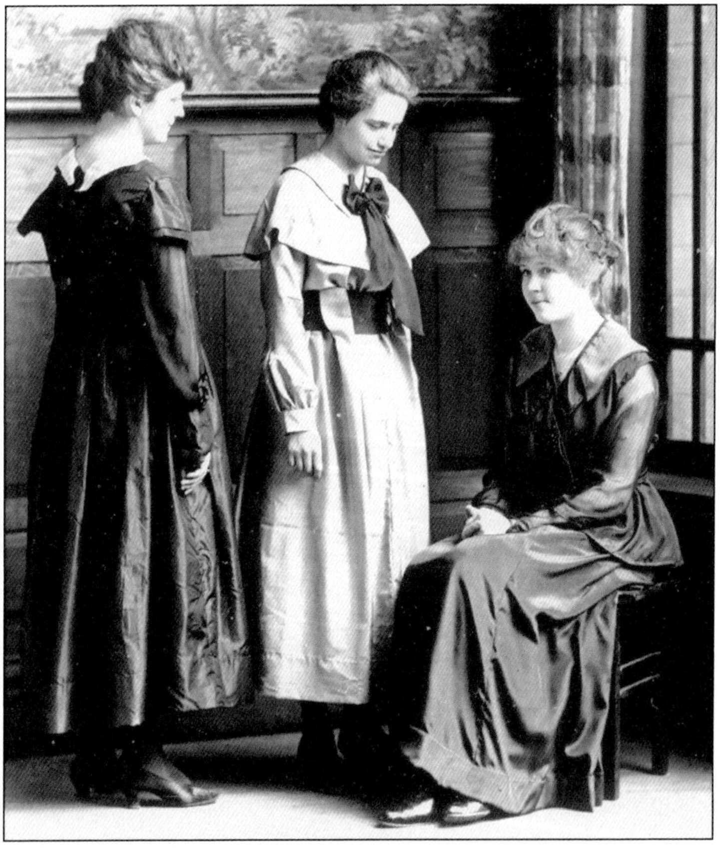

A clothing construction class at Stout, around 1900, provided a venue for students to create garments that reflected ingenuity and fashion. (Courtesy of UWSA.)

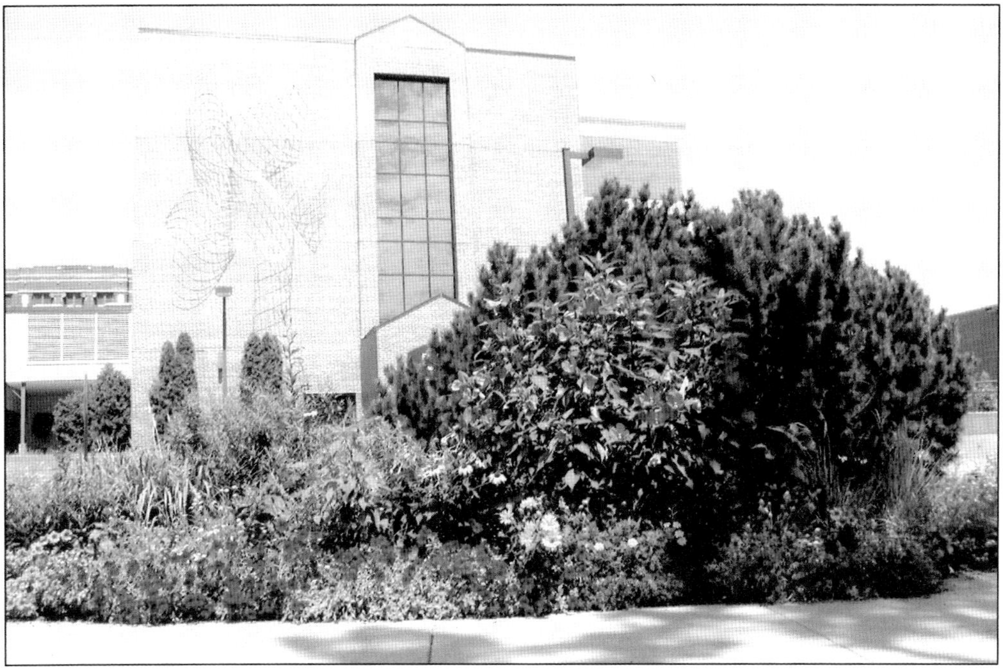

Campus landscaping adds to the integrity and beauty of the campus. This arrangement is in front of Fryklund Hall, where students can access labs to learn technology, graphic arts, materials and design, printing, and other hands-on education opportunities. (Courtesy of Bruce Dybvik.)

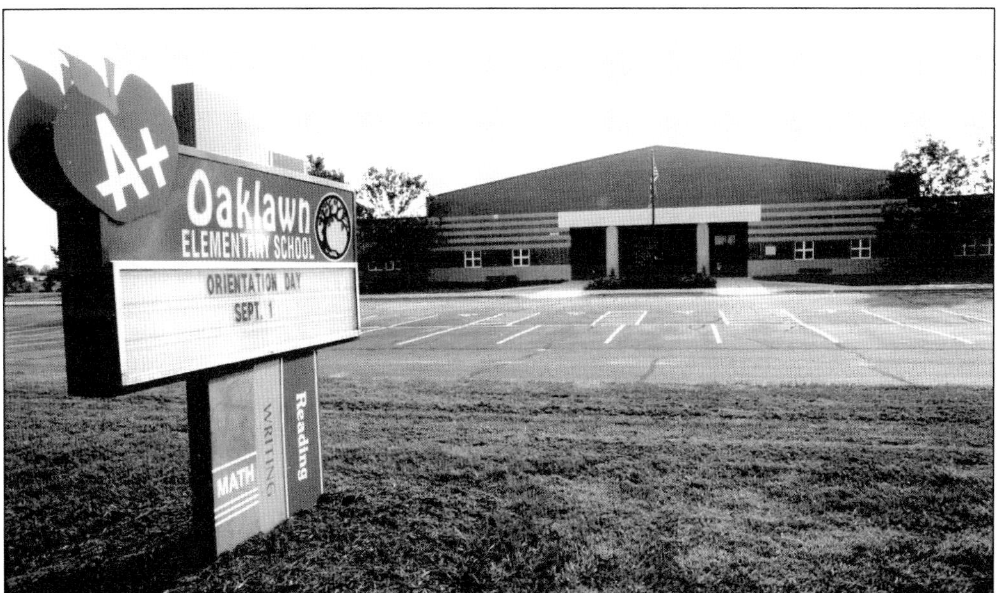

Oaklawn Elementary School is on the east side of Menomonie, across from Dunn County Recreation Park. Oaklawn is the newest school in Menomonie, located on the east side of town. A new middle school sits immediately to the south of Oaklawn Elementary School. (Courtesy of Bruce Dybvik.)

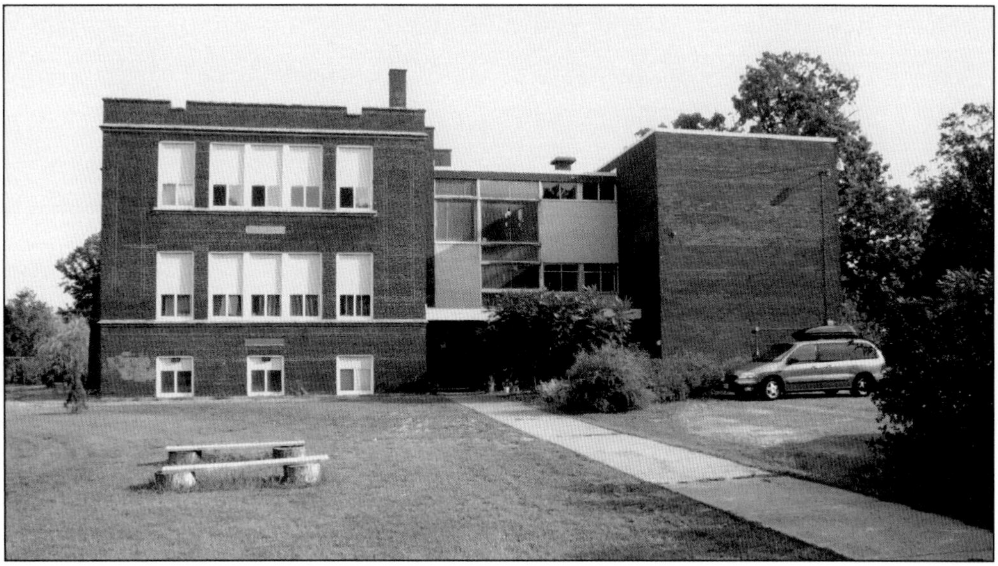

The old East School was an integral part of Menomonie's east side neighborhood. It was replaced by Oaklawn Elementary School and now hosts a Tibetan community, serving as apartments for students and families. In the past, yoga classes and a labyrinth have been offered to the community at the school. (Courtesy of Bruce Dybvik.)

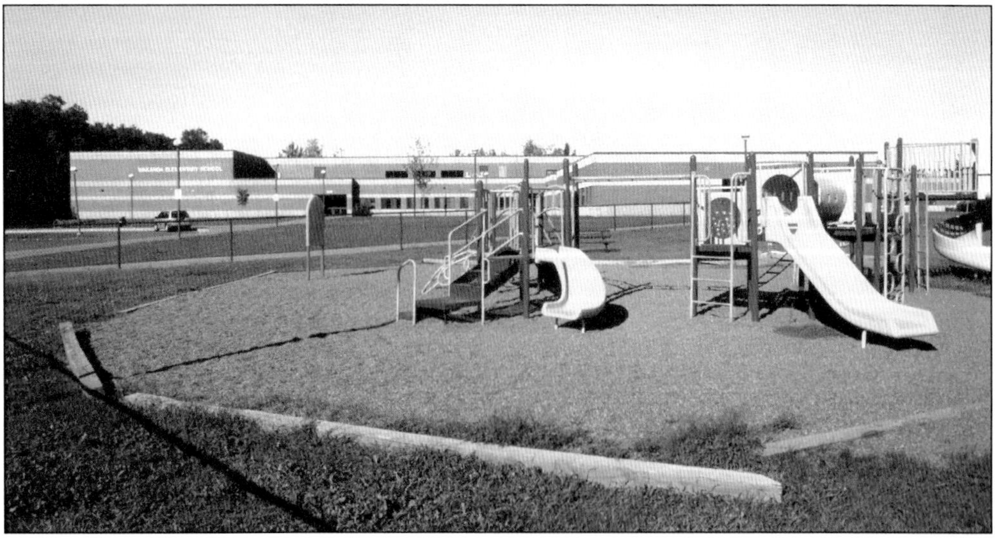

Wakanda Elementary School, located in Wakanda Park, sits next to a community water park and Wakanda park, providing opportunities for a multitude of community activities. (Courtesy of Bruce Dybvik.)

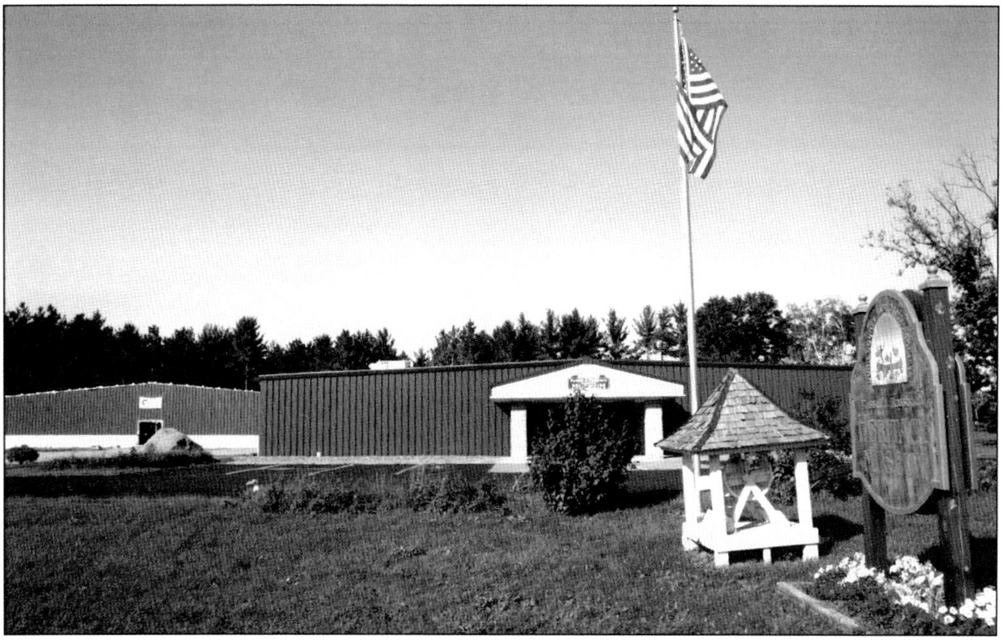

The Dunn County Historical Society, located in Wakanda Park, plays an active role in the community, offering exhibits, brochures, videos, gifts, books, and information tours. The Russell J. Rassbac Heritage Museum hosts their headquarters and includes such exhibits as the interactive display of the Kraft State Bank Robbery, the Caddie Woodlawn children's discovery room, and the Harry Miller Automotive Genius display. (Courtesy of Bruce Dybvik.)

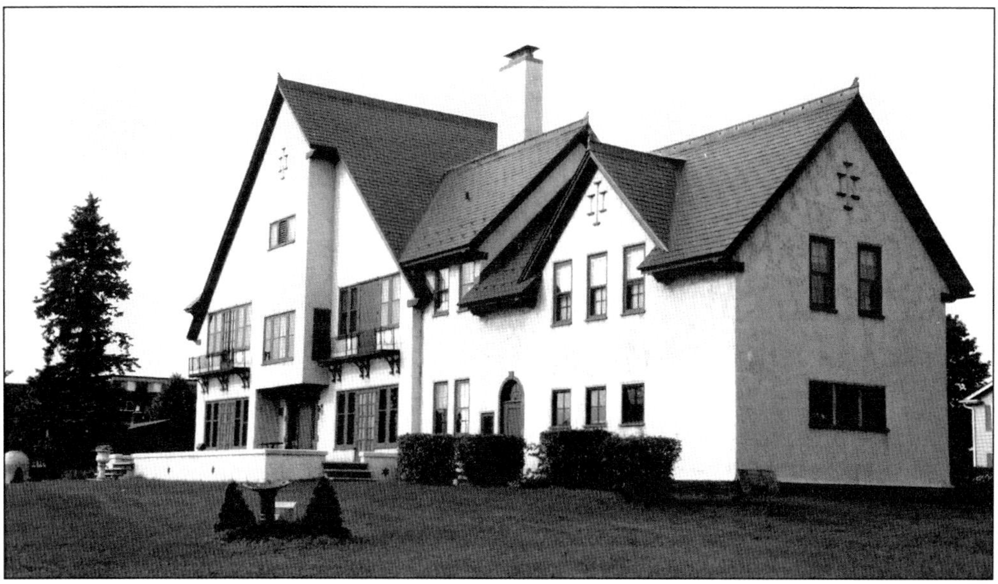

The Wilson Place Museum in 2006 is as majestic as it was in the 1800s. This lovely home, built in 1859 by Capt. William Wilson, founder of the city of Menomonie and the Knapp, Stout and Co. Company, has been restored, and guided tours are offered on Friday through Sunday. John and Jackie Dotseth, along with their son, Tim, completed restoration of the home in 1976. They now open it to the public as a means of sharing their knowledge and interests with the community and tourists. It is located at 101 Wilson Circle, off Broadway Street. (Courtesy of Bruce Dybvik.)

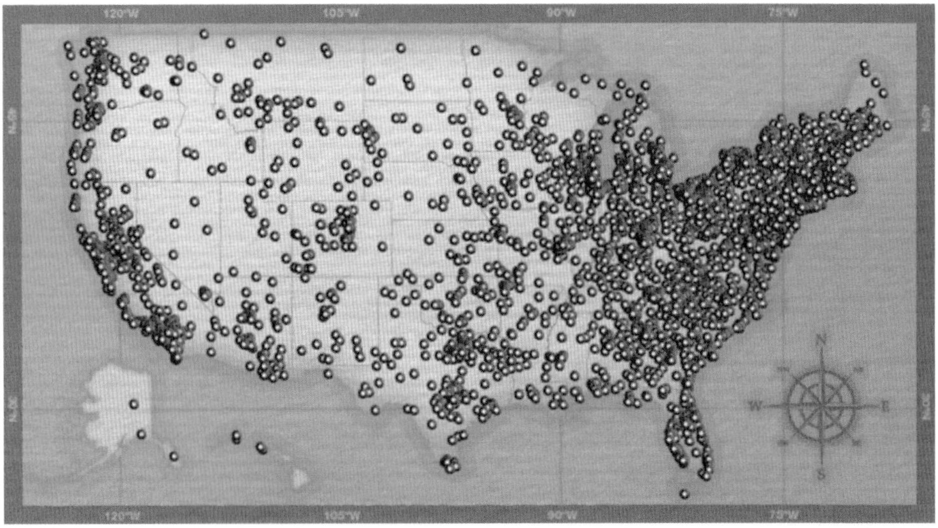